STAR WARS
DOCTOR APHRA

FORTUNE AND FATE

Writer
ALYSSA WONG

Artist
MARIKA CRESTA

Color Artist
RACHELLE ROSENBERG

Letterer
VC's JOE CARAMAGNA

Cover Art
VALENTINA REMENAR

Recap Design
CARLOS LAO

Assistant Editor
TOM GRONEMAN

Editor
MARK PANICCIA

		For Lucasfilm:	
Collection Editor	**JENNIFER GRÜNWALD**	Senior Editor	**ROBERT SIMPSON**
Assistant Managing Editor	**MAIA LOY**	Creative Director	**MICHAEL SIGLAIN**
Assistant Managing Editor	**LISA MONTALBANO**	Art Director	**TROY ALDERS**
VP Production & Special Projects	**JEFF YOUNGQUIST**	Lucasfilm Story Group	**MATT MARTIN**
Book Designer	**ADAM DEL RE**		**PABLO HIDALGO**
SVP Print, Sales & Marketing	**DAVID GABRIEL**		**EMILY SHKOUKANI**
Editor in Chief	**C.B. CEBULSKI**	Lucasfilm Art Department	**PHIL SZOSTAK**

STAR WARS: DOCTOR APHRA VOL. 1 — FORTUNE AND FATE. Contains material originally published in magazine form as STAR WARS: DOCTOR APHRA (2020) #1-5. First printing 2020. ISBN 978-1-302-92304-4. Published by MARVEL WORLDWIDE, INC., a subsidiary of MARVEL ENTERTAINMENT, LLC. OFFICE OF PUBLICATION: 1290 Avenue of the Americas, New York, NY 10104. STAR WARS and related text and illustrations are trademarks and/or copyrights, in the United States and other countries, of Lucasfilm Ltd. and/or its affiliates. © & TM Lucasfilm Ltd. No similarity between any of the names, characters, persons, and/or institutions in this magazine with those of any living or dead person or institution is intended, and any such similarity which may exist is purely coincidental. Marvel and its logos are TM Marvel Characters, Inc. **Printed in Canada.** KEVIN FEIGE, Chief Creative Officer; DAN BUCKLEY, President, Marvel Entertainment; JOHN NEE, Publisher; JOE QUESADA, EVP & Creative Director; TOM BREVOORT, SVP of Publishing; DAVID BOGART, Associate Publisher & SVP of Talent Affairs; Publishing & Partnership; DAVID GABRIEL, VP of Print & Digital Publishing; JEFF YOUNGQUIST, VP of Production & Special Projects; DAN CARR, Executive Director of Publishing Technology; ALEX MORALES, Director of Publishing Operations; DAN EDINGTON, Managing Editor; RICKEY PURDIN, Director of Talent Relations; SUSAN CRESPI, Production Manager; STAN LEE, Chairman Emeritus. For information regarding advertising in Marvel Comics or on Marvel.com, please contact Vit DeBellis, Custom Solutions & Integrated Advertising Manager, at vdebellis@marvel.com. For Marvel subscription inquiries, please call 888-511-5480. **Manufactured between 11/20/2020 and 12/22/2020 by SOLISCO PRINTERS, SCOTT, QC, CANADA.**

10 9 8 7 6 5 4 3 2 1

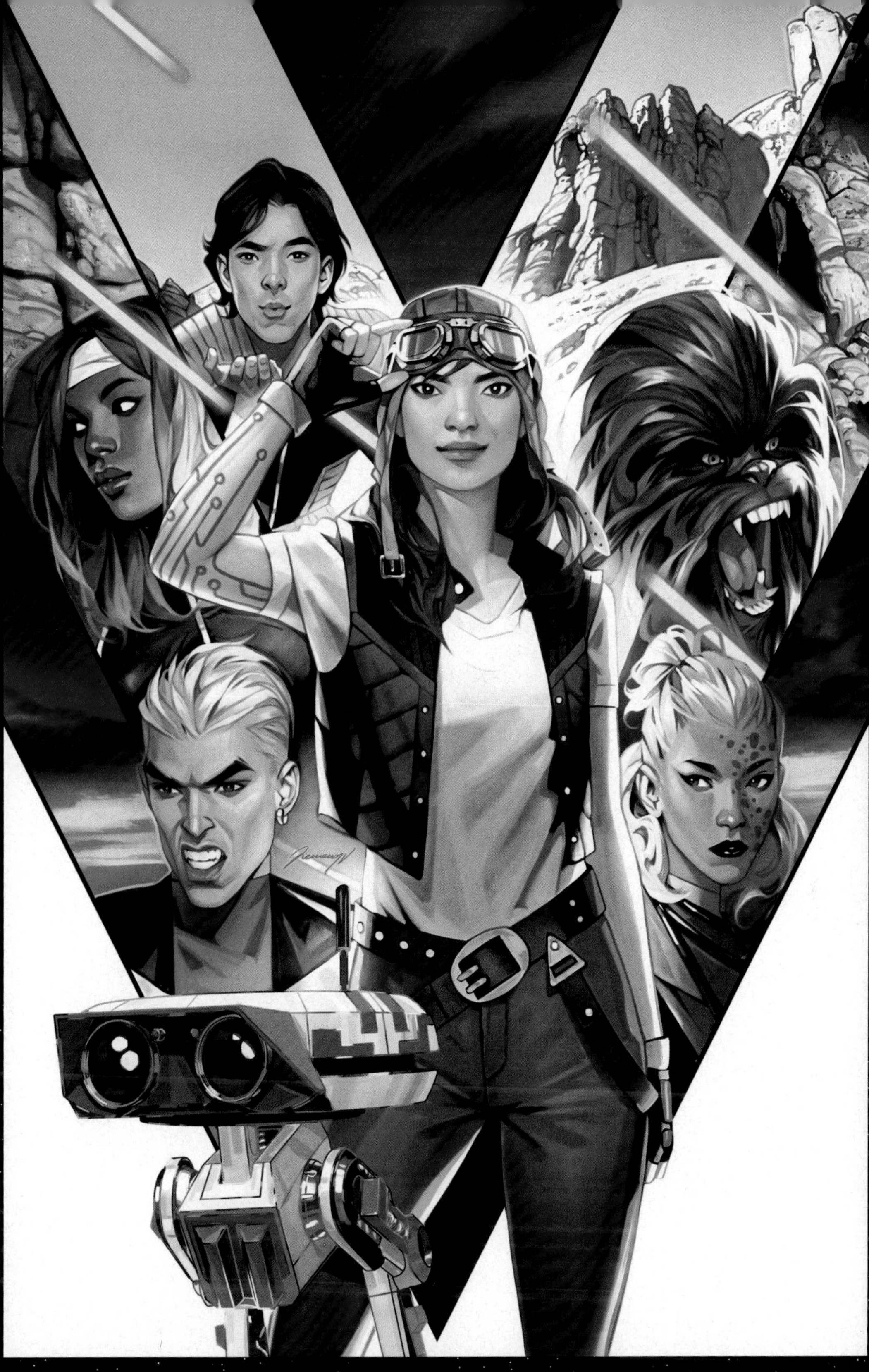

1 — THE RINGS OF VAALE

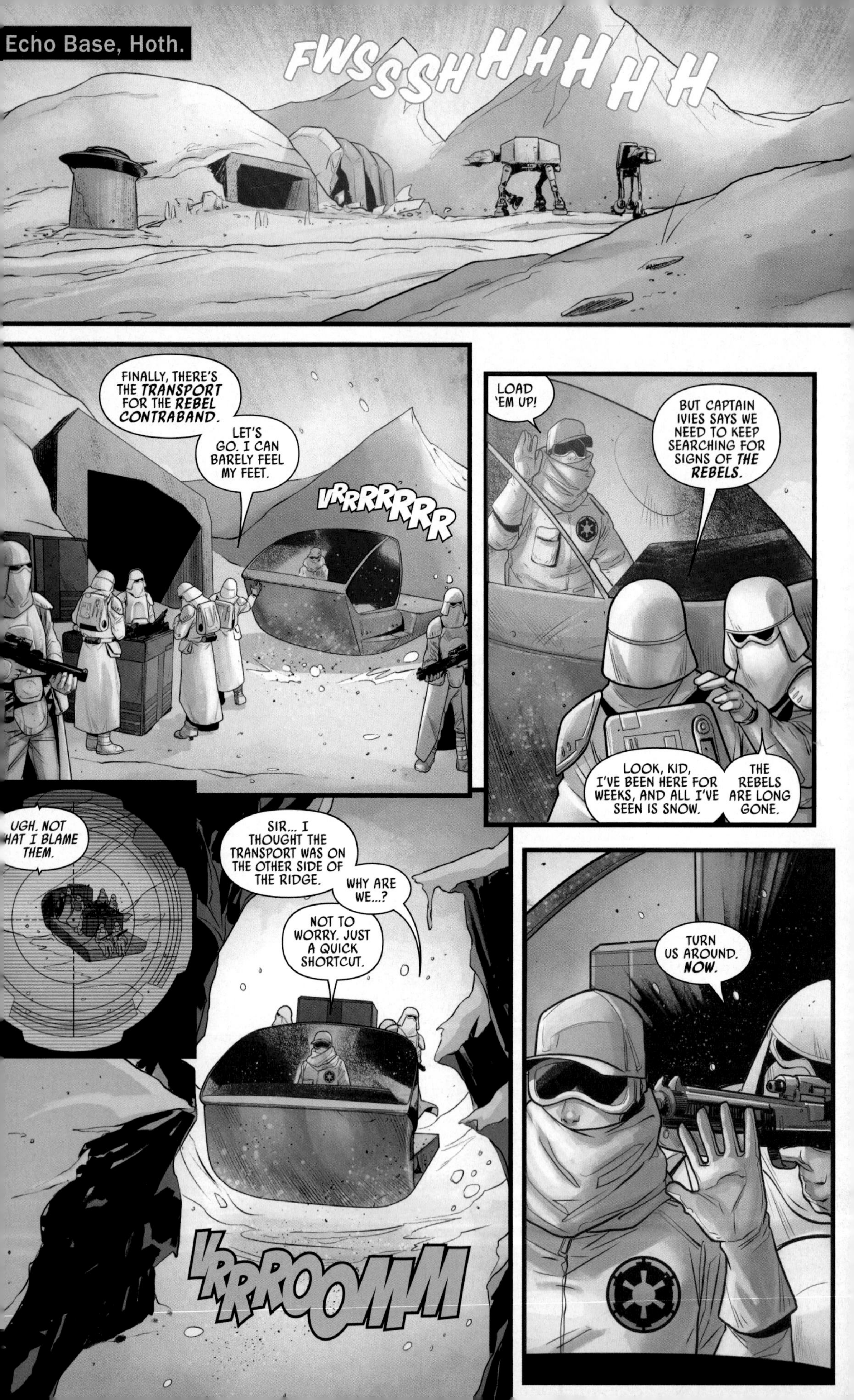
Echo Base, Hoth.
FWSSSHHHHHHH
FINALLY, THERE'S THE TRANSPORT FOR THE REBEL CONTRABAND.
LET'S GO. I CAN BARELY FEEL MY FEET.
VRRRRRRR
LOAD 'EM UP!
BUT CAPTAIN IVIES SAYS WE NEED TO KEEP SEARCHING FOR SIGNS OF THE REBELS.
LOOK, KID, I'VE BEEN HERE FOR WEEKS, AND ALL I'VE SEEN IS SNOW.
THE REBELS ARE LONG GONE.
UGH. NOT HAT I BLAME THEM.
SIR... I THOUGHT THE TRANSPORT WAS ON THE OTHER SIDE OF THE RIDGE.
WHY ARE WE...?
NOT TO WORRY. JUST A QUICK SHORTCUT.
VRRROOMM
TURN US AROUND. NOW.

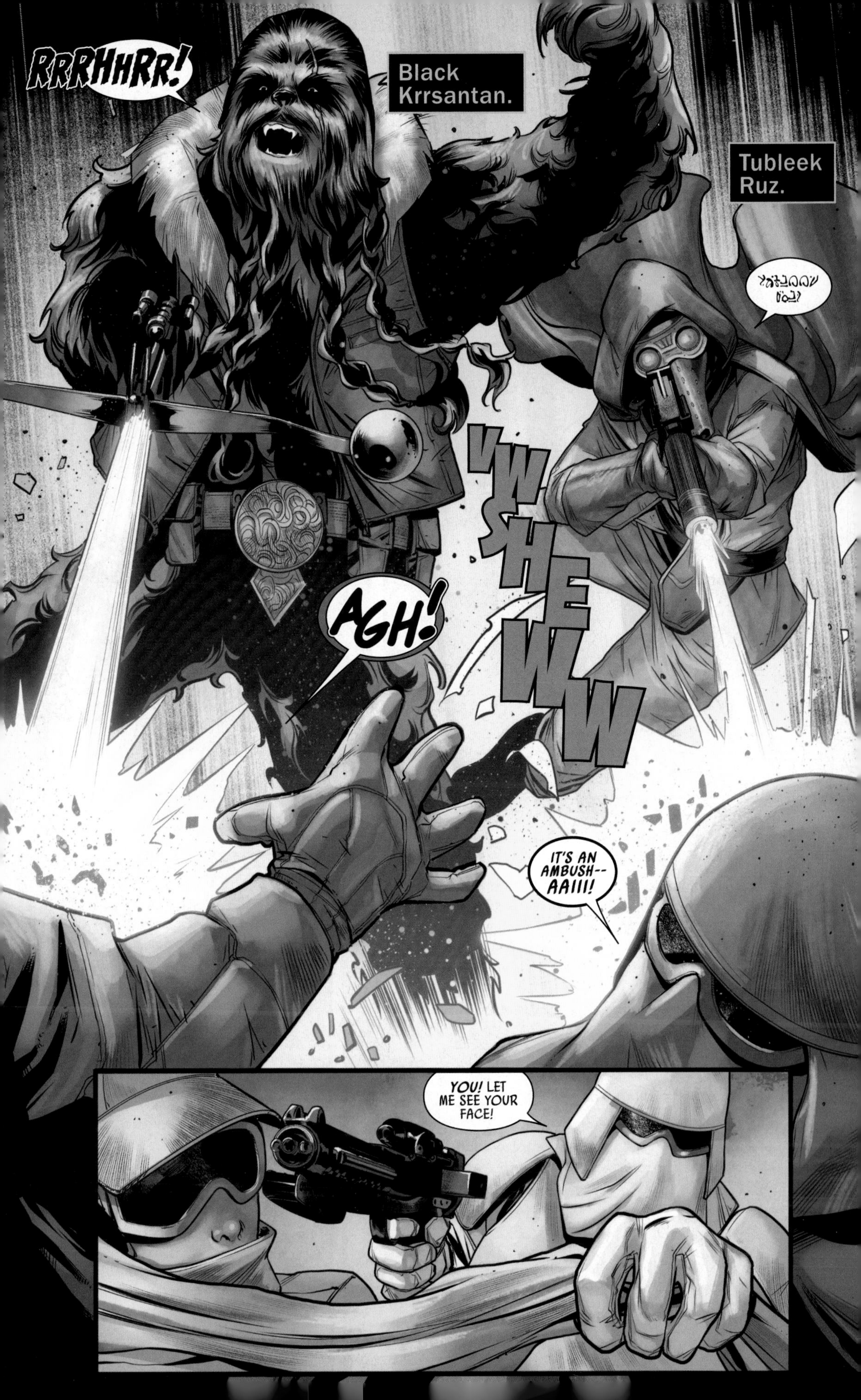
RRRHHRR!
Black Krrsantan.
Tubleek Ruz.
VWSHEWW
AGH!
IT'S AN AMBUSH-- AAIII!
YOU! LET ME SEE YOUR FACE!

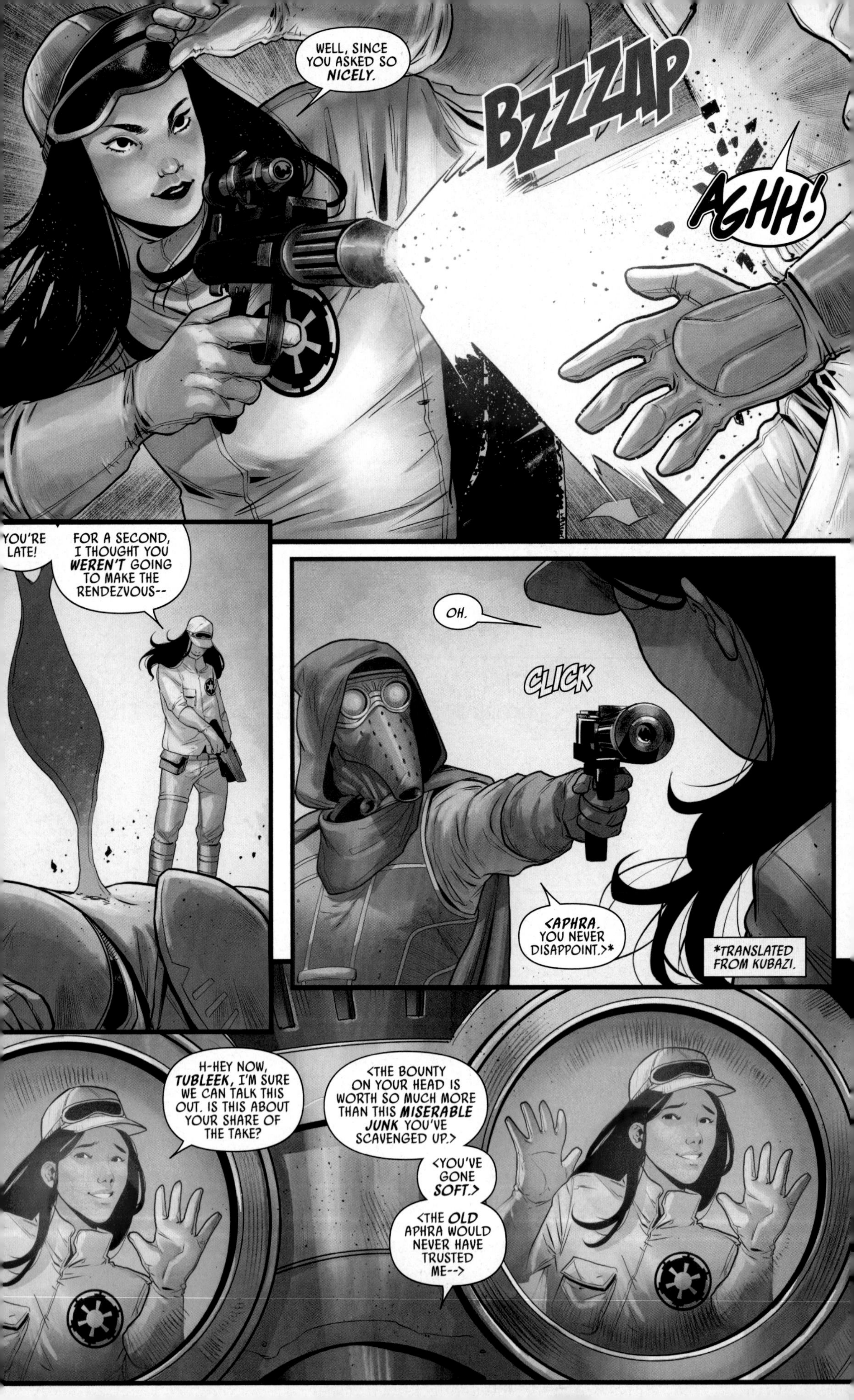
WELL, SINCE YOU ASKED SO NICELY.
BZZZAP
AGHH!
YOU'RE LATE!
FOR A SECOND, I THOUGHT YOU WEREN'T GOING TO MAKE THE RENDEZVOUS--
OH.
CLICK
<APHRA. YOU NEVER DISAPPOINT.>*
*TRANSLATED FROM KUBAZI.
H-HEY NOW, TUBLEEK, I'M SURE WE CAN TALK THIS OUT. IS THIS ABOUT YOUR SHARE OF THE TAKE?
<THE BOUNTY ON YOUR HEAD IS WORTH SO MUCH MORE THAN THIS MISERABLE JUNK YOU'VE SCAVENGED UP.>
<YOU'VE GONE SOFT.>
<THE OLD APHRA WOULD NEVER HAVE TRUSTED ME-->

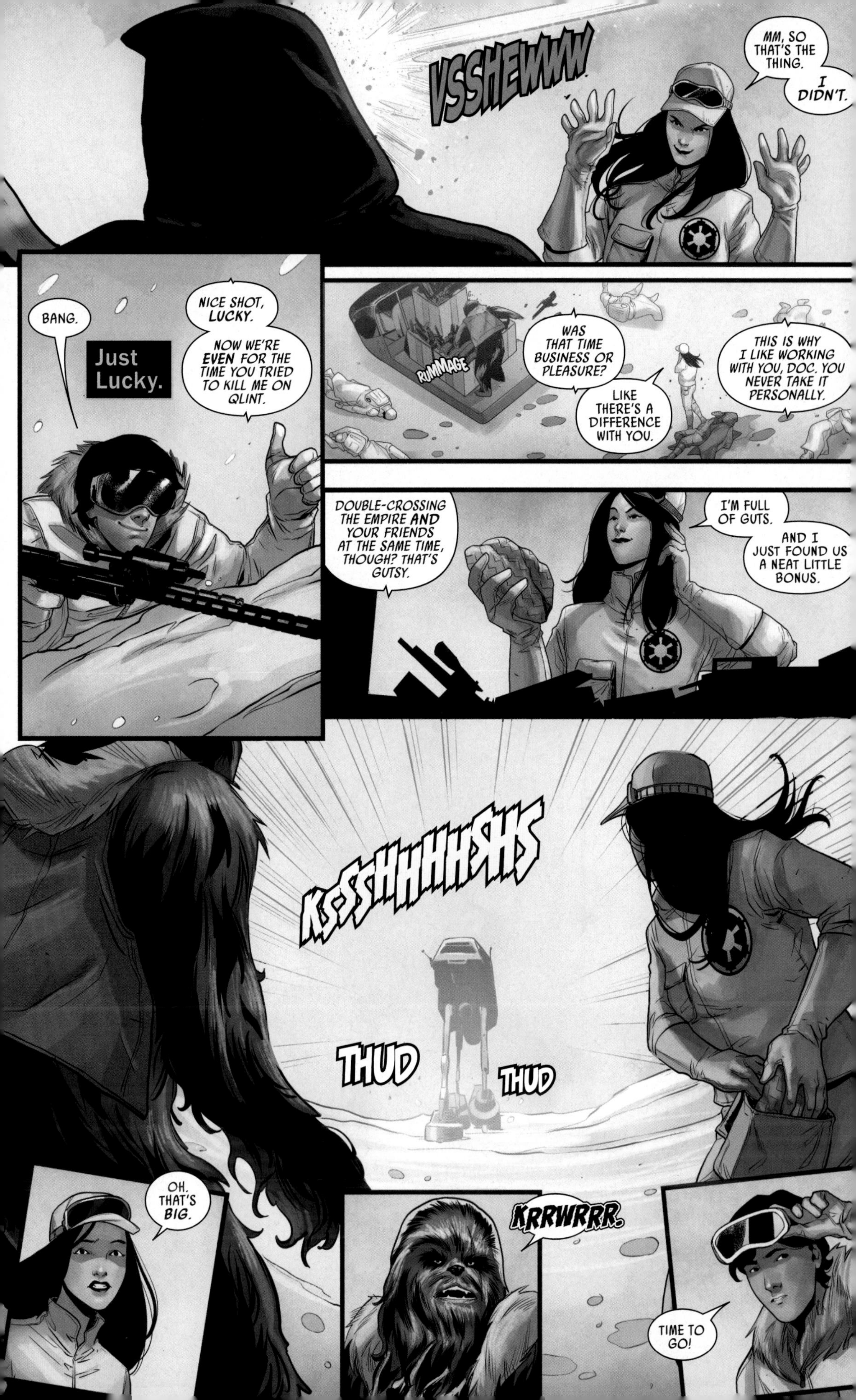
VSSHEWWW
MM, SO THAT'S THE THING.
I DIDN'T.
BANG.
Just Lucky.
NICE SHOT, LUCKY.
NOW WE'RE EVEN FOR THE TIME YOU TRIED TO KILL ME ON QLINT.
RUMMAGE
WAS THAT TIME BUSINESS OR PLEASURE?
LIKE THERE'S A DIFFERENCE WITH YOU.
THIS IS WHY I LIKE WORKING WITH YOU, DOC. YOU NEVER TAKE IT PERSONALLY.
DOUBLE-CROSSING THE EMPIRE AND YOUR FRIENDS AT THE SAME TIME, THOUGH? THAT'S GUTSY.
I'M FULL OF GUTS.
AND I JUST FOUND US A NEAT LITTLE BONUS.
KS-SSHHHHSHS
THUD
THUD
OH. THAT'S BIG.
KRRWRRR.
TIME TO GO!

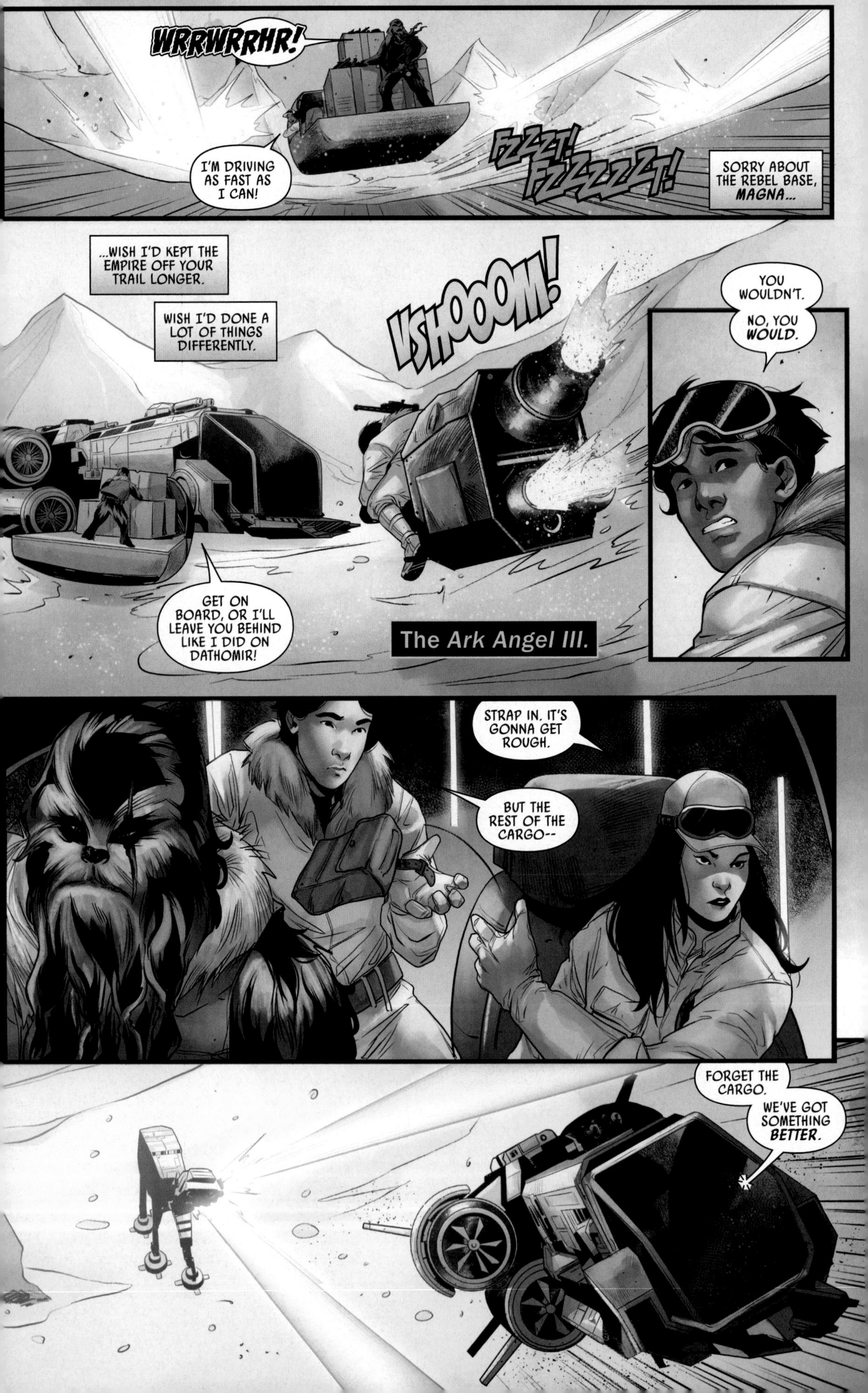
WRRWRRHR!
I'M DRIVING AS FAST AS I CAN!
FZZZT! FZZZZZZT!
SORRY ABOUT THE REBEL BASE, MAGNA...
...WISH I'D KEPT THE EMPIRE OFF YOUR TRAIL LONGER.
WISH I'D DONE A LOT OF THINGS DIFFERENTLY.
VSHOOOM!
YOU WOULDN'T.
NO, YOU WOULD.
GET ON BOARD, OR I'LL LEAVE YOU BEHIND LIKE I DID ON DATHOMIR!
The Ark Angel III.
STRAP IN. IT'S GONNA GET ROUGH.
BUT THE REST OF THE CARGO--
FORGET THE CARGO.
WE'VE GOT SOMETHING BETTER.

STAR WARS

DOCTOR APHRA

The heroic Rebel Alliance is scattered and on the run after their defeat by the Empire at the Battle of Hoth.

After narrowly escaping the vengeful Darth Vader and cutting all ties to her past, rogue archaeologist Doctor Chelli Aphra is back on the hunt for the rarest, most valuable treasures in the galaxy.

With Aphra's cunning intellect and flexible moral compass (plus a new, highly skilled team), the next huge payday is just around the corner. But there are some secrets in the dark corners of the galaxy that not even Doctor Aphra is prepared to uncover...

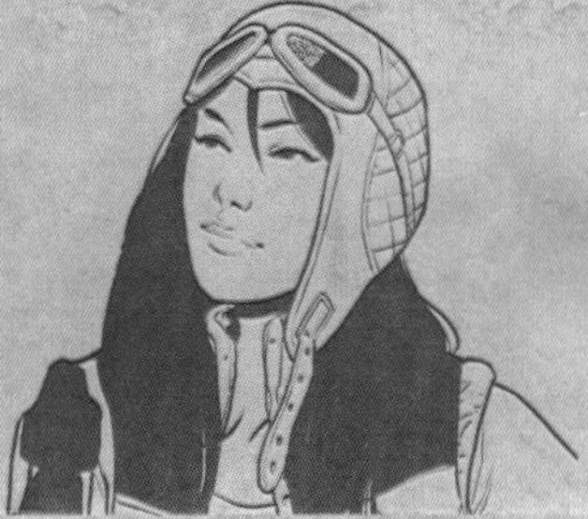

DOCTOR CHELLI APHRA

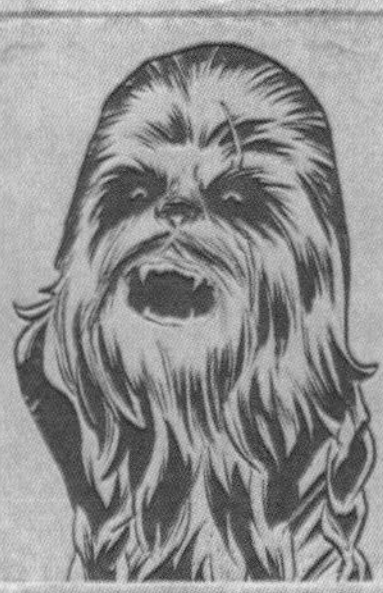

BLACK KRRSANTAN

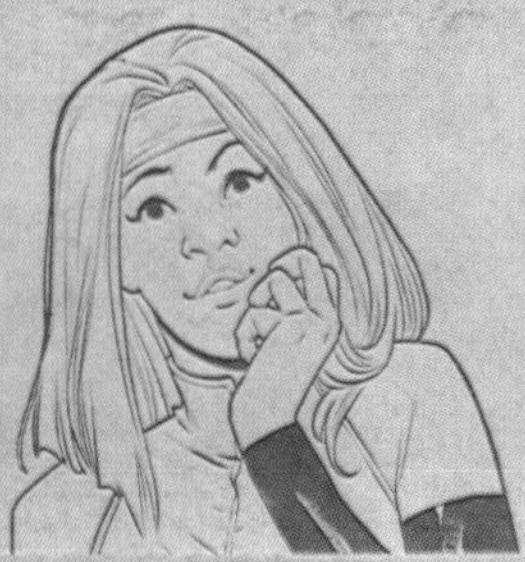

DETTA YAO

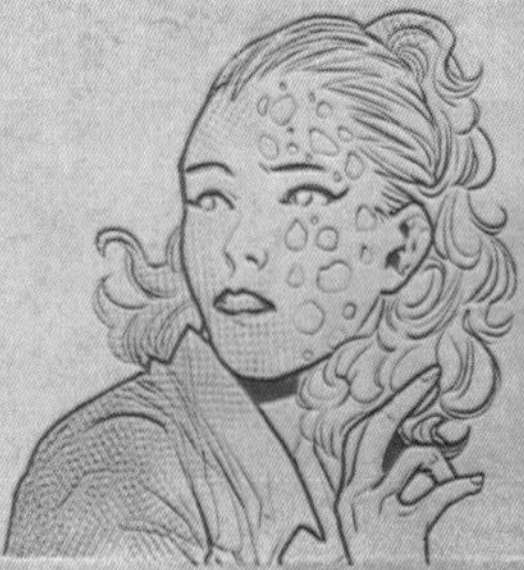

DOCTOR EUSTACIA OKKA

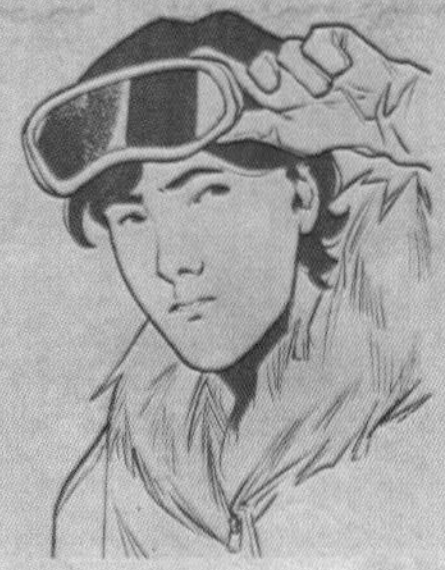

JUST LUCKY

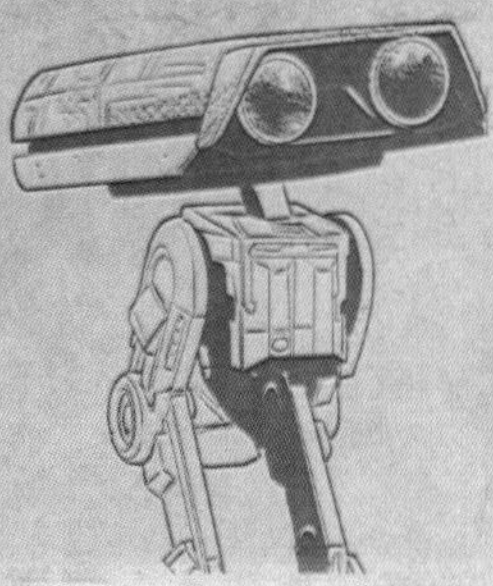

TA-418

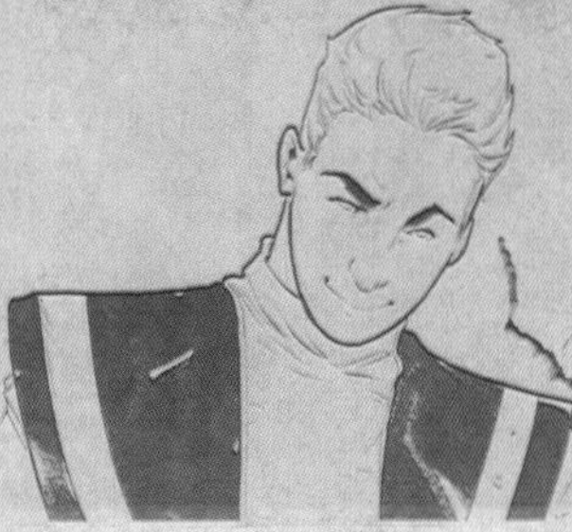

RONEN TAGGE

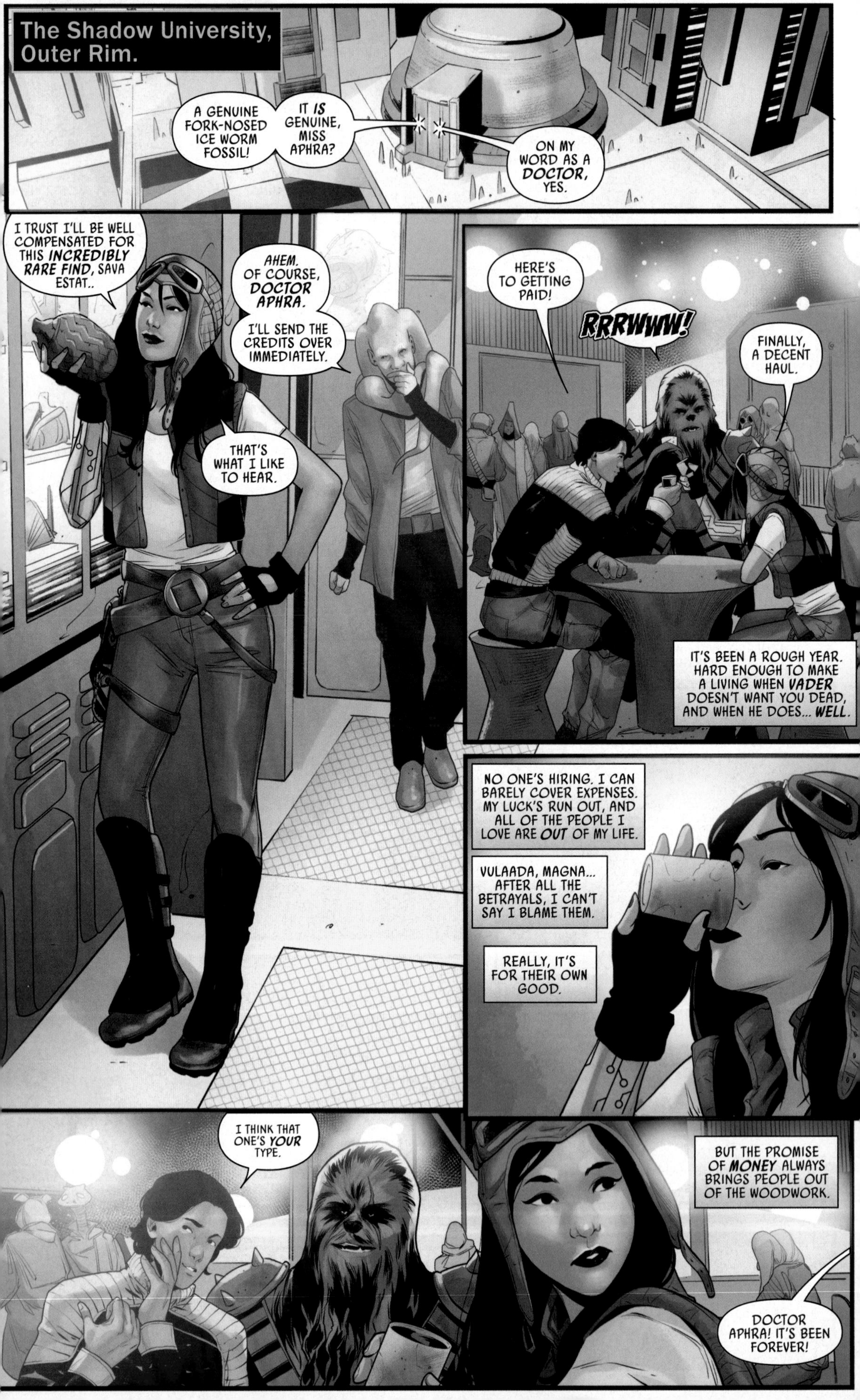
The Shadow University, Outer Rim.
A GENUINE FORK-NOSED ICE WORM FOSSIL!
IT IS GENUINE, MISS APHRA?
ON MY WORD AS A DOCTOR, YES.
I TRUST I'LL BE WELL COMPENSATED FOR THIS INCREDIBLY RARE FIND, SAVA ESTAT..
AHEM. OF COURSE, DOCTOR APHRA.
I'LL SEND THE CREDITS OVER IMMEDIATELY.
THAT'S WHAT I LIKE TO HEAR.
HERE'S TO GETTING PAID!
RRRWWW!
FINALLY, A DECENT HAUL.
IT'S BEEN A ROUGH YEAR. HARD ENOUGH TO MAKE A LIVING WHEN VADER DOESN'T WANT YOU DEAD, AND WHEN HE DOES... WELL.
NO ONE'S HIRING. I CAN BARELY COVER EXPENSES. MY LUCK'S RUN OUT, AND ALL OF THE PEOPLE I LOVE ARE OUT OF MY LIFE.
VULAADA, MAGNA... AFTER ALL THE BETRAYALS, I CAN'T SAY I BLAME THEM.
REALLY, IT'S FOR THEIR OWN GOOD.
I THINK THAT ONE'S YOUR TYPE.
BUT THE PROMISE OF MONEY ALWAYS BRINGS PEOPLE OUT OF THE WOODWORK.
DOCTOR APHRA! IT'S BEEN FOREVER!

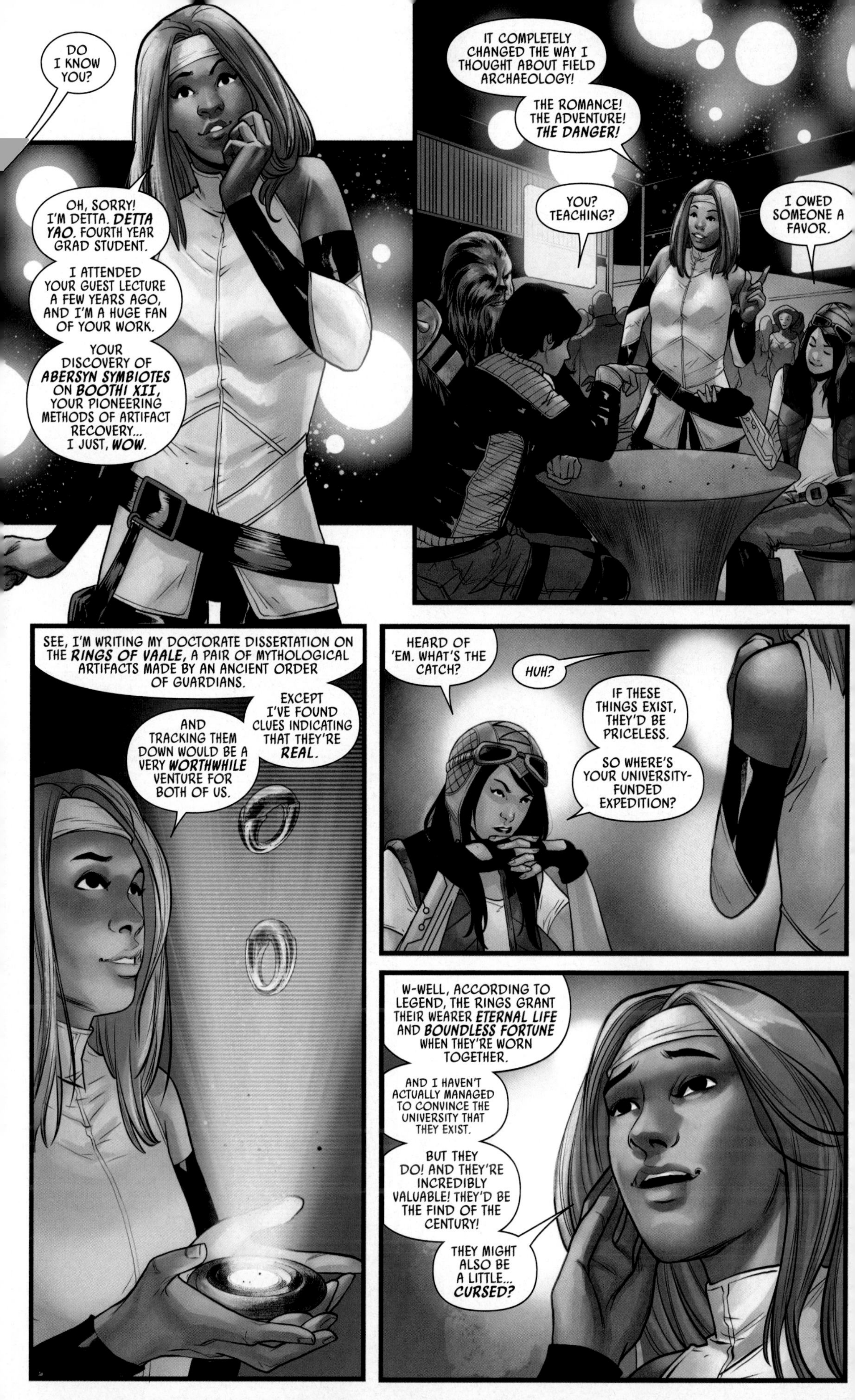
DO I KNOW YOU?
OH, SORRY! I'M DETTA. DETTA YAO. FOURTH YEAR GRAD STUDENT.
I ATTENDED YOUR GUEST LECTURE A FEW YEARS AGO, AND I'M A HUGE FAN OF YOUR WORK.
YOUR DISCOVERY OF ABERSYN SYMBIOTES ON BOOTHI XII, YOUR PIONEERING METHODS OF ARTIFACT RECOVERY... I JUST, WOW.
IT COMPLETELY CHANGED THE WAY I THOUGHT ABOUT FIELD ARCHAEOLOGY!
THE ROMANCE! THE ADVENTURE! THE DANGER!
YOU? TEACHING?
I OWED SOMEONE A FAVOR.
SEE, I'M WRITING MY DOCTORATE DISSERTATION ON THE RINGS OF VAALE, A PAIR OF MYTHOLOGICAL ARTIFACTS MADE BY AN ANCIENT ORDER OF GUARDIANS.
EXCEPT I'VE FOUND CLUES INDICATING THAT THEY'RE REAL.
AND TRACKING THEM DOWN WOULD BE A VERY WORTHWHILE VENTURE FOR BOTH OF US.
HEARD OF 'EM. WHAT'S THE CATCH?
HUH?
IF THESE THINGS EXIST, THEY'D BE PRICELESS.
SO WHERE'S YOUR UNIVERSITY-FUNDED EXPEDITION?
W-WELL, ACCORDING TO LEGEND, THE RINGS GRANT THEIR WEARER ETERNAL LIFE AND BOUNDLESS FORTUNE WHEN THEY'RE WORN TOGETHER.
AND I HAVEN'T ACTUALLY MANAGED TO CONVINCE THE UNIVERSITY THAT THEY EXIST.
BUT THEY DO! AND THEY'RE INCREDIBLY VALUABLE! THEY'D BE THE FIND OF THE CENTURY!
THEY MIGHT ALSO BE A LITTLE... CURSED?

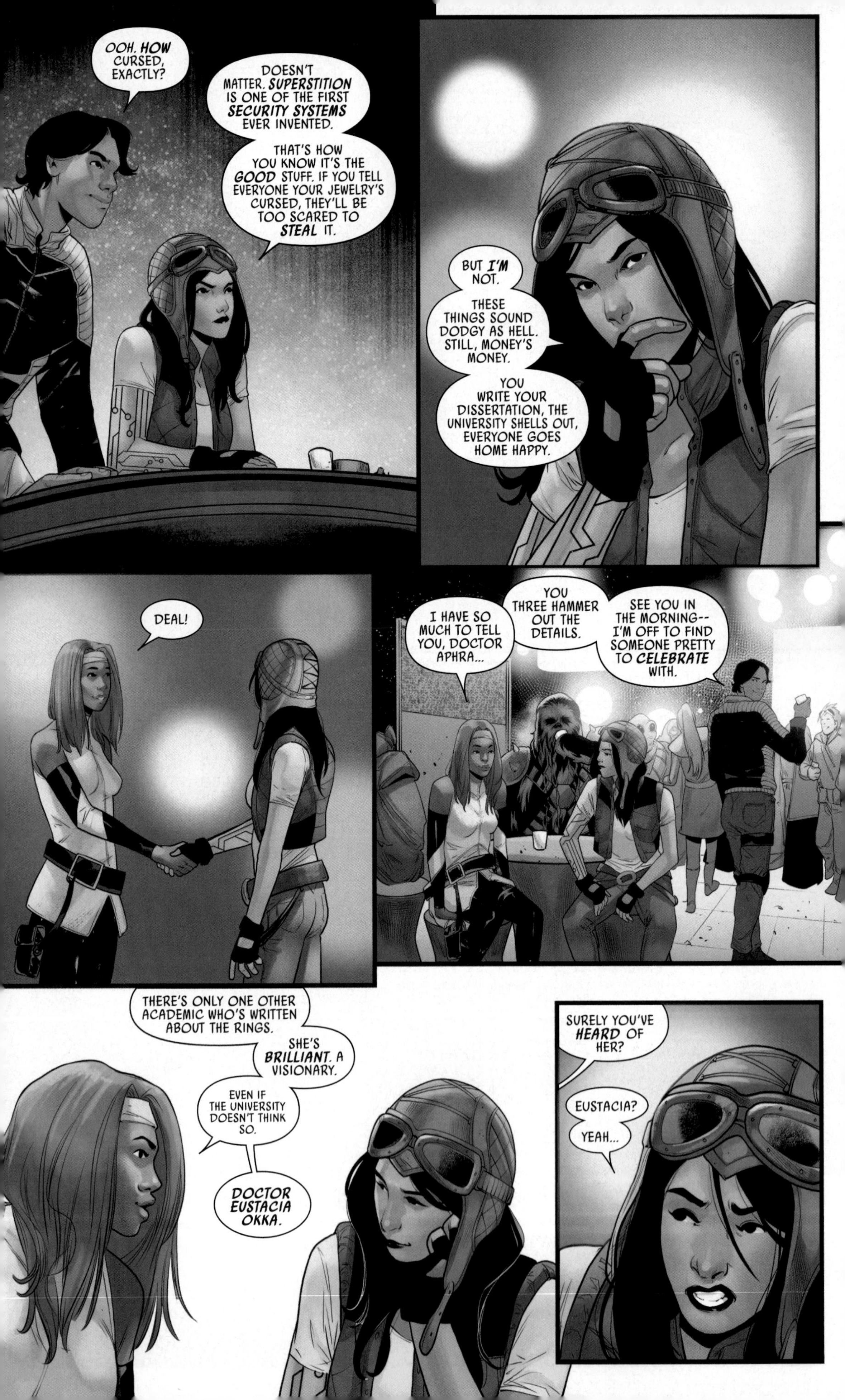
OOH. HOW CURSED, EXACTLY?
DOESN'T MATTER. SUPERSTITION IS ONE OF THE FIRST SECURITY SYSTEMS EVER INVENTED.
THAT'S HOW YOU KNOW IT'S THE GOOD STUFF. IF YOU TELL EVERYONE YOUR JEWELRY'S CURSED, THEY'LL BE TOO SCARED TO STEAL IT.
BUT I'M NOT.
THESE THINGS SOUND DODGY AS HELL. STILL, MONEY'S MONEY.
YOU WRITE YOUR DISSERTATION, THE UNIVERSITY SHELLS OUT, EVERYONE GOES HOME HAPPY.
DEAL!
I HAVE SO MUCH TO TELL YOU, DOCTOR APHRA...
YOU THREE HAMMER OUT THE DETAILS.
SEE YOU IN THE MORNING-- I'M OFF TO FIND SOMEONE PRETTY TO CELEBRATE WITH.
THERE'S ONLY ONE OTHER ACADEMIC WHO'S WRITTEN ABOUT THE RINGS.
SHE'S BRILLIANT. A VISIONARY.
EVEN IF THE UNIVERSITY DOESN'T THINK SO.
DOCTOR EUSTACIA OKKA.
SURELY YOU'VE HEARD OF HER?
EUSTACIA?
YEAH...

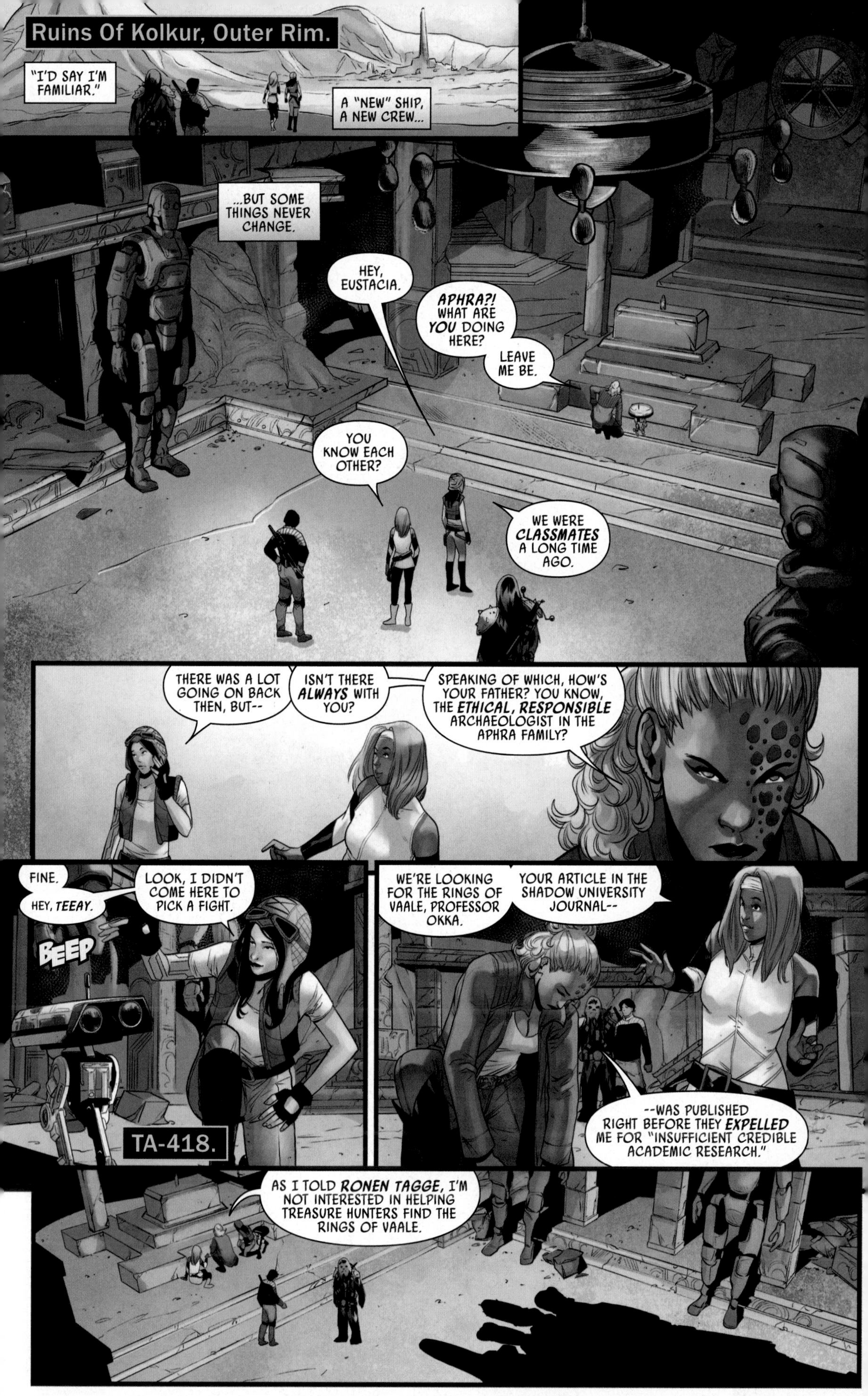

Ruins Of Kolkur, Outer Rim.
"I'D SAY I'M FAMILIAR."
A "NEW" SHIP, A NEW CREW...
...BUT SOME THINGS NEVER CHANGE.
HEY, EUSTACIA.
APHRA?! WHAT ARE YOU DOING HERE?
LEAVE ME BE.
YOU KNOW EACH OTHER?
WE WERE CLASSMATES A LONG TIME AGO.
THERE WAS A LOT GOING ON BACK THEN, BUT--
ISN'T THERE ALWAYS WITH YOU?
SPEAKING OF WHICH, HOW'S YOUR FATHER? YOU KNOW, THE ETHICAL, RESPONSIBLE ARCHAEOLOGIST IN THE APHRA FAMILY?
FINE.
HEY, TEEAY.
LOOK, I DIDN'T COME HERE TO PICK A FIGHT.
BEEP
TA-418.
WE'RE LOOKING FOR THE RINGS OF VAALE, PROFESSOR OKKA.
YOUR ARTICLE IN THE SHADOW UNIVERSITY JOURNAL--
--WAS PUBLISHED RIGHT BEFORE THEY EXPELLED ME FOR "INSUFFICIENT CREDIBLE ACADEMIC RESEARCH."
AS I TOLD RONEN TAGGE, I'M NOT INTERESTED IN HELPING TREASURE HUNTERS FIND THE RINGS OF VAALE.

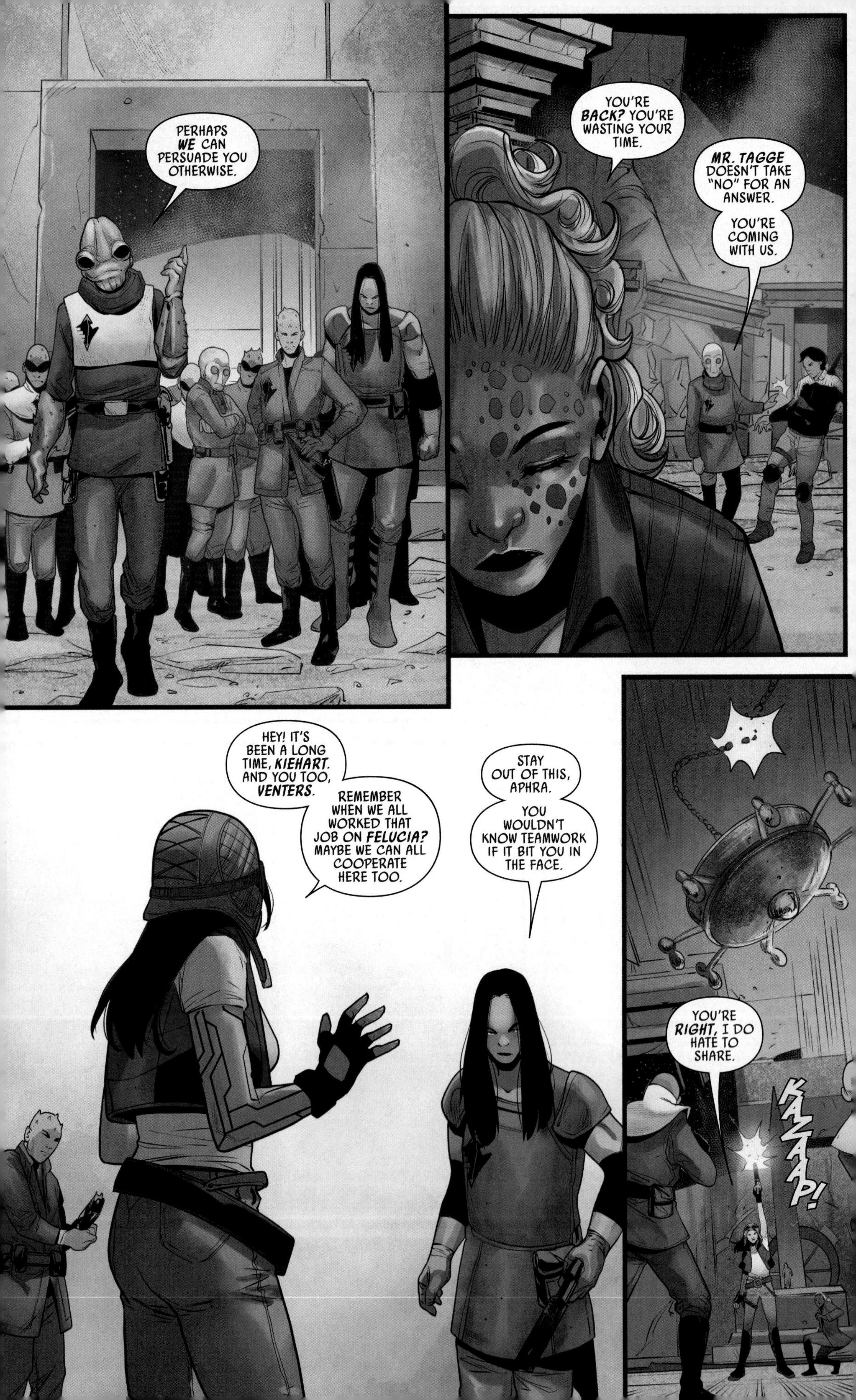
PERHAPS WE CAN PERSUADE YOU OTHERWISE.
YOU'RE BACK? YOU'RE WASTING YOUR TIME.
MR. TAGGE DOESN'T TAKE "NO" FOR AN ANSWER.
YOU'RE COMING WITH US.
HEY! IT'S BEEN A LONG TIME, KIEHART. AND YOU TOO, VENTERS.
REMEMBER WHEN WE ALL WORKED THAT JOB ON FELUCIA? MAYBE WE CAN ALL COOPERATE HERE TOO.
STAY OUT OF THIS, APHRA.
YOU WOULDN'T KNOW TEAMWORK IF IT BIT YOU IN THE FACE.
YOU'RE RIGHT, I DO HATE TO SHARE.
KAZAAP!

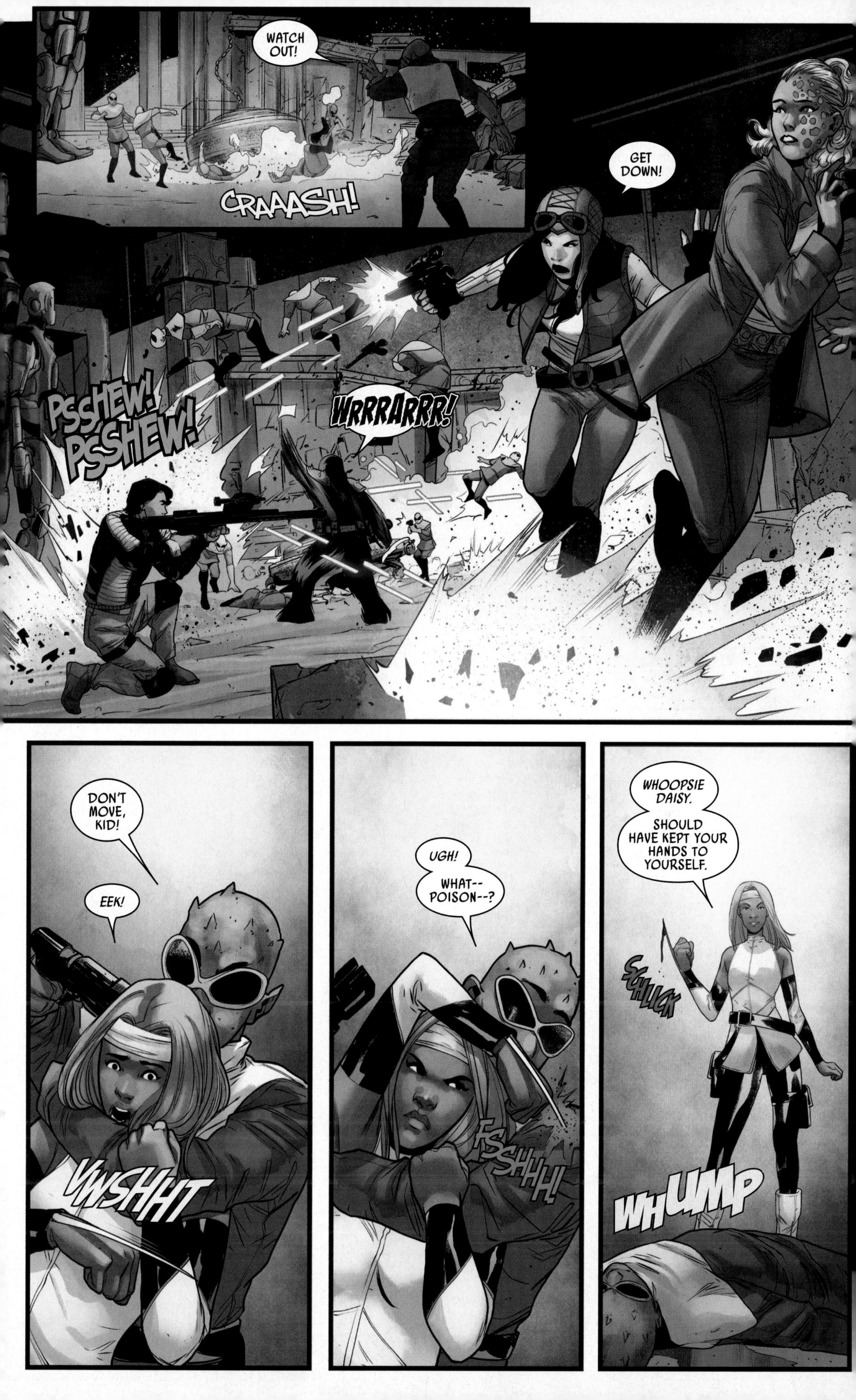
WATCH OUT!
CRAAASH!
GET DOWN!
PSSHEW! PSSHEW!
WRRRARRR!
DON'T MOVE, KID!
EEK!
VWSHHT
UGH!
WHAT-- POISON--?
FSSHHH!
WHOOPSIE DAISY.
SHOULD HAVE KEPT YOUR HANDS TO YOURSELF.
SCHLICK
WHUMP

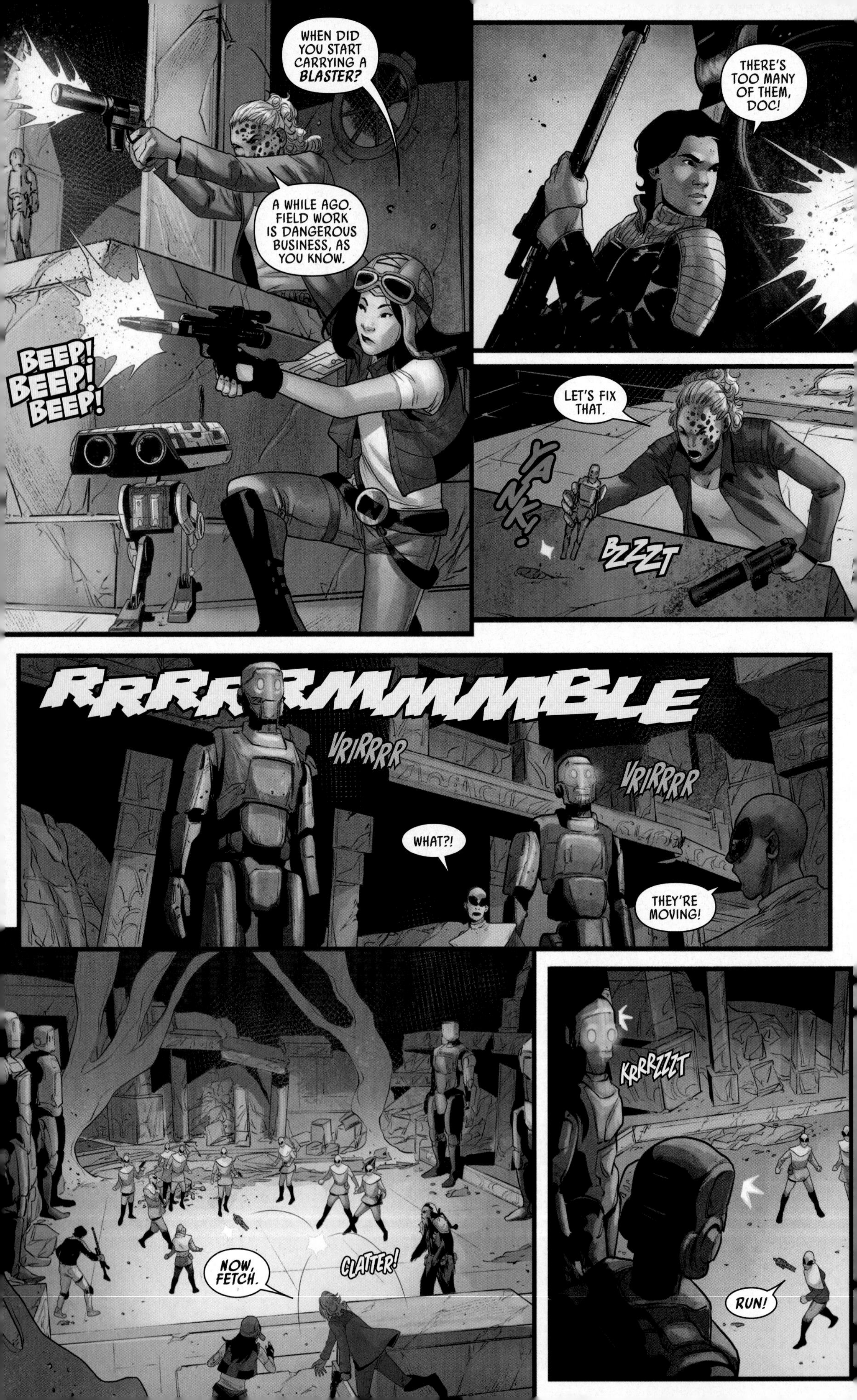

WHEN DID YOU START CARRYING A BLASTER?
A WHILE AGO. FIELD WORK IS DANGEROUS BUSINESS, AS YOU KNOW.
BEEP! BEEP! BEEP!
THERE'S TOO MANY OF THEM, DOC!
LET'S FIX THAT.
YANK!
BZZZT
RRRRRMMMMBLE
VRIRRRR
VRIRRRR
WHAT?!
THEY'RE MOVING!
NOW, FETCH.
CLATTER!
KRRRZZZT
RUN!

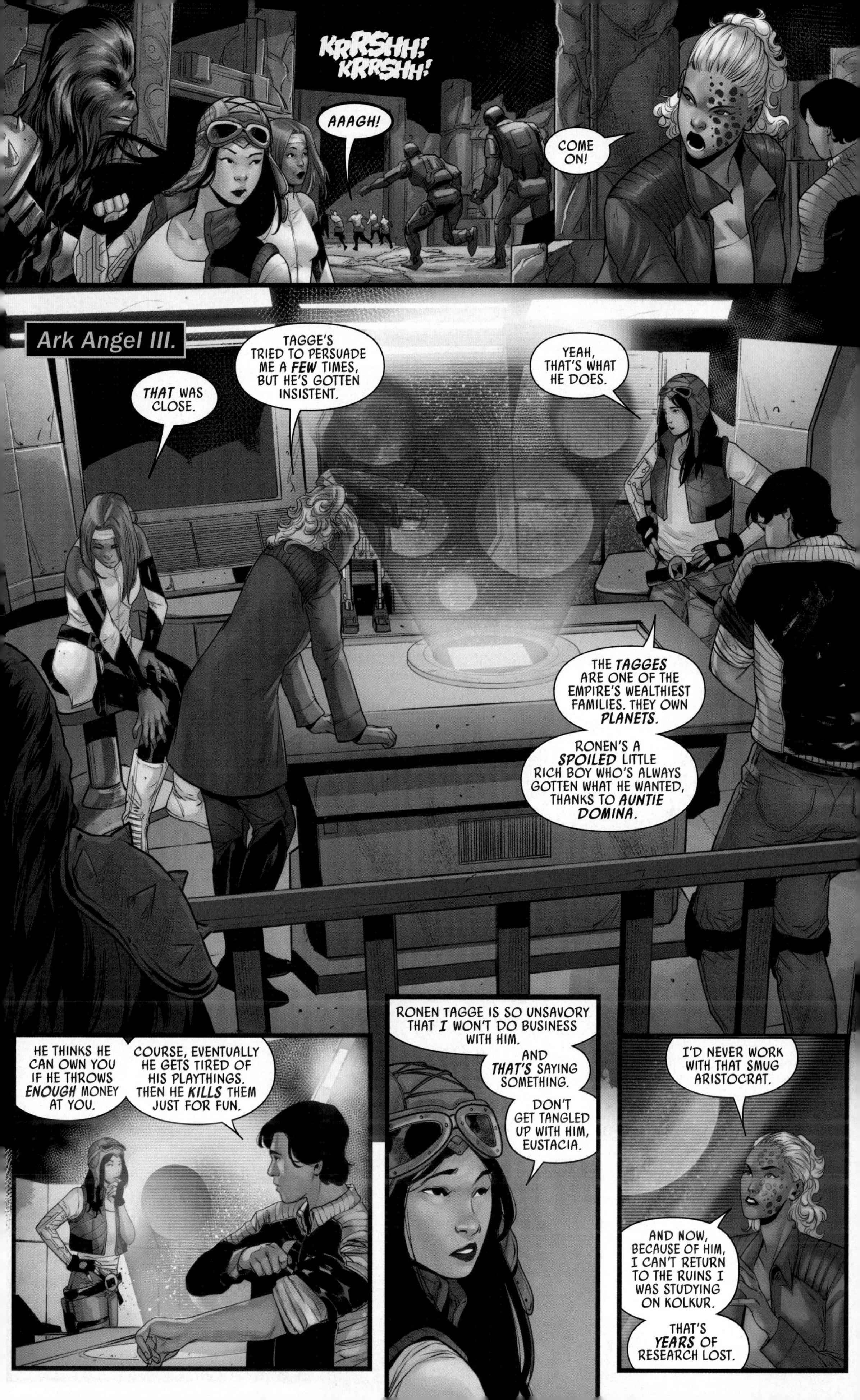

KRRSHH! KRRSHH!
AAAGH!
COME ON!
Ark Angel III.
THAT WAS CLOSE.
TAGGE'S TRIED TO PERSUADE ME A FEW TIMES, BUT HE'S GOTTEN INSISTENT.
YEAH, THAT'S WHAT HE DOES.
THE TAGGES ARE ONE OF THE EMPIRE'S WEALTHIEST FAMILIES. THEY OWN PLANETS.
RONEN'S A SPOILED LITTLE RICH BOY WHO'S ALWAYS GOTTEN WHAT HE WANTED, THANKS TO AUNTIE DOMINA.
HE THINKS HE CAN OWN YOU IF HE THROWS ENOUGH MONEY AT YOU.
COURSE, EVENTUALLY HE GETS TIRED OF HIS PLAYTHINGS. THEN HE KILLS THEM JUST FOR FUN.
RONEN TAGGE IS SO UNSAVORY THAT I WON'T DO BUSINESS WITH HIM.
AND THAT'S SAYING SOMETHING.
DON'T GET TANGLED UP WITH HIM, EUSTACIA.
I'D NEVER WORK WITH THAT SMUG ARISTOCRAT.
AND NOW, BECAUSE OF HIM, I CAN'T RETURN TO THE RUINS I WAS STUDYING ON KOLKUR.
THAT'S YEARS OF RESEARCH LOST.

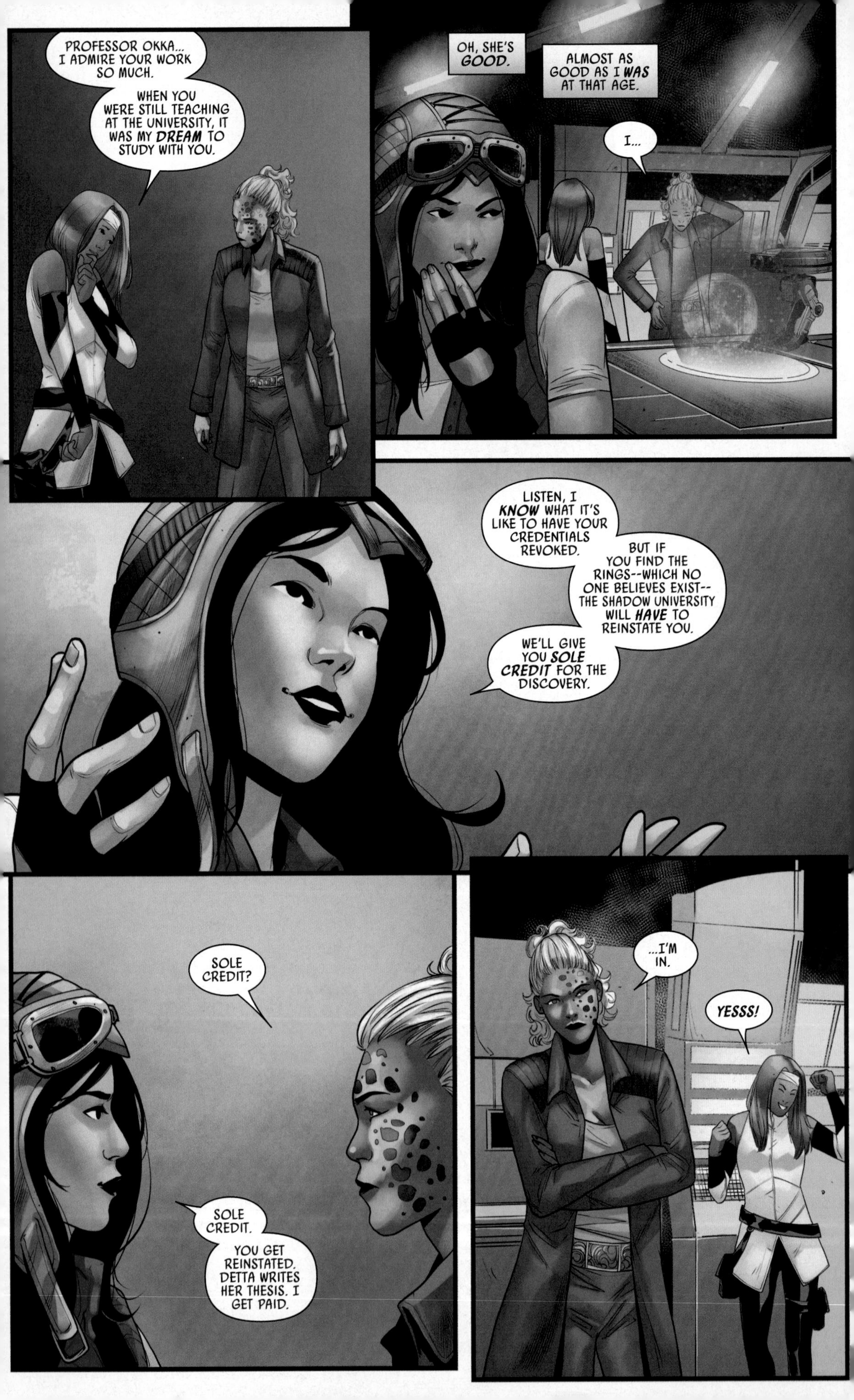
PROFESSOR OKKA... I ADMIRE YOUR WORK SO MUCH.
WHEN YOU WERE STILL TEACHING AT THE UNIVERSITY, IT WAS MY DREAM TO STUDY WITH YOU.
OH, SHE'S GOOD.
ALMOST AS GOOD AS I WAS AT THAT AGE.
I...
LISTEN, I KNOW WHAT IT'S LIKE TO HAVE YOUR CREDENTIALS REVOKED.
BUT IF YOU FIND THE RINGS--WHICH NO ONE BELIEVES EXIST--THE SHADOW UNIVERSITY WILL HAVE TO REINSTATE YOU.
WE'LL GIVE YOU SOLE CREDIT FOR THE DISCOVERY.
SOLE CREDIT?
SOLE CREDIT.
YOU GET REINSTATED. DETTA WRITES HER THESIS. I GET PAID.
...I'M IN.
YESSS!

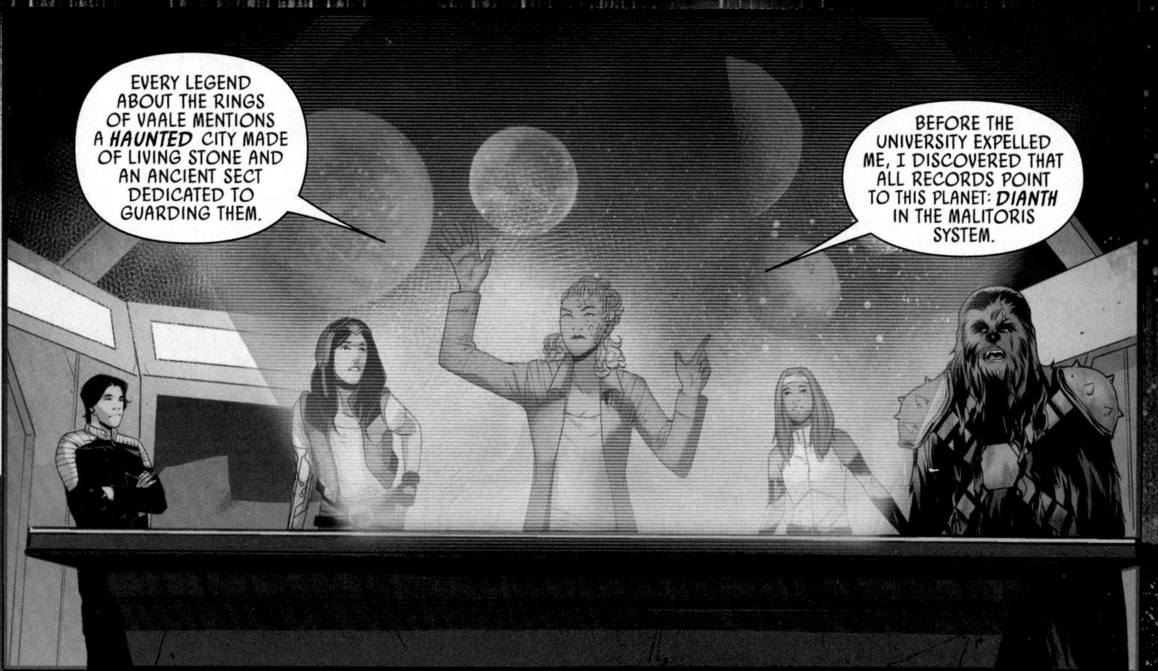
EVERY LEGEND ABOUT THE RINGS OF VAALE MENTIONS A HAUNTED CITY MADE OF LIVING STONE AND AN ANCIENT SECT DEDICATED TO GUARDING THEM.
BEFORE THE UNIVERSITY EXPELLED ME, I DISCOVERED THAT ALL RECORDS POINT TO THIS PLANET: DIANTH IN THE MALITORIS SYSTEM.

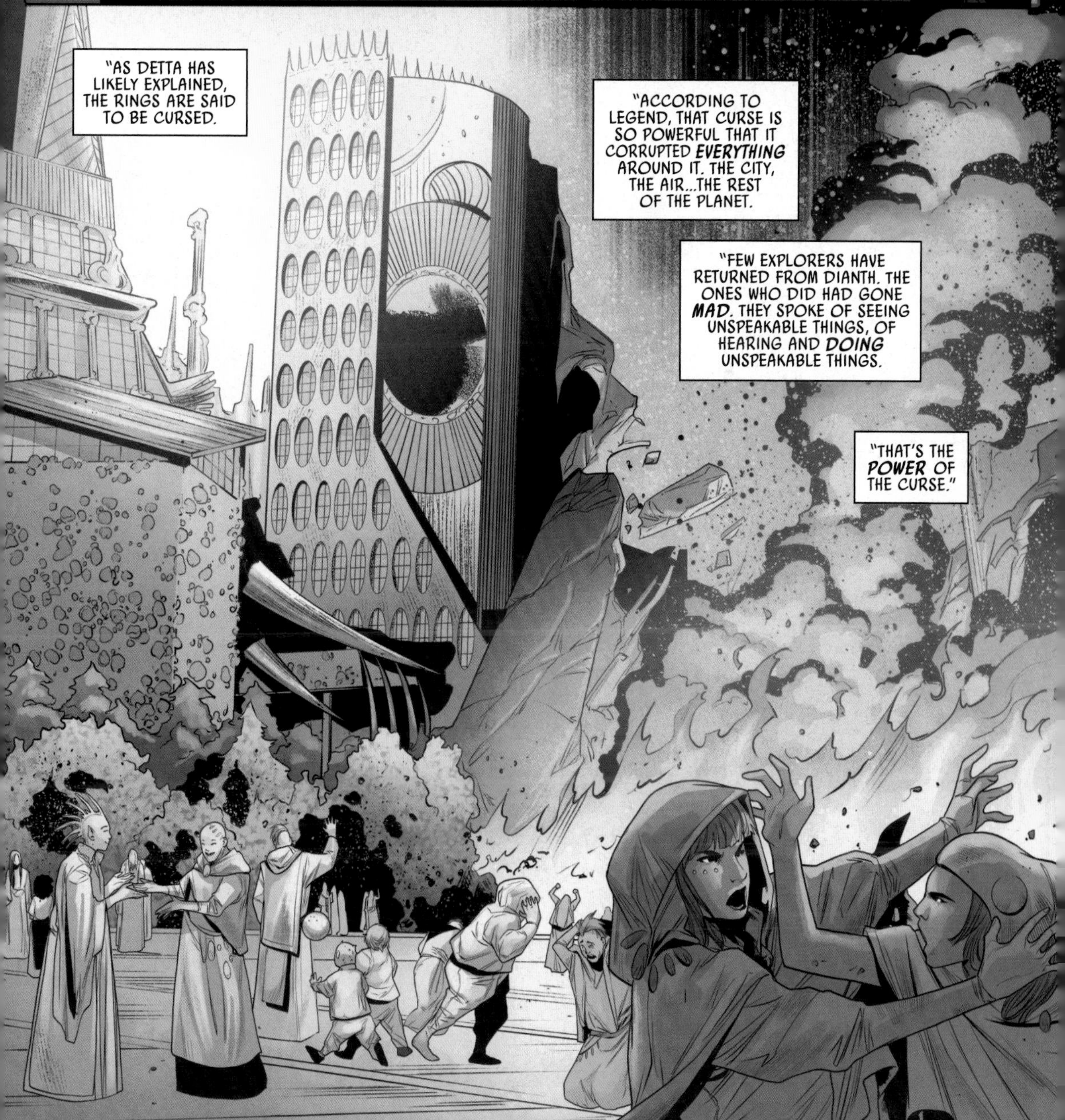
"AS DETTA HAS LIKELY EXPLAINED, THE RINGS ARE SAID TO BE CURSED.
"ACCORDING TO LEGEND, THAT CURSE IS SO POWERFUL THAT IT CORRUPTED EVERYTHING AROUND IT. THE CITY, THE AIR...THE REST OF THE PLANET.
"FEW EXPLORERS HAVE RETURNED FROM DIANTH. THE ONES WHO DID HAD GONE MAD. THEY SPOKE OF SEEING UNSPEAKABLE THINGS, OF HEARING AND DOING UNSPEAKABLE THINGS.
"THAT'S THE POWER OF THE CURSE."

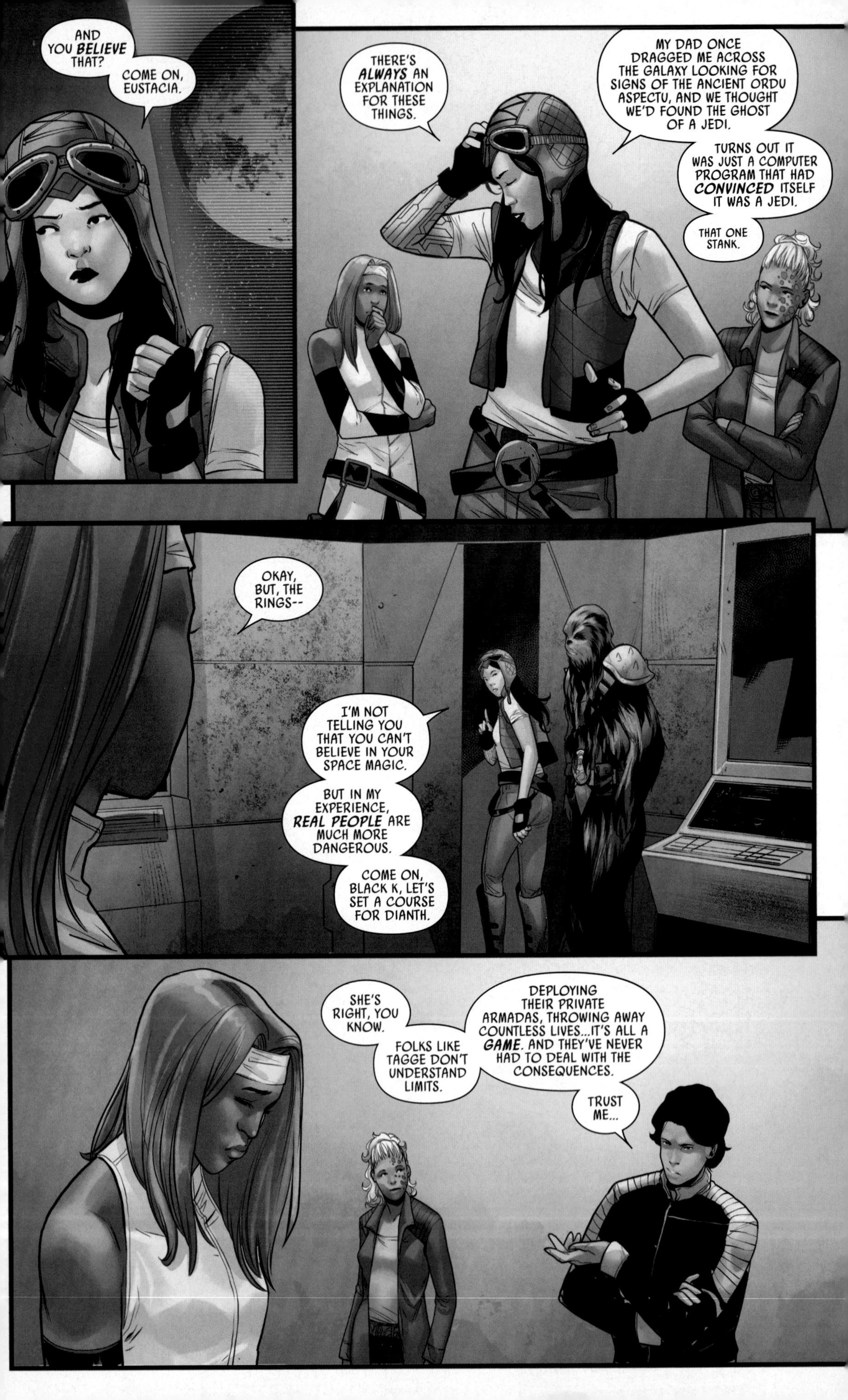
AND YOU *BELIEVE* THAT?
COME ON, EUSTACIA.
THERE'S *ALWAYS* AN EXPLANATION FOR THESE THINGS.
MY DAD ONCE DRAGGED ME ACROSS THE GALAXY LOOKING FOR SIGNS OF THE ANCIENT ORDU ASPECTU, AND WE THOUGHT WE'D FOUND THE GHOST OF A JEDI.
TURNS OUT IT WAS JUST A COMPUTER PROGRAM THAT HAD *CONVINCED* ITSELF IT WAS A JEDI.
THAT ONE STANK.
OKAY, BUT, THE RINGS--
I'M NOT TELLING YOU THAT YOU CAN'T BELIEVE IN YOUR SPACE MAGIC.
BUT IN MY EXPERIENCE, *REAL PEOPLE* ARE MUCH MORE DANGEROUS.
COME ON, BLACK K, LET'S SET A COURSE FOR DIANTH.
SHE'S RIGHT, YOU KNOW.
FOLKS LIKE TAGGE DON'T UNDERSTAND LIMITS.
DEPLOYING THEIR PRIVATE ARMADAS, THROWING AWAY COUNTLESS LIVES...IT'S ALL A *GAME*. AND THEY'VE NEVER HAD TO DEAL WITH THE CONSEQUENCES.
TRUST ME...

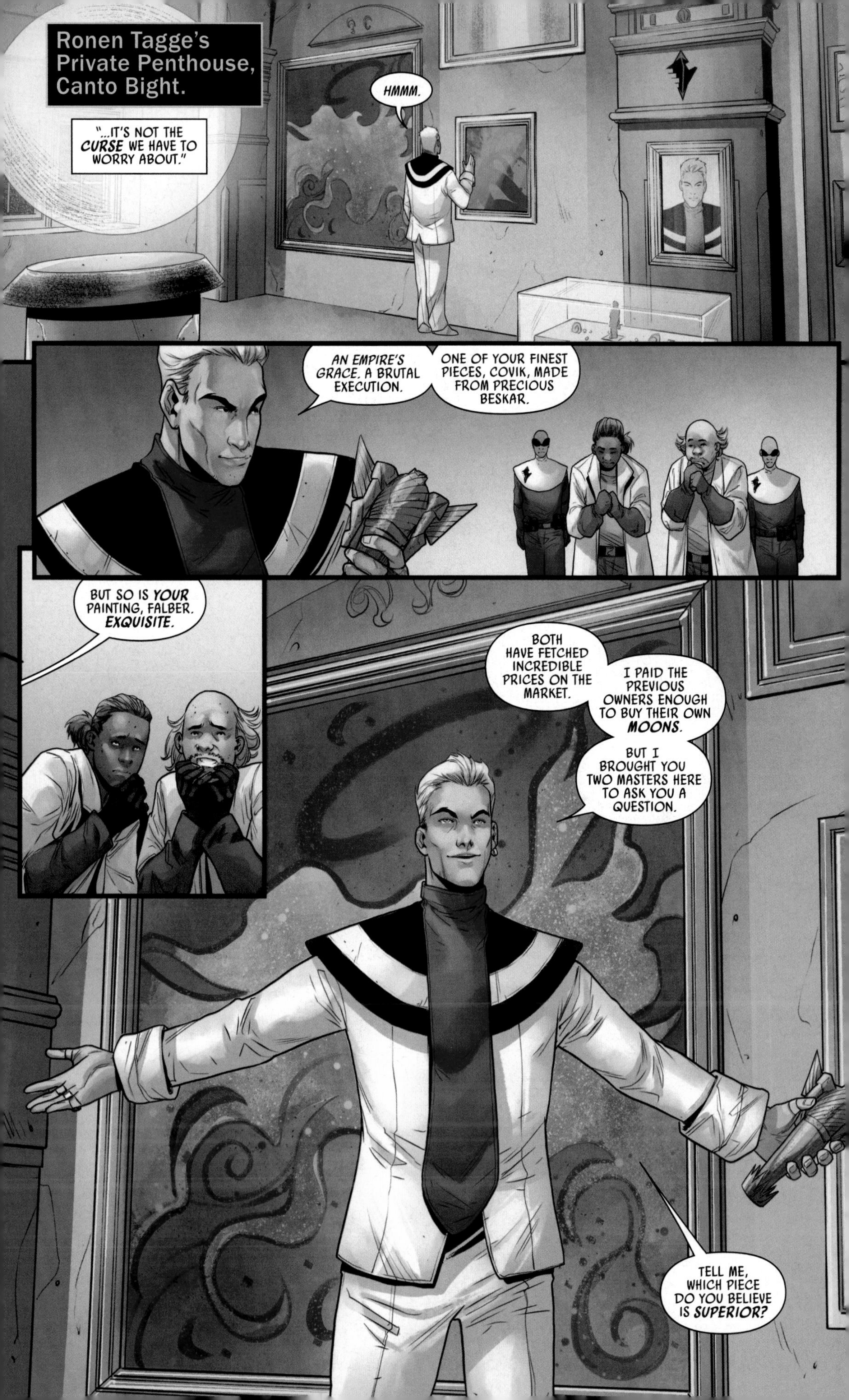
Ronen Tagge's Private Penthouse, Canto Bight.
"...IT'S NOT THE CURSE WE HAVE TO WORRY ABOUT."
HMMM.
AN EMPIRE'S GRACE. A BRUTAL EXECUTION.
ONE OF YOUR FINEST PIECES, COVIK, MADE FROM PRECIOUS BESKAR.
BUT SO IS YOUR PAINTING, FALBER. EXQUISITE.
BOTH HAVE FETCHED INCREDIBLE PRICES ON THE MARKET.
I PAID THE PREVIOUS OWNERS ENOUGH TO BUY THEIR OWN MOONS.
BUT I BROUGHT YOU TWO MASTERS HERE TO ASK YOU A QUESTION.
TELL ME, WHICH PIECE DO YOU BELIEVE IS SUPERIOR?

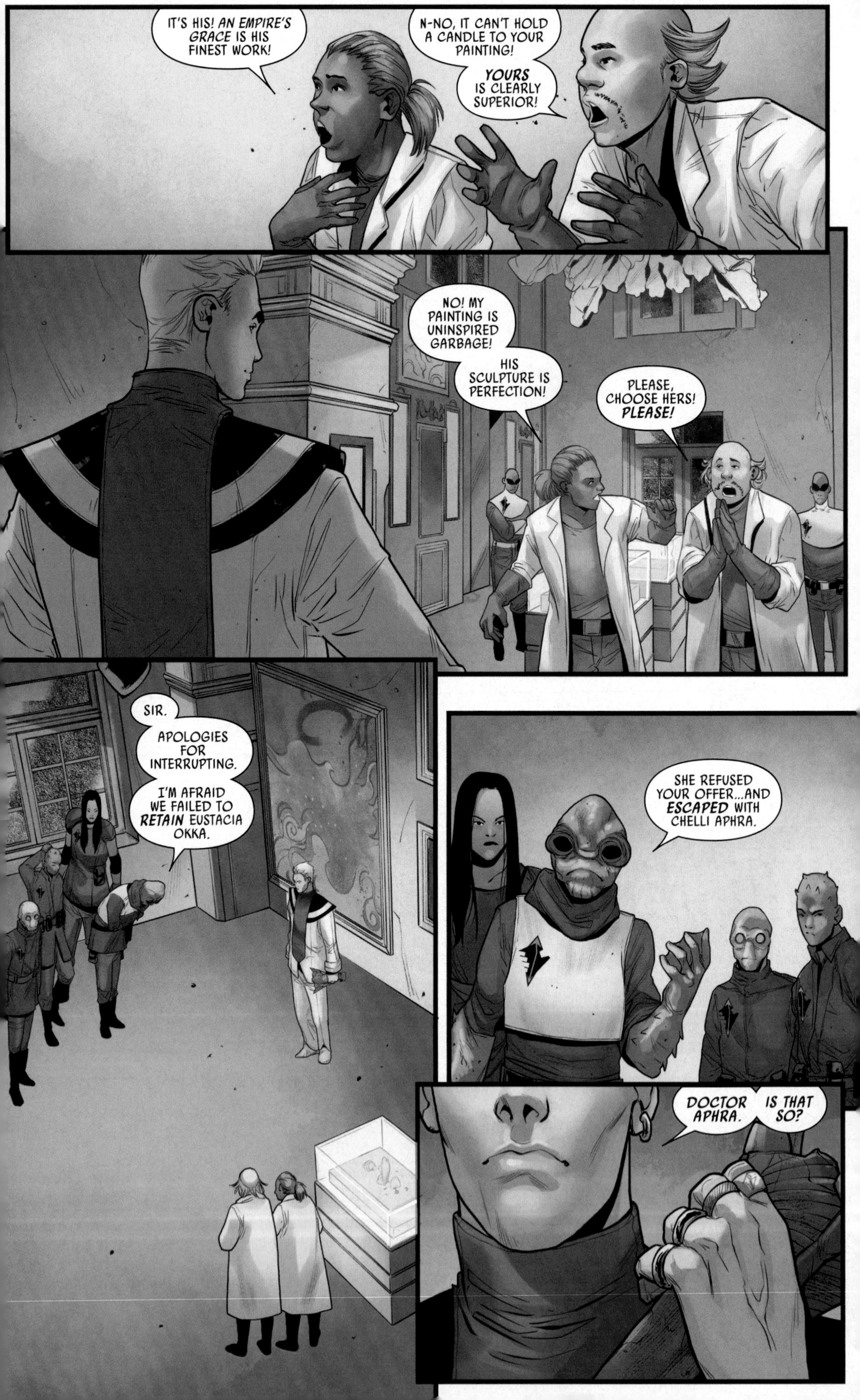
IT'S HIS! *AN EMPIRE'S GRACE* IS HIS FINEST WORK!
N-NO, IT CAN'T HOLD A CANDLE TO YOUR PAINTING!
YOURS IS CLEARLY SUPERIOR!
NO! MY PAINTING IS UNINSPIRED GARBAGE!
HIS SCULPTURE IS PERFECTION!
PLEASE, CHOOSE HERS! ***PLEASE!***
SIR.
APOLOGIES FOR INTERRUPTING.
I'M AFRAID WE FAILED TO ***RETAIN*** EUSTACIA OKKA.
SHE REFUSED YOUR OFFER...AND ***ESCAPED*** WITH CHELLI APHRA.
DOCTOR APHRA.
IS THAT SO?

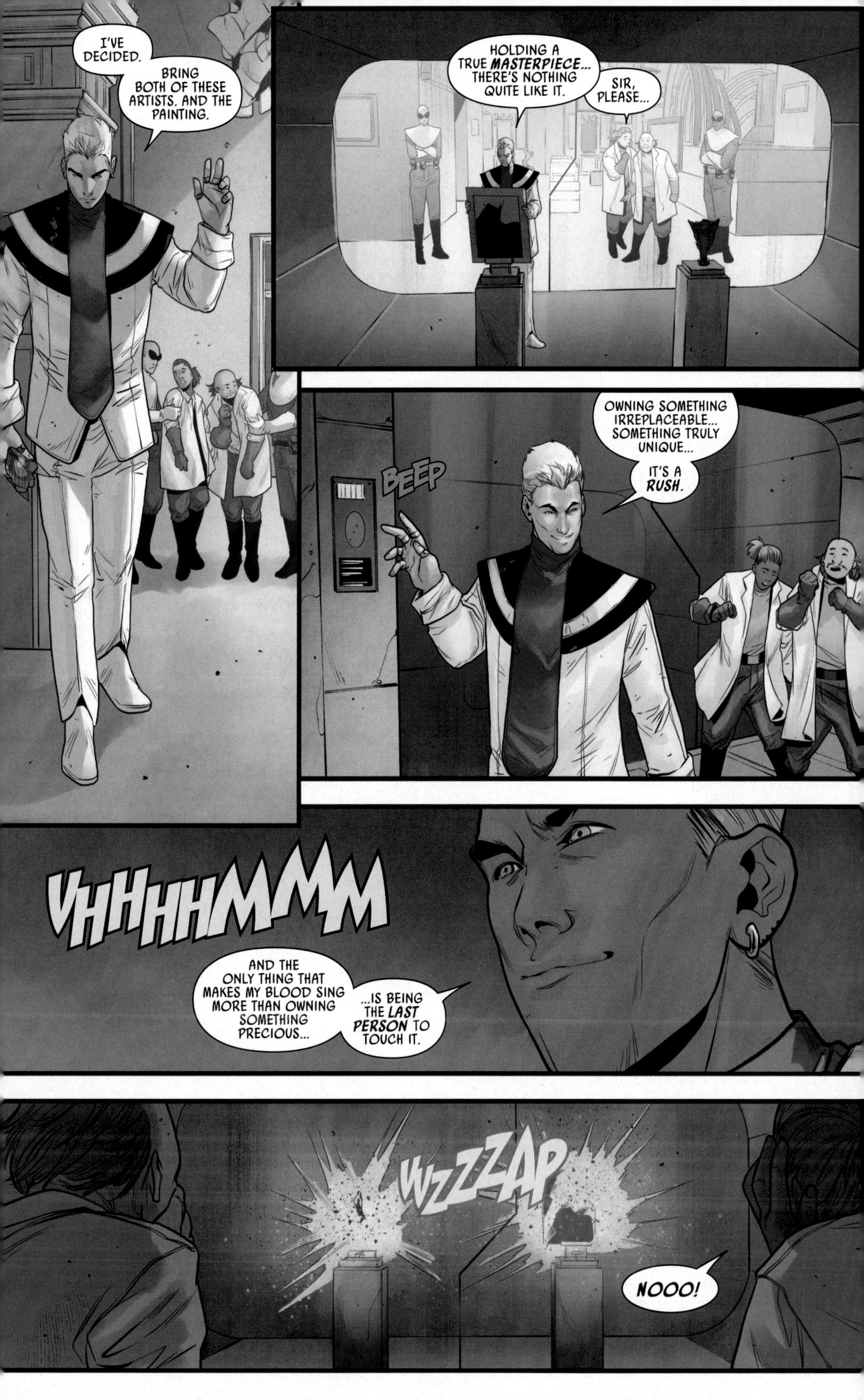
I'VE DECIDED.
BRING BOTH OF THESE ARTISTS. AND THE PAINTING.
HOLDING A TRUE MASTERPIECE... THERE'S NOTHING QUITE LIKE IT.
SIR, PLEASE...
OWNING SOMETHING IRREPLACEABLE... SOMETHING TRULY UNIQUE...
IT'S A RUSH.
BEEP
VHHHHMMMM
AND THE ONLY THING THAT MAKES MY BLOOD SING MORE THAN OWNING SOMETHING PRECIOUS...
...IS BEING THE LAST PERSON TO TOUCH IT.
VVZZZAP
NOOO!

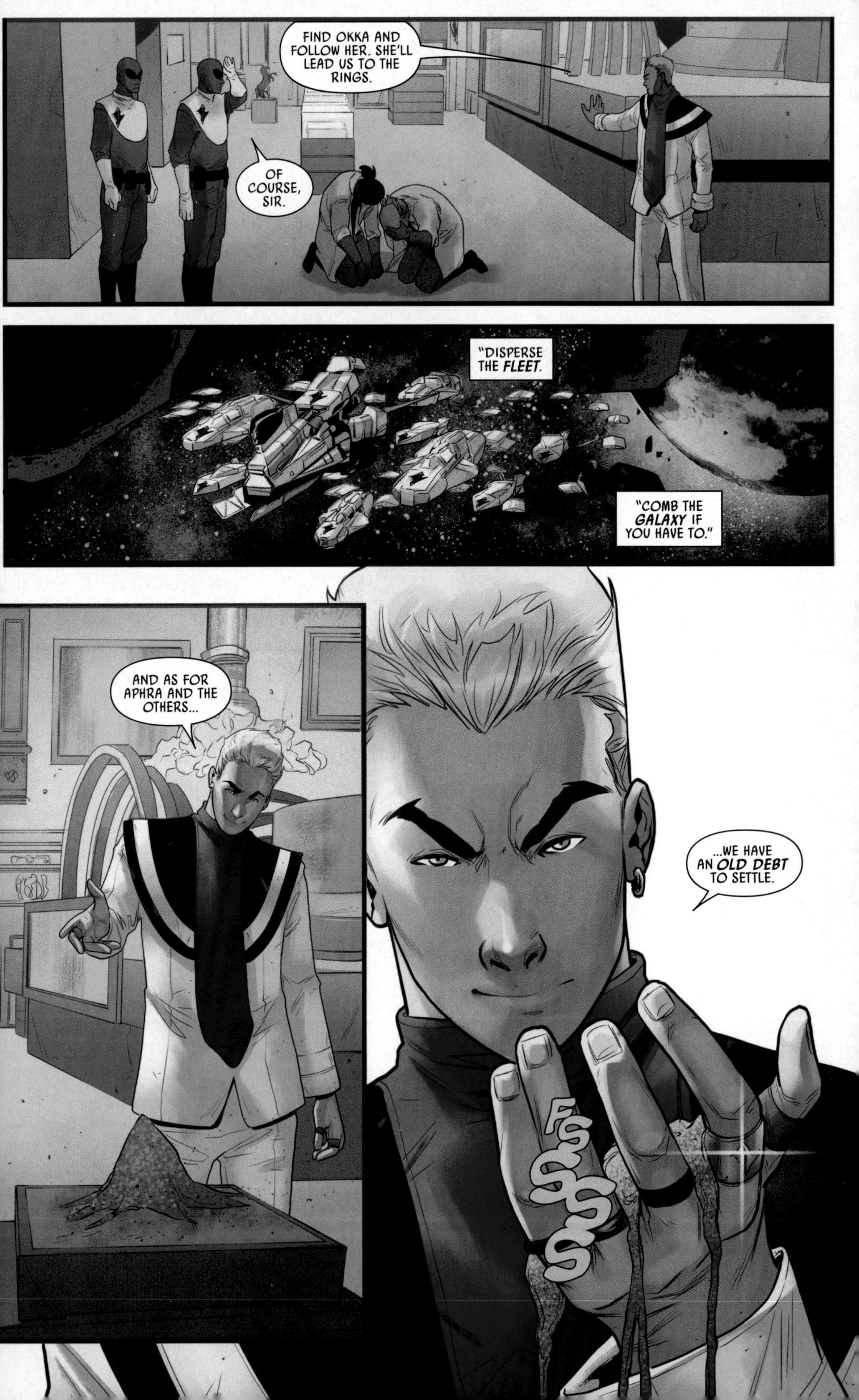
FIND OKKA AND FOLLOW HER. SHE'LL LEAD US TO THE RINGS.
OF COURSE, SIR.
"DISPERSE THE *FLEET*.
"COMB THE *GALAXY* IF YOU HAVE TO."
AND AS FOR APHRA AND THE OTHERS...
...WE HAVE AN *OLD DEBT* TO SETTLE.
FSSSS

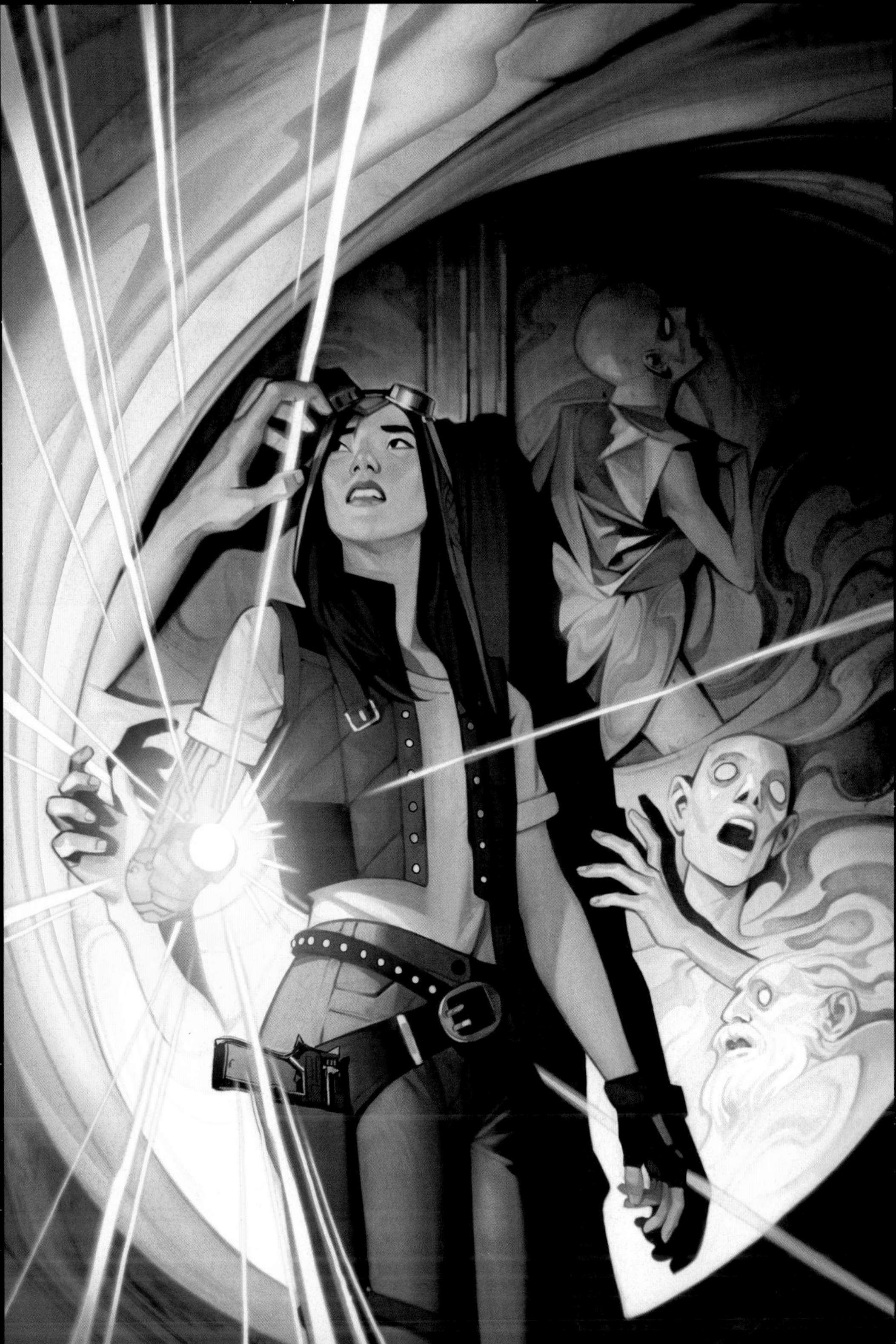

2 — HAUNTED

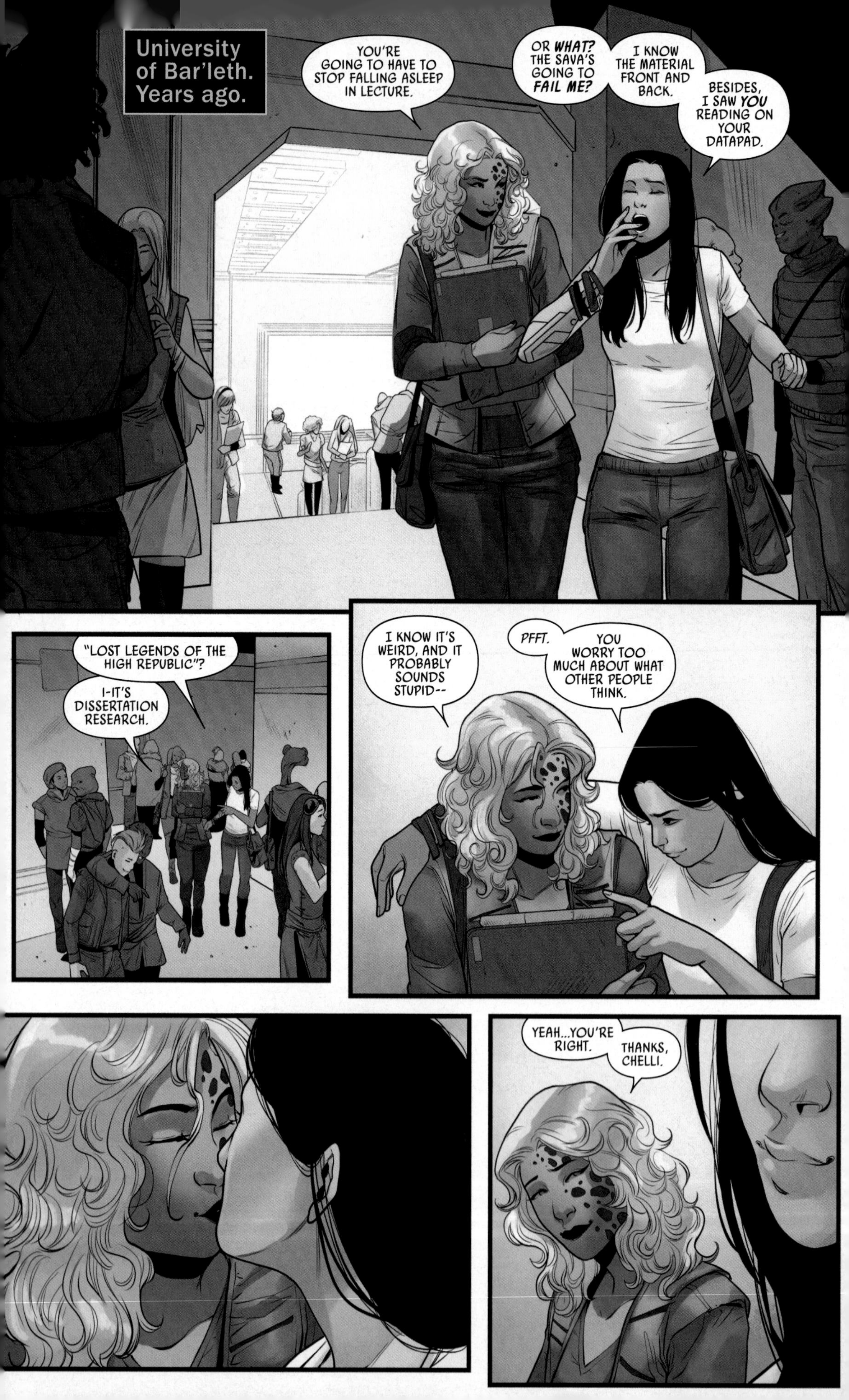
University of Bar'leth. Years ago.
YOU'RE GOING TO HAVE TO STOP FALLING ASLEEP IN LECTURE.
OR *WHAT?* THE SAVA'S GOING TO *FAIL ME?*
I KNOW THE MATERIAL FRONT AND BACK.
BESIDES, I SAW *YOU* READING ON YOUR DATAPAD.
"LOST LEGENDS OF THE HIGH REPUBLIC"?
I-IT'S DISSERTATION RESEARCH.
I KNOW IT'S WEIRD, AND IT PROBABLY SOUNDS STUPID--
PFFT.
YOU WORRY TOO MUCH ABOUT WHAT OTHER PEOPLE THINK.
YEAH...YOU'RE RIGHT.
THANKS, CHELLI.

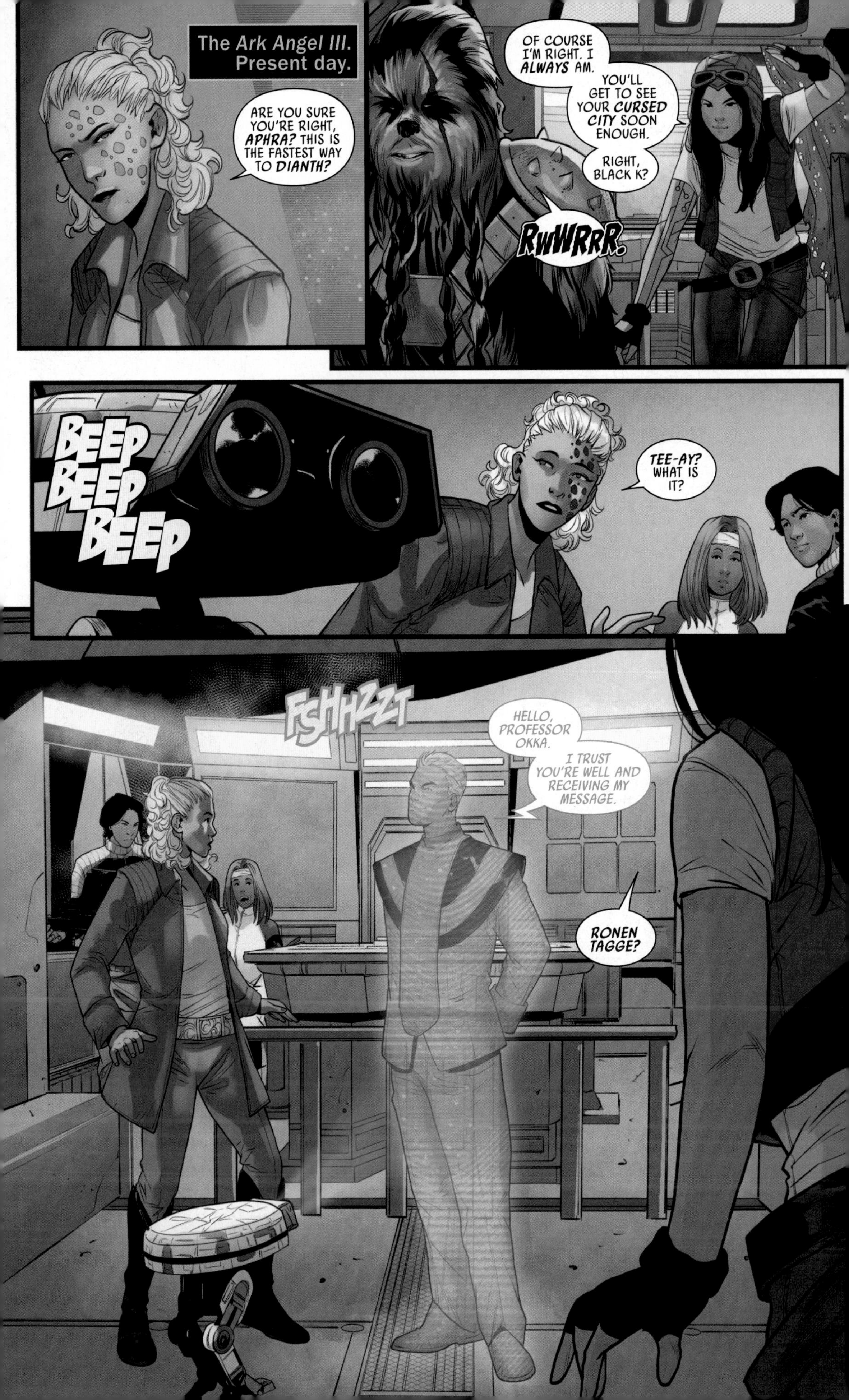

The *Ark Angel III*. Present day.
ARE YOU SURE YOU'RE RIGHT, **APHRA?** THIS IS THE FASTEST WAY TO **DIANTH?**
OF COURSE I'M RIGHT. I **ALWAYS** AM.
YOU'LL GET TO SEE YOUR **CURSED CITY** SOON ENOUGH.
RIGHT, BLACK K?
RWWRRR.
BEEP BEEP BEEP
TEE-AY? WHAT IS IT?
FSHHZZT
HELLO, PROFESSOR OKKA.
I TRUST YOU'RE WELL AND RECEIVING MY MESSAGE.
RONEN TAGGE?

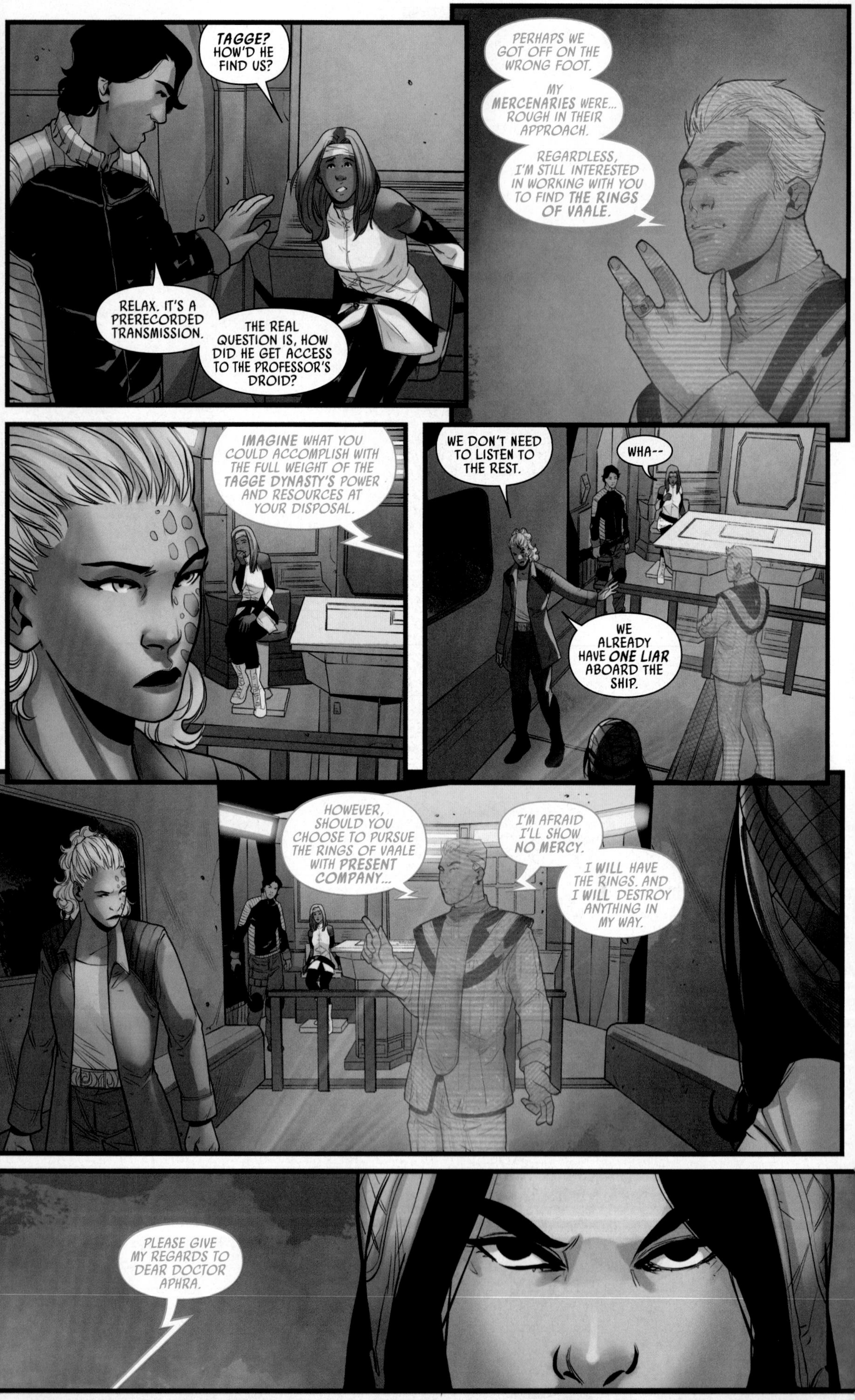
TAGGE? HOW'D HE FIND US?
RELAX. IT'S A PRERECORDED TRANSMISSION.
THE REAL QUESTION IS, HOW DID HE GET ACCESS TO THE PROFESSOR'S DROID?
PERHAPS WE GOT OFF ON THE WRONG FOOT.
MY MERCENARIES WERE... ROUGH IN THEIR APPROACH.
REGARDLESS, I'M STILL INTERESTED IN WORKING WITH YOU TO FIND THE RINGS OF VAALE.
IMAGINE WHAT YOU COULD ACCOMPLISH WITH THE FULL WEIGHT OF THE TAGGE DYNASTY'S POWER AND RESOURCES AT YOUR DISPOSAL.
WE DON'T NEED TO LISTEN TO THE REST.
WHA--
WE ALREADY HAVE ONE LIAR ABOARD THE SHIP.
HOWEVER, SHOULD YOU CHOOSE TO PURSUE THE RINGS OF VAALE WITH PRESENT COMPANY...
I'M AFRAID I'LL SHOW NO MERCY.
I WILL HAVE THE RINGS. AND I WILL DESTROY ANYTHING IN MY WAY.
PLEASE GIVE MY REGARDS TO DEAR DOCTOR APHRA.

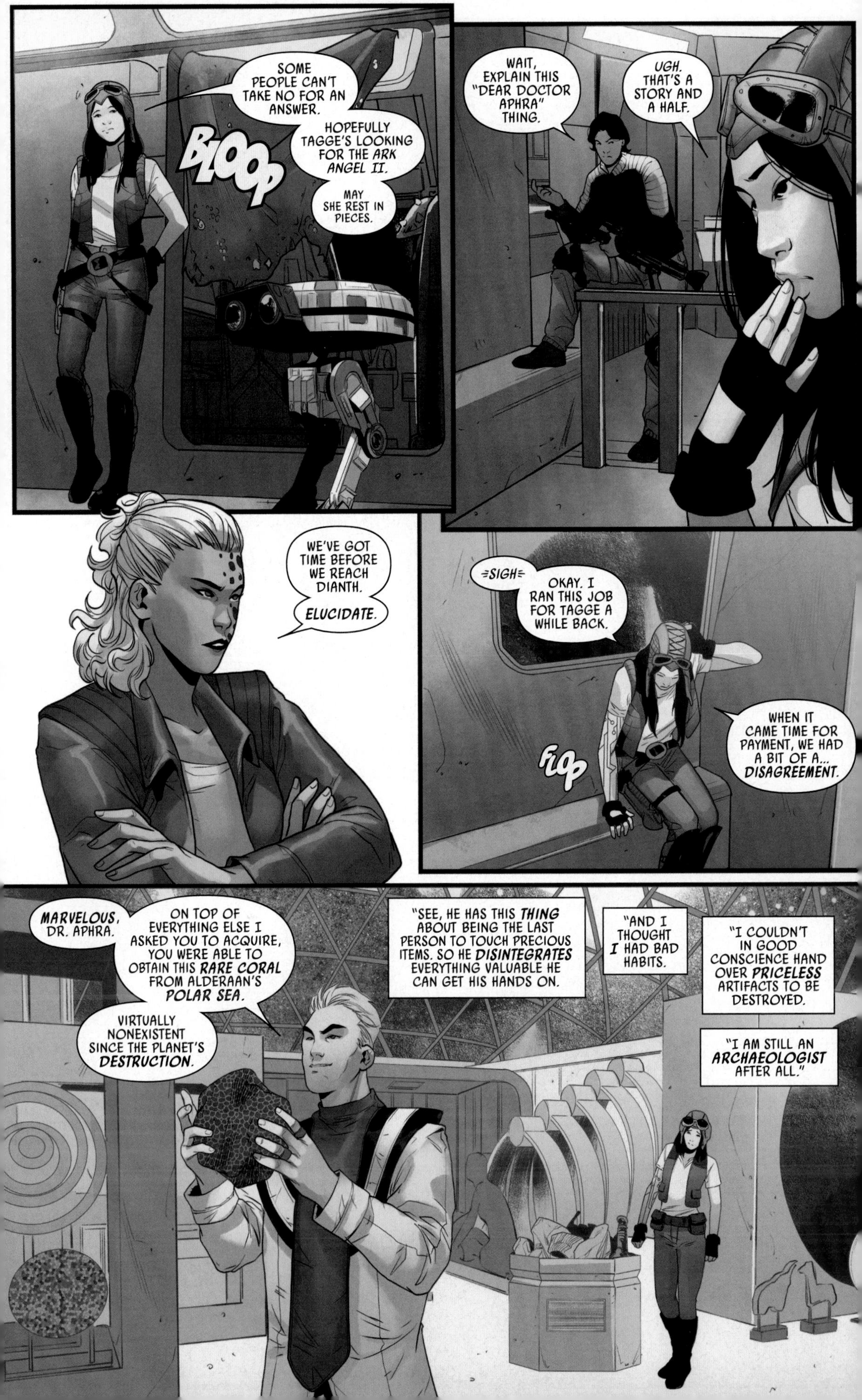
SOME PEOPLE CAN'T TAKE NO FOR AN ANSWER.
BLOOP
HOPEFULLY TAGGE'S LOOKING FOR THE ARK ANGEL II.
MAY SHE REST IN PIECES.
WAIT, EXPLAIN THIS "DEAR DOCTOR APHRA" THING.
UGH. THAT'S A STORY AND A HALF.
WE'VE GOT TIME BEFORE WE REACH DIANTH.
ELUCIDATE.
=SIGH=
OKAY. I RAN THIS JOB FOR TAGGE A WHILE BACK.
FLOP
WHEN IT CAME TIME FOR PAYMENT, WE HAD A BIT OF A... DISAGREEMENT.
MARVELOUS, DR. APHRA.
ON TOP OF EVERYTHING ELSE I ASKED YOU TO ACQUIRE, YOU WERE ABLE TO OBTAIN THIS RARE CORAL FROM ALDERAAN'S POLAR SEA.
VIRTUALLY NONEXISTENT SINCE THE PLANET'S DESTRUCTION.
"SEE, HE HAS THIS THING ABOUT BEING THE LAST PERSON TO TOUCH PRECIOUS ITEMS. SO HE DISINTEGRATES EVERYTHING VALUABLE HE CAN GET HIS HANDS ON.
"AND I THOUGHT I HAD BAD HABITS.
"I COULDN'T IN GOOD CONSCIENCE HAND OVER PRICELESS ARTIFACTS TO BE DESTROYED.
"I AM STILL AN ARCHAEOLOGIST AFTER ALL."

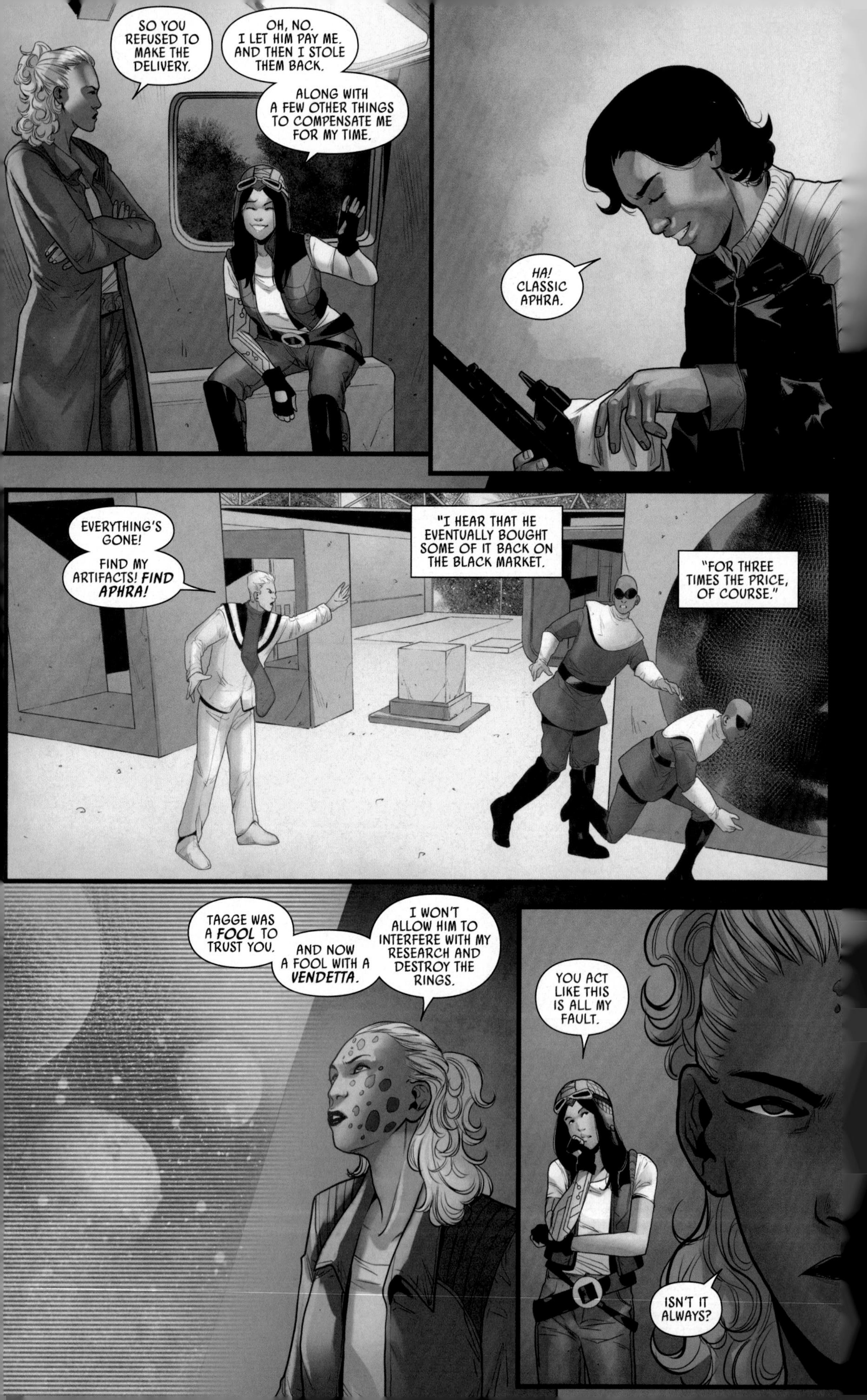
SO YOU REFUSED TO MAKE THE DELIVERY.
OH, NO. I LET HIM PAY ME. AND THEN I STOLE THEM BACK.
ALONG WITH A FEW OTHER THINGS TO COMPENSATE ME FOR MY TIME.
HA! CLASSIC APHRA.
EVERYTHING'S GONE!
FIND MY ARTIFACTS! FIND APHRA!
"I HEAR THAT HE EVENTUALLY BOUGHT SOME OF IT BACK ON THE BLACK MARKET.
"FOR THREE TIMES THE PRICE, OF COURSE."
TAGGE WAS A FOOL TO TRUST YOU.
AND NOW A FOOL WITH A VENDETTA.
I WON'T ALLOW HIM TO INTERFERE WITH MY RESEARCH AND DESTROY THE RINGS.
YOU ACT LIKE THIS IS ALL MY FAULT.
ISN'T IT ALWAYS?

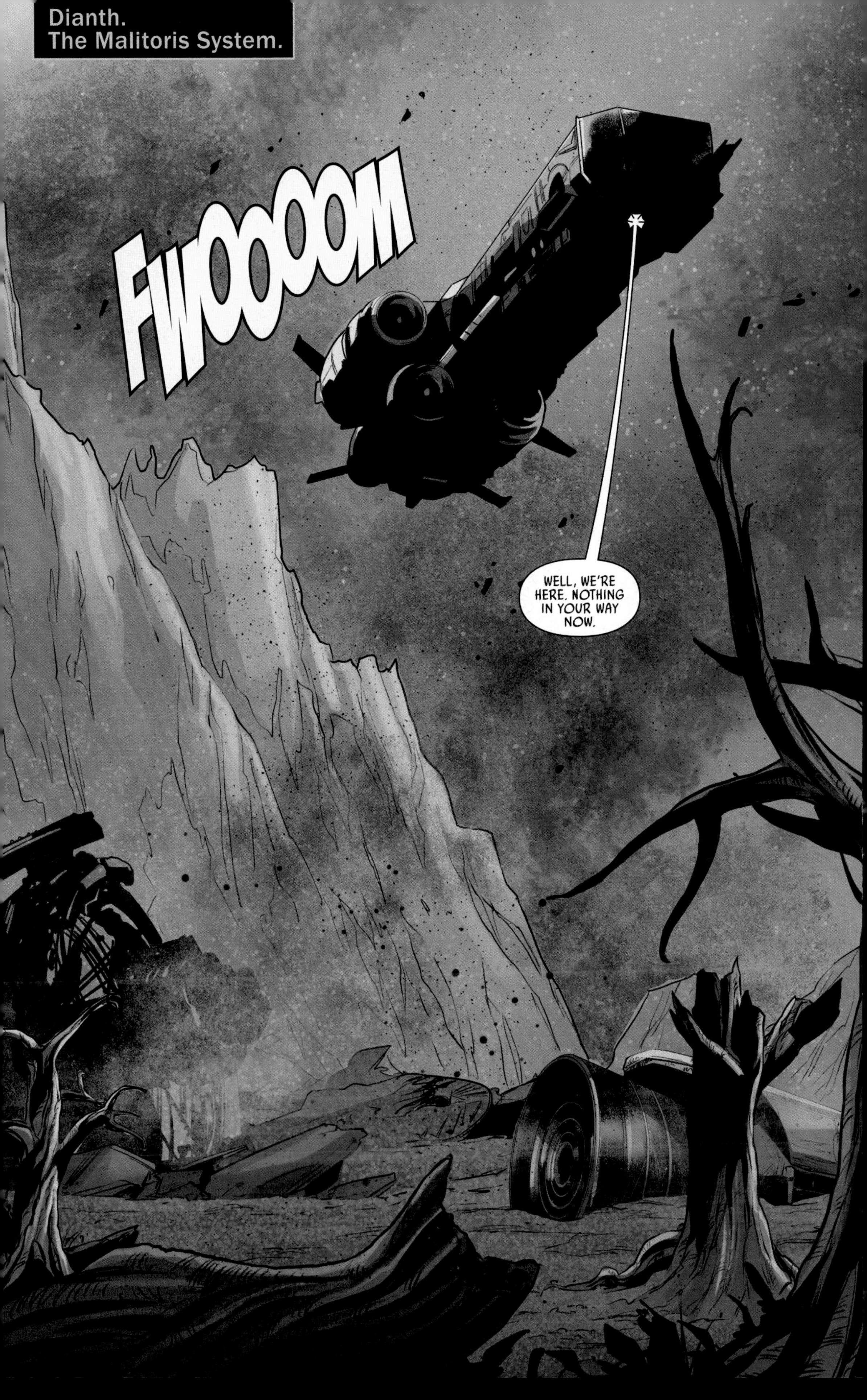
Dianth.
The Malitoris System.
FWOOOOM
WELL, WE'RE HERE. NOTHING IN YOUR WAY NOW.

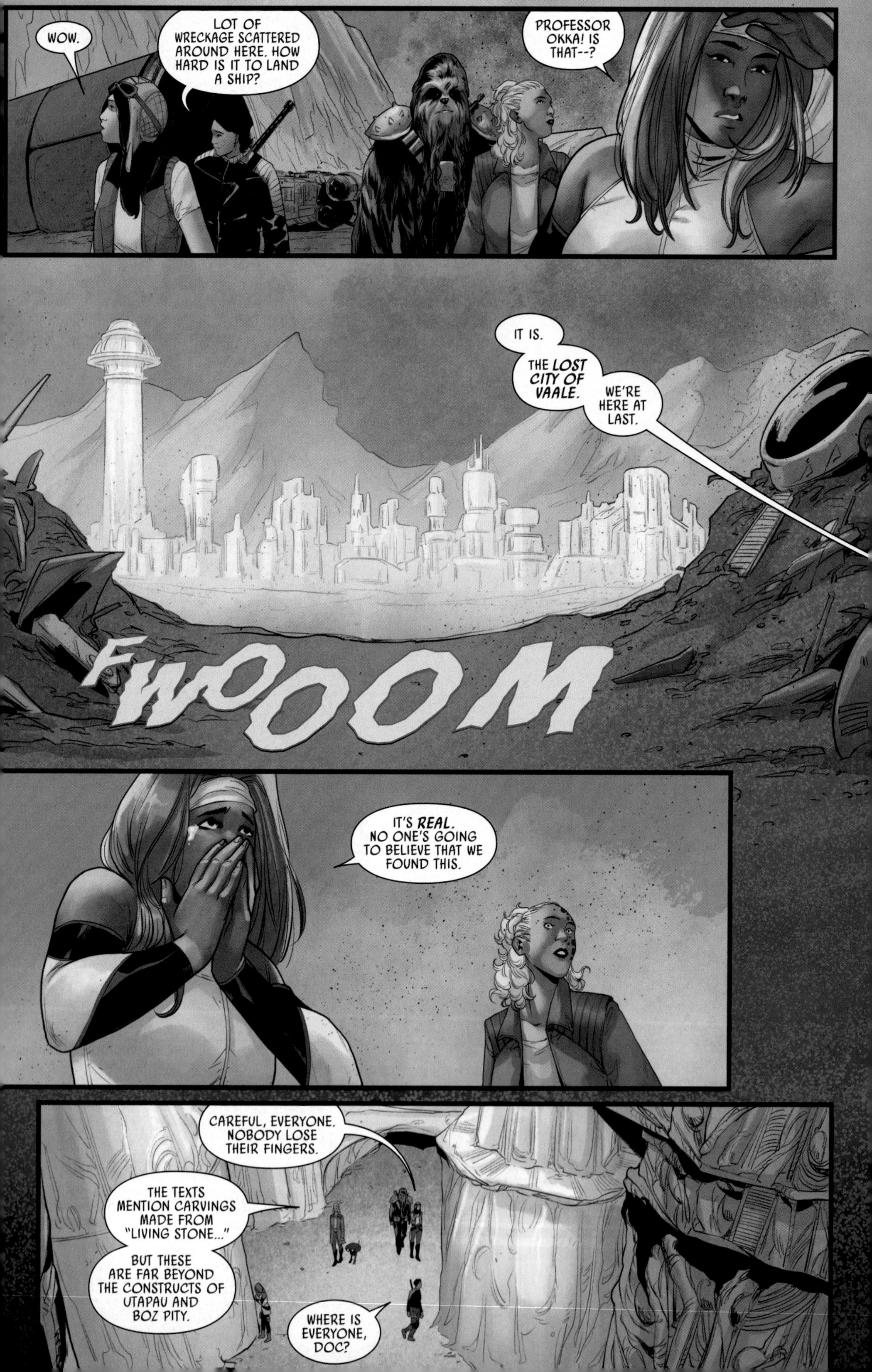

WOW.
LOT OF WRECKAGE SCATTERED AROUND HERE. HOW HARD IS IT TO LAND A SHIP?
PROFESSOR OKKA! IS THAT--?
IT IS.
THE LOST CITY OF VAALE.
WE'RE HERE AT LAST.
FWOOOM
IT'S REAL. NO ONE'S GOING TO BELIEVE THAT WE FOUND THIS.
CAREFUL, EVERYONE. NOBODY LOSE THEIR FINGERS.
THE TEXTS MENTION CARVINGS MADE FROM "LIVING STONE..."
BUT THESE ARE FAR BEYOND THE CONSTRUCTS OF UTAPAU AND BOZ PITY.
WHERE IS EVERYONE, DOC?

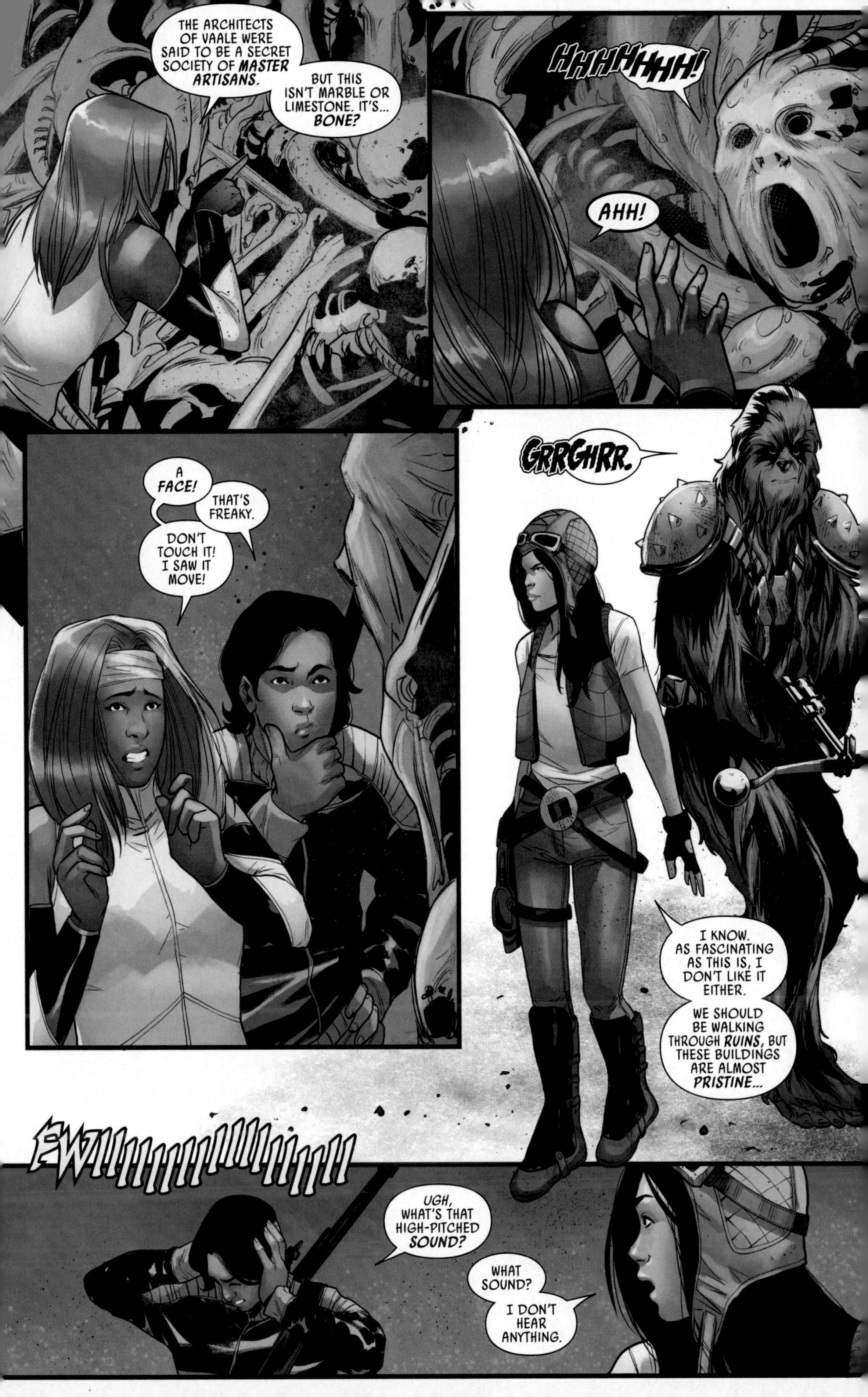
THE ARCHITECTS OF VAALE WERE SAID TO BE A SECRET SOCIETY OF MASTER ARTISANS.
BUT THIS ISN'T MARBLE OR LIMESTONE. IT'S... BONE?
HHHHHHHH!
AHH!
A FACE!
THAT'S FREAKY.
DON'T TOUCH IT! I SAW IT MOVE!
GRRGHRR.
I KNOW. AS FASCINATING AS THIS IS, I DON'T LIKE IT EITHER.
WE SHOULD BE WALKING THROUGH RUINS, BUT THESE BUILDINGS ARE ALMOST PRISTINE...
EWIIIIIIIIIIIIIIIIIIII
UGH, WHAT'S THAT HIGH-PITCHED SOUND?
WHAT SOUND?
I DON'T HEAR ANYTHING.

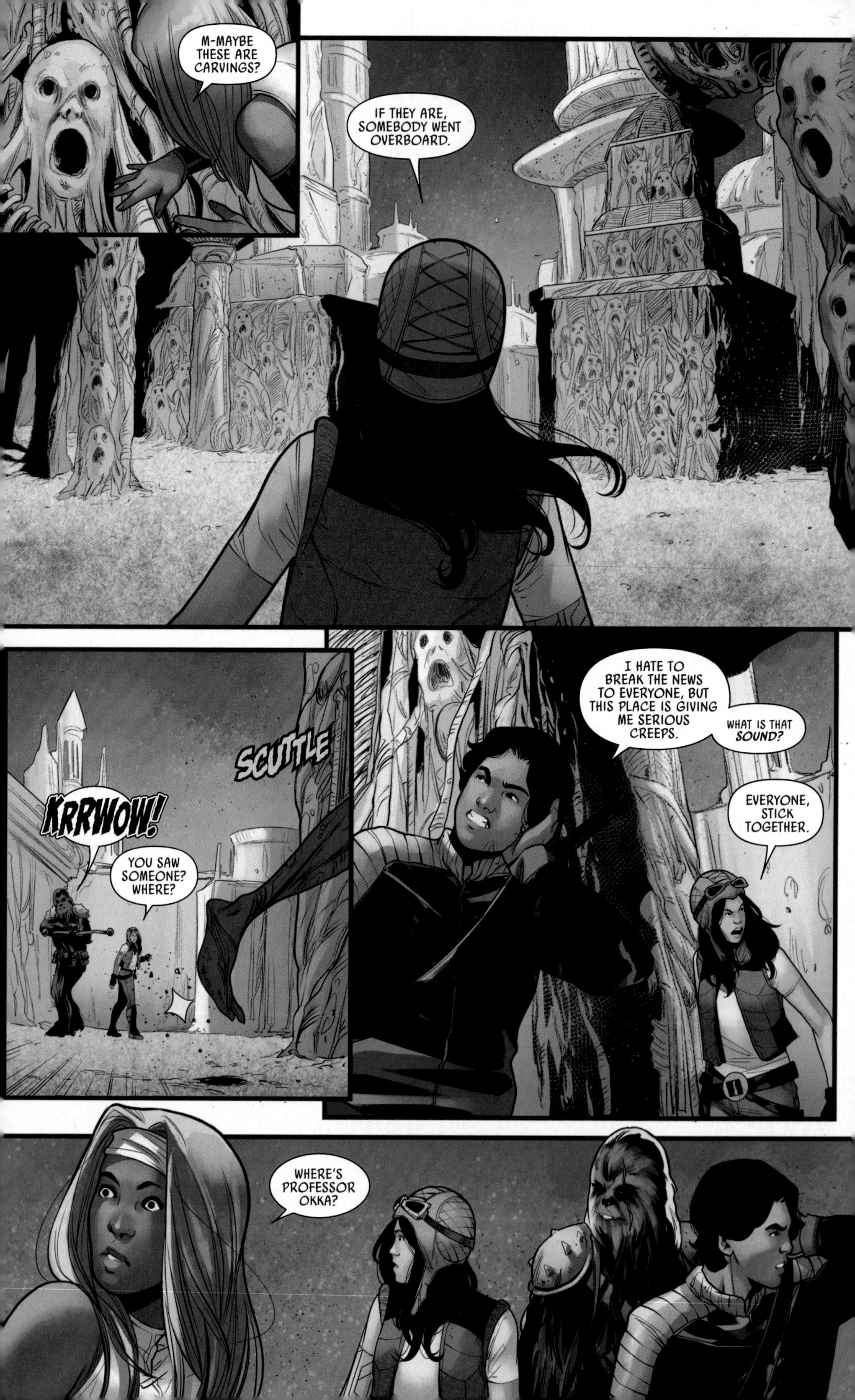
M-MAYBE THESE ARE CARVINGS?
IF THEY ARE, SOMEBODY WENT OVERBOARD.
KRRWOW!
YOU SAW SOMEONE? WHERE?
SCUTTLE
I HATE TO BREAK THE NEWS TO EVERYONE, BUT THIS PLACE IS GIVING ME SERIOUS CREEPS.
WHAT IS THAT SOUND?
EVERYONE, STICK TOGETHER.
WHERE'S PROFESSOR OKKA?

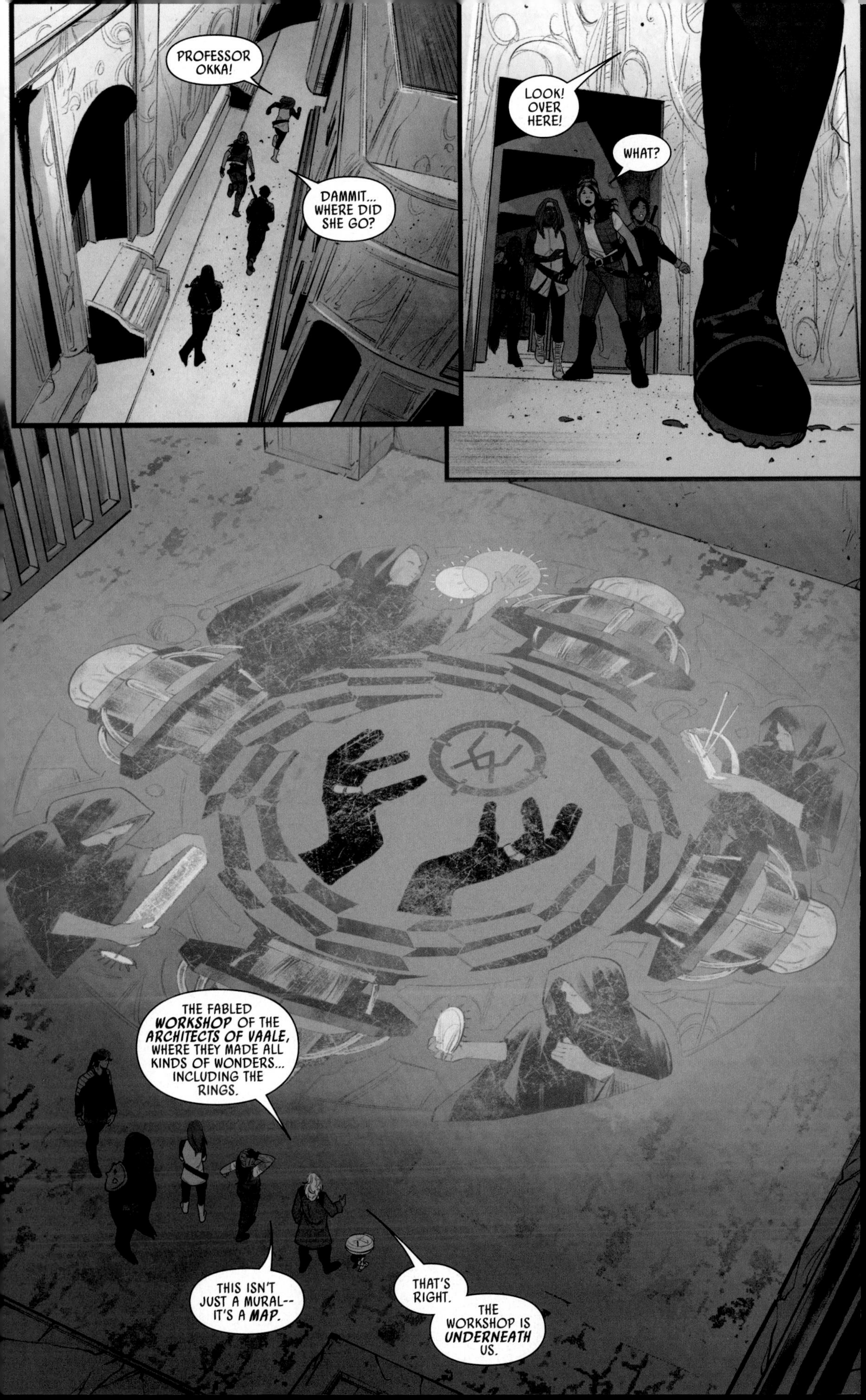
PROFESSOR OKKA!
DAMMIT... WHERE DID SHE GO?
LOOK! OVER HERE!
WHAT?
THE FABLED WORKSHOP OF THE ARCHITECTS OF VAALE, WHERE THEY MADE ALL KINDS OF WONDERS... INCLUDING THE RINGS.
THIS ISN'T JUST A MURAL-- IT'S A MAP.
THAT'S RIGHT.
THE WORKSHOP IS UNDERNEATH US.

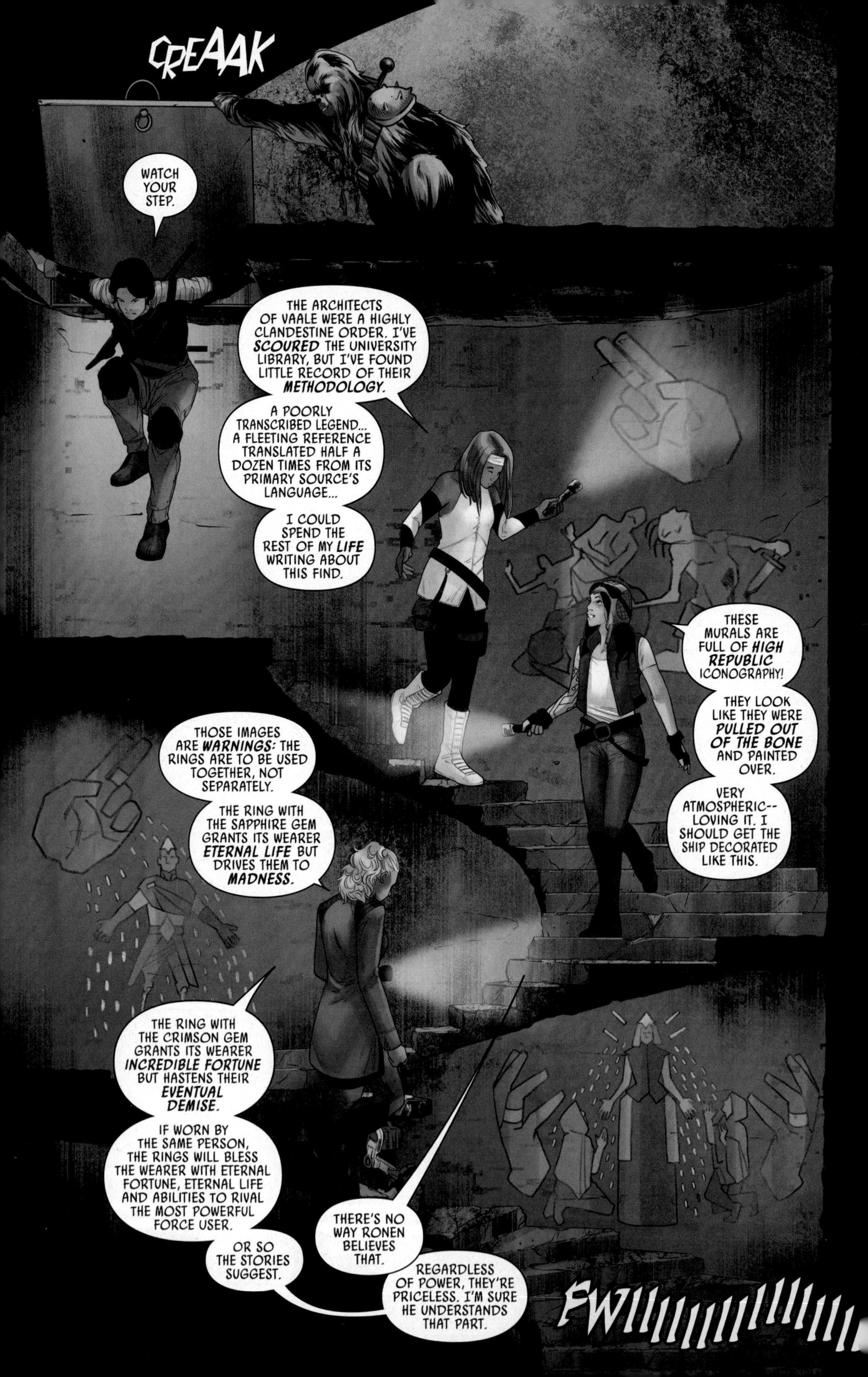
CREAAK
WATCH YOUR STEP.
THE ARCHITECTS OF VAALE WERE A HIGHLY CLANDESTINE ORDER. I'VE SCOURED THE UNIVERSITY LIBRARY, BUT I'VE FOUND LITTLE RECORD OF THEIR METHODOLOGY.
A POORLY TRANSCRIBED LEGEND... A FLEETING REFERENCE TRANSLATED HALF A DOZEN TIMES FROM ITS PRIMARY SOURCE'S LANGUAGE...
I COULD SPEND THE REST OF MY LIFE WRITING ABOUT THIS FIND.
THESE MURALS ARE FULL OF HIGH REPUBLIC ICONOGRAPHY!
THEY LOOK LIKE THEY WERE PULLED OUT OF THE BONE AND PAINTED OVER.
VERY ATMOSPHERIC--LOVING IT. I SHOULD GET THE SHIP DECORATED LIKE THIS.
THOSE IMAGES ARE WARNINGS: THE RINGS ARE TO BE USED TOGETHER, NOT SEPARATELY.
THE RING WITH THE SAPPHIRE GEM GRANTS ITS WEARER ETERNAL LIFE BUT DRIVES THEM TO MADNESS.
THE RING WITH THE CRIMSON GEM GRANTS ITS WEARER INCREDIBLE FORTUNE BUT HASTENS THEIR EVENTUAL DEMISE.
IF WORN BY THE SAME PERSON, THE RINGS WILL BLESS THE WEARER WITH ETERNAL FORTUNE, ETERNAL LIFE AND ABILITIES TO RIVAL THE MOST POWERFUL FORCE USER.
OR SO THE STORIES SUGGEST.
THERE'S NO WAY RONEN BELIEVES THAT.
REGARDLESS OF POWER, THEY'RE PRICELESS. I'M SURE HE UNDERSTANDS THAT PART.
FWIIIIIIIIIIIIIIII

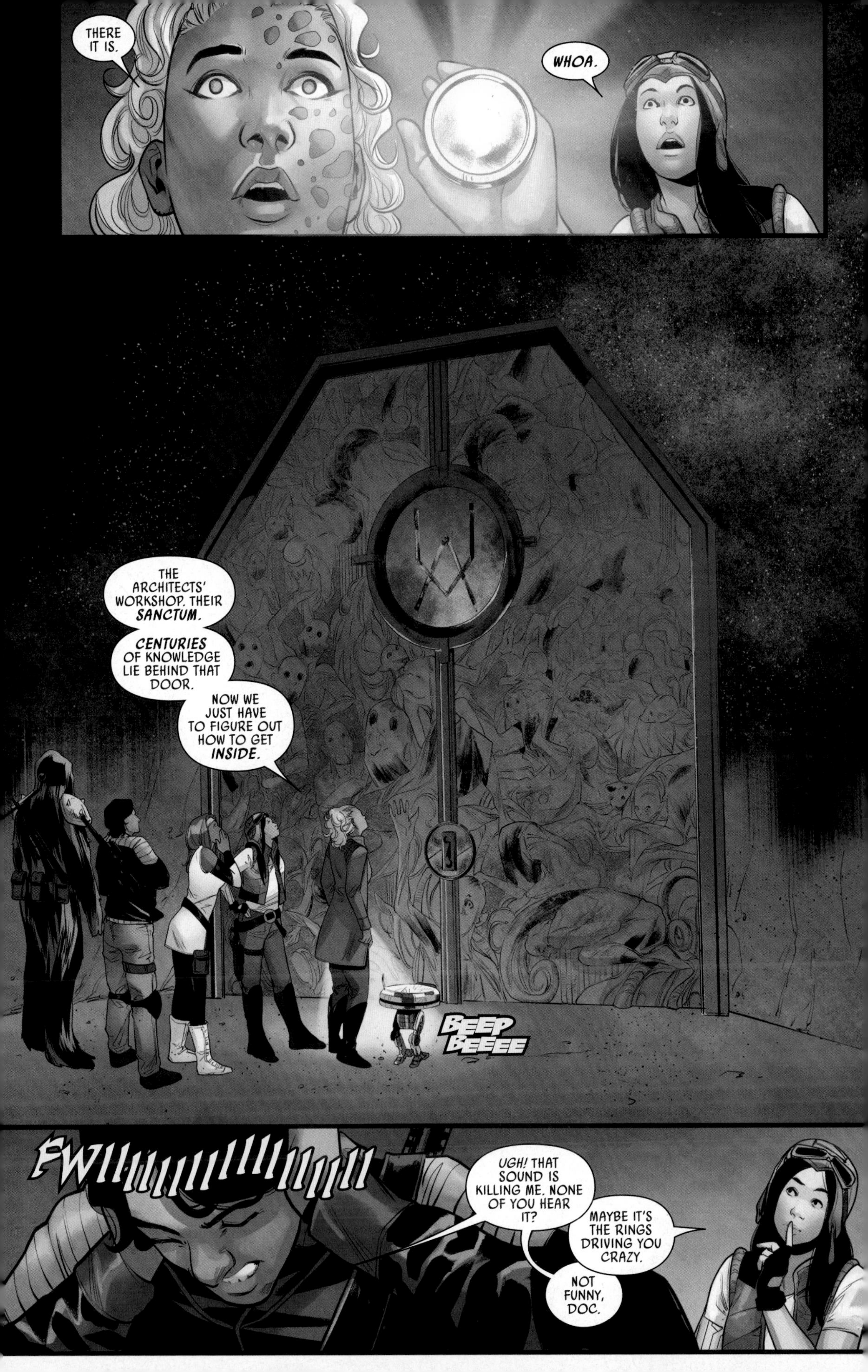
THERE IT IS.
WHOA.
THE ARCHITECTS' WORKSHOP. THEIR SANCTUM.
CENTURIES OF KNOWLEDGE LIE BEHIND THAT DOOR.
NOW WE JUST HAVE TO FIGURE OUT HOW TO GET INSIDE.
BEEP BEEEE
FWIIIIIIIIIIIIIIIII
UGH! THAT SOUND IS KILLING ME. NONE OF YOU HEAR IT?
MAYBE IT'S THE RINGS DRIVING YOU CRAZY.
NOT FUNNY, DOC.

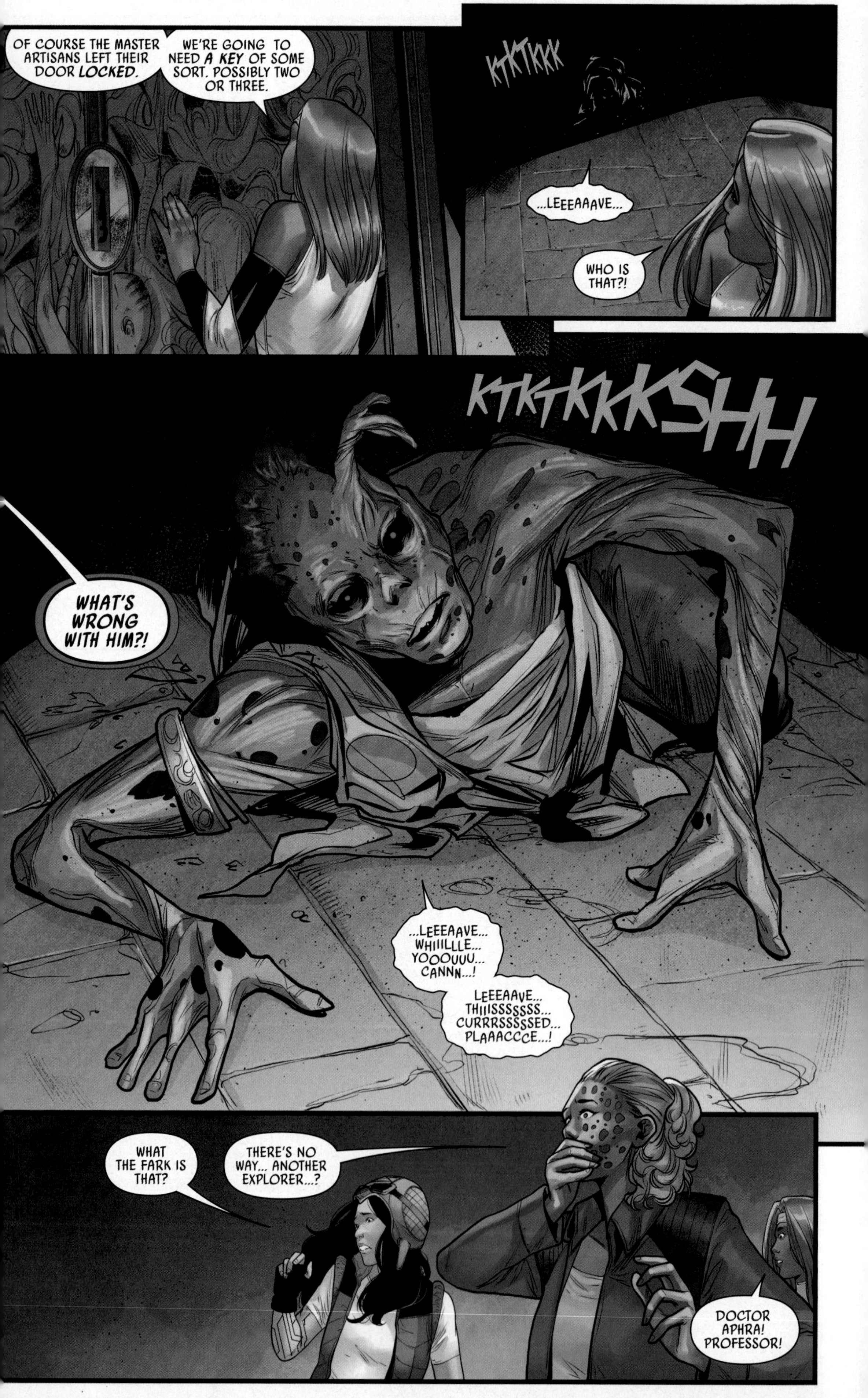
OF COURSE THE MASTER ARTISANS LEFT THEIR DOOR LOCKED.
WE'RE GOING TO NEED A KEY OF SOME SORT. POSSIBLY TWO OR THREE.
KTKTKKK
...LEEEAAAVE...
WHO IS THAT?!
KTKTKKKSHH
WHAT'S WRONG WITH HIM?!
...LEEEAAVE... WHIIILLLE... YOOOUUU... CANNN...!
LEEEAAVE... THIIISSSSSSS... CURRRSSSSSSED... PLAAACCCE...!
WHAT THE FARK IS THAT?
THERE'S NO WAY... ANOTHER EXPLORER...?
DOCTOR APHRA! PROFESSOR!

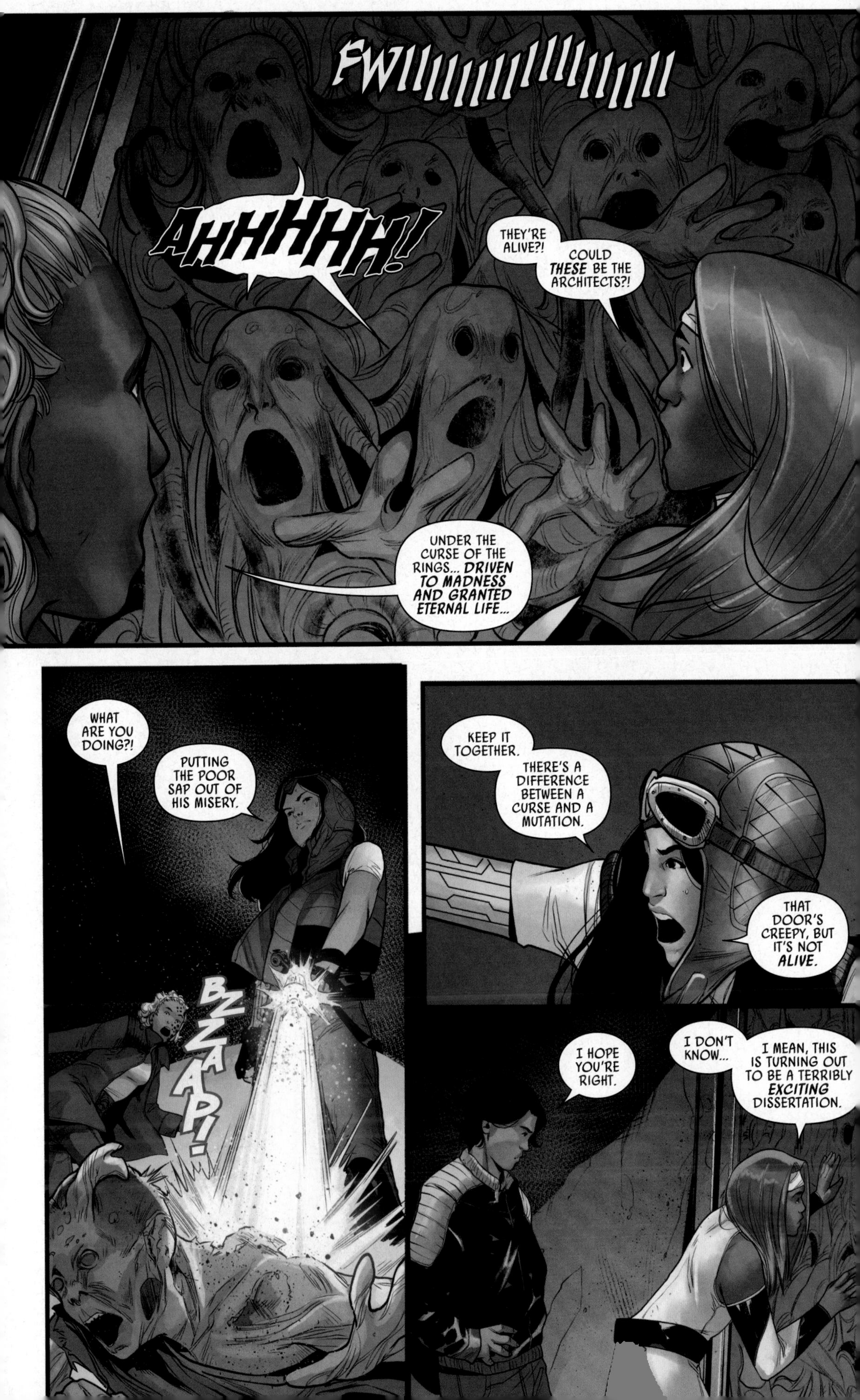
FWIIIIIIIIIIIIIIIIIIIII
AHHHHH!!
THEY'RE ALIVE?!
COULD THESE BE THE ARCHITECTS?!
UNDER THE CURSE OF THE RINGS... DRIVEN TO MADNESS AND GRANTED ETERNAL LIFE...
WHAT ARE YOU DOING?!
PUTTING THE POOR SAP OUT OF HIS MISERY.
BZZAAP!
KEEP IT TOGETHER.
THERE'S A DIFFERENCE BETWEEN A CURSE AND A MUTATION.
THAT DOOR'S CREEPY, BUT IT'S NOT ALIVE.
I HOPE YOU'RE RIGHT.
I DON'T KNOW...
I MEAN, THIS IS TURNING OUT TO BE A TERRIBLY EXCITING DISSERTATION.

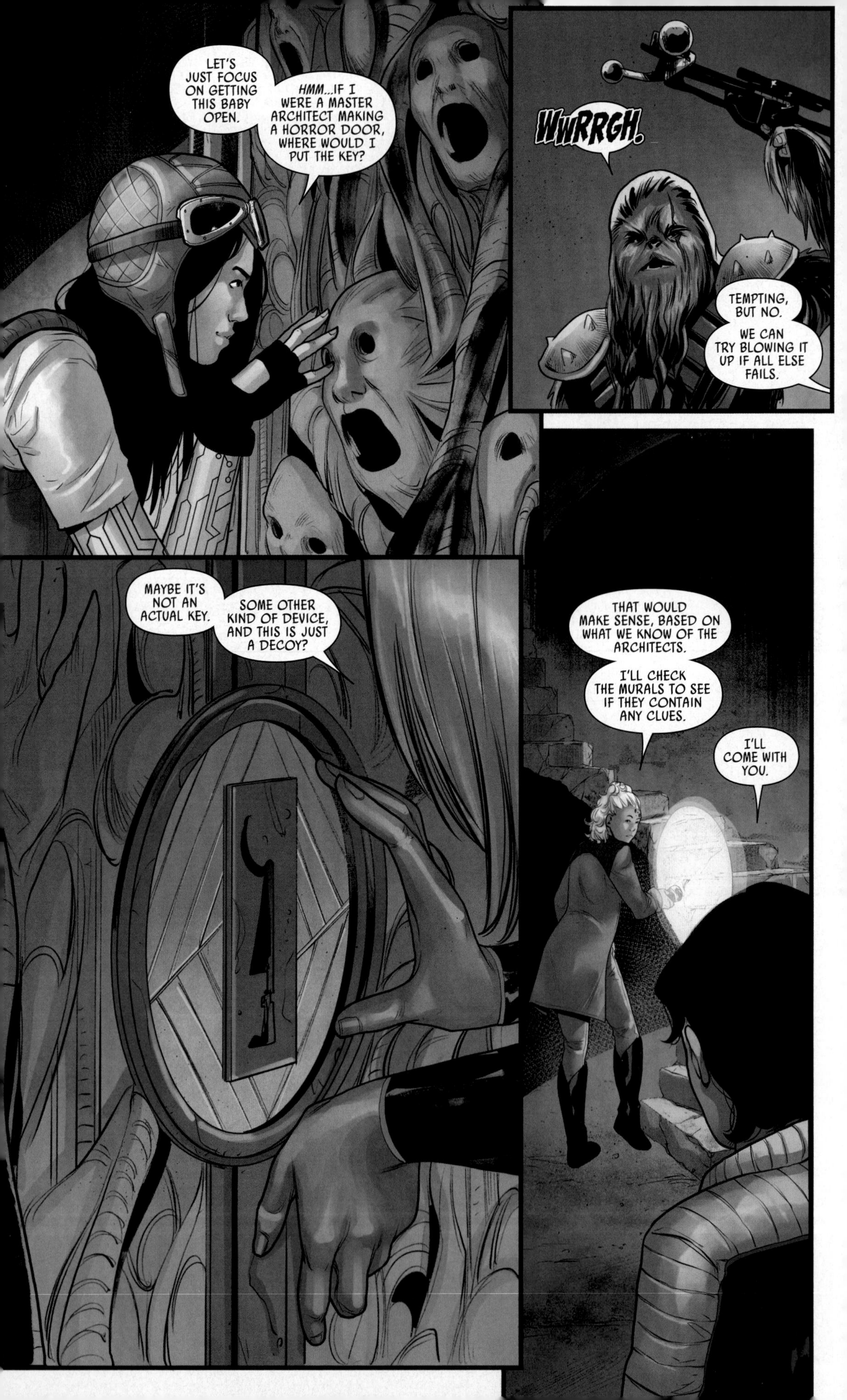
LET'S JUST FOCUS ON GETTING THIS BABY OPEN.
HMM...IF I WERE A MASTER ARCHITECT MAKING A HORROR DOOR, WHERE WOULD I PUT THE KEY?
WWRRGH.
TEMPTING, BUT NO.
WE CAN TRY BLOWING IT UP IF ALL ELSE FAILS.
MAYBE IT'S NOT AN ACTUAL KEY.
SOME OTHER KIND OF DEVICE, AND THIS IS JUST A DECOY?
THAT WOULD MAKE SENSE, BASED ON WHAT WE KNOW OF THE ARCHITECTS.
I'LL CHECK THE MURALS TO SEE IF THEY CONTAIN ANY CLUES.
I'LL COME WITH YOU.

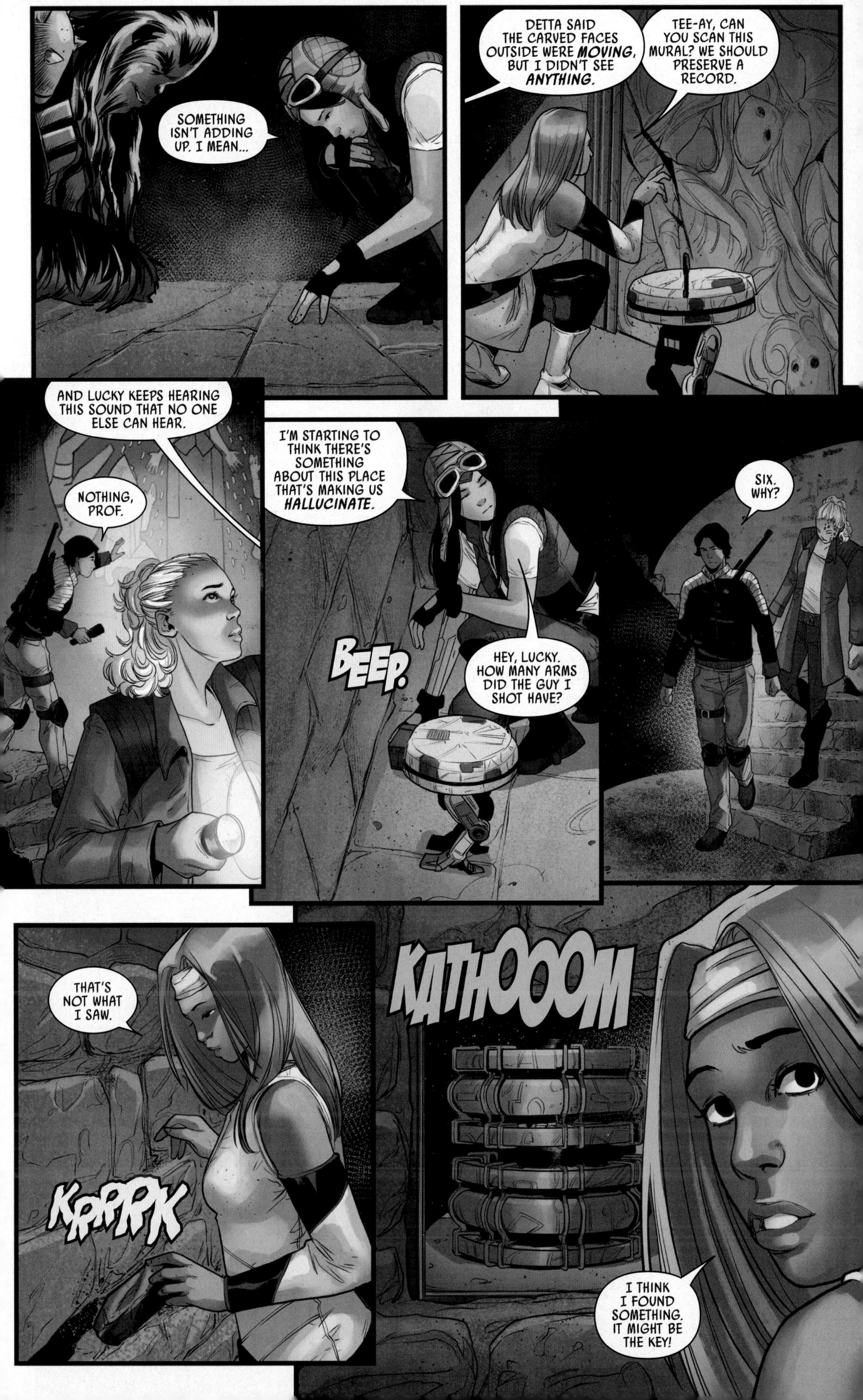
SOMETHING ISN'T ADDING UP. I MEAN...
DETTA SAID THE CARVED FACES OUTSIDE WERE MOVING, BUT I DIDN'T SEE ANYTHING.
TEE-AY, CAN YOU SCAN THIS MURAL? WE SHOULD PRESERVE A RECORD.
AND LUCKY KEEPS HEARING THIS SOUND THAT NO ONE ELSE CAN HEAR.
NOTHING, PROF.
I'M STARTING TO THINK THERE'S SOMETHING ABOUT THIS PLACE THAT'S MAKING US HALLUCINATE.
BEEP.
HEY, LUCKY. HOW MANY ARMS DID THE GUY I SHOT HAVE?
SIX. WHY?
THAT'S NOT WHAT I SAW.
KRRRK
KATHOOOM
I THINK I FOUND SOMETHING. IT MIGHT BE THE KEY!

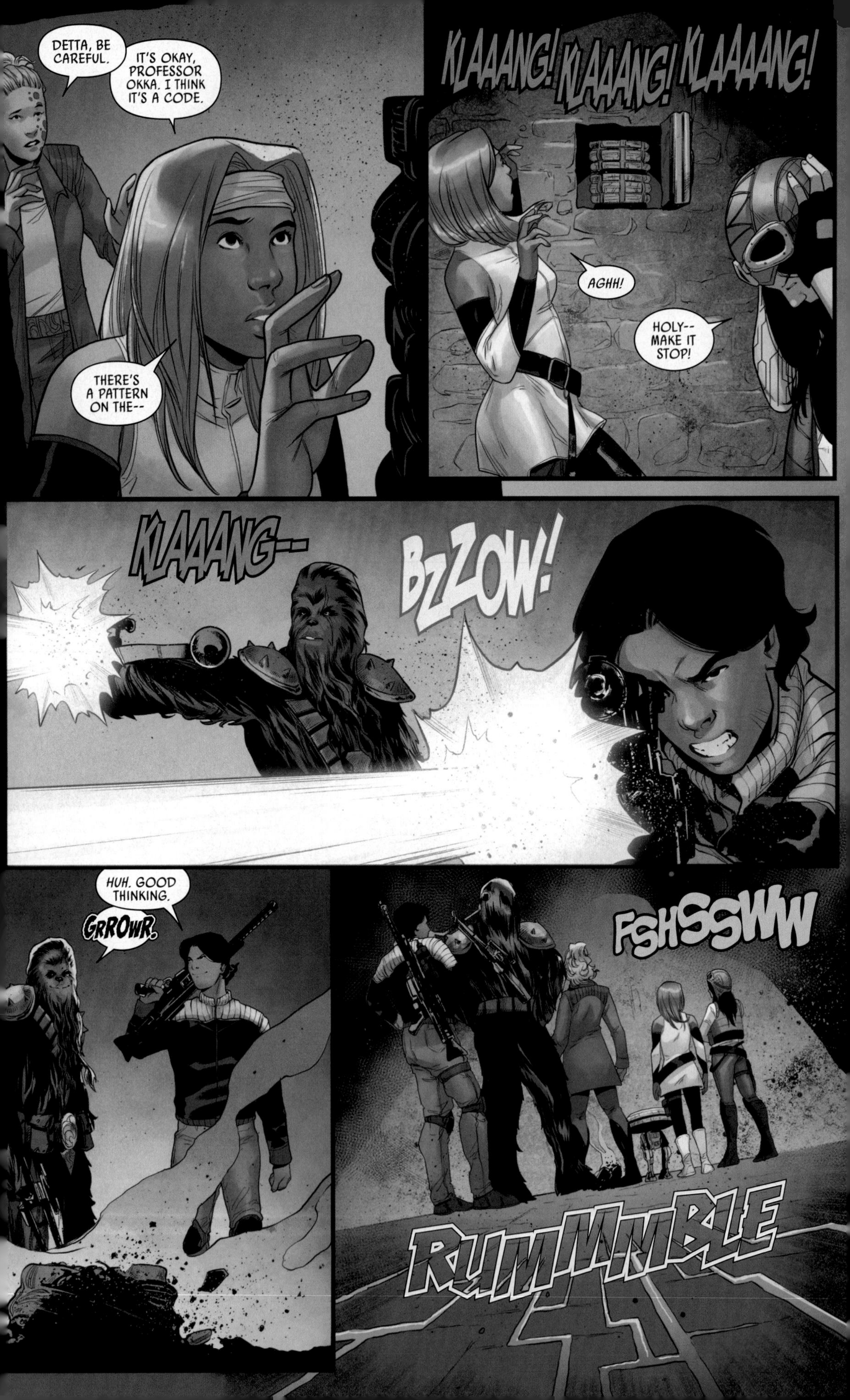
DETTA, BE CAREFUL.
IT'S OKAY, PROFESSOR OKKA. I THINK IT'S A CODE.
THERE'S A PATTERN ON THE--
KLAAANG! KLAAANG! KLAAAANG!
AGHH!
HOLY-- MAKE IT STOP!
KLAAANG--
BZZOW!
HUH. GOOD THINKING.
GRROWR.
FSHSSWW
RUMMMMBLE

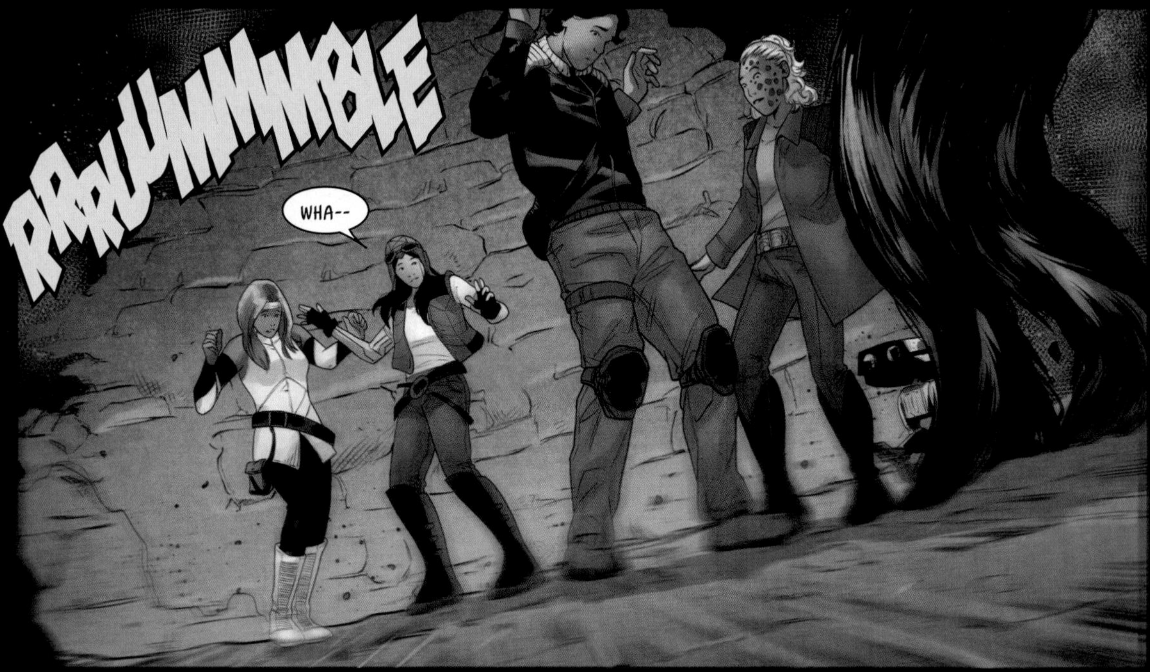
RRRUMMMMBLE
WHA--
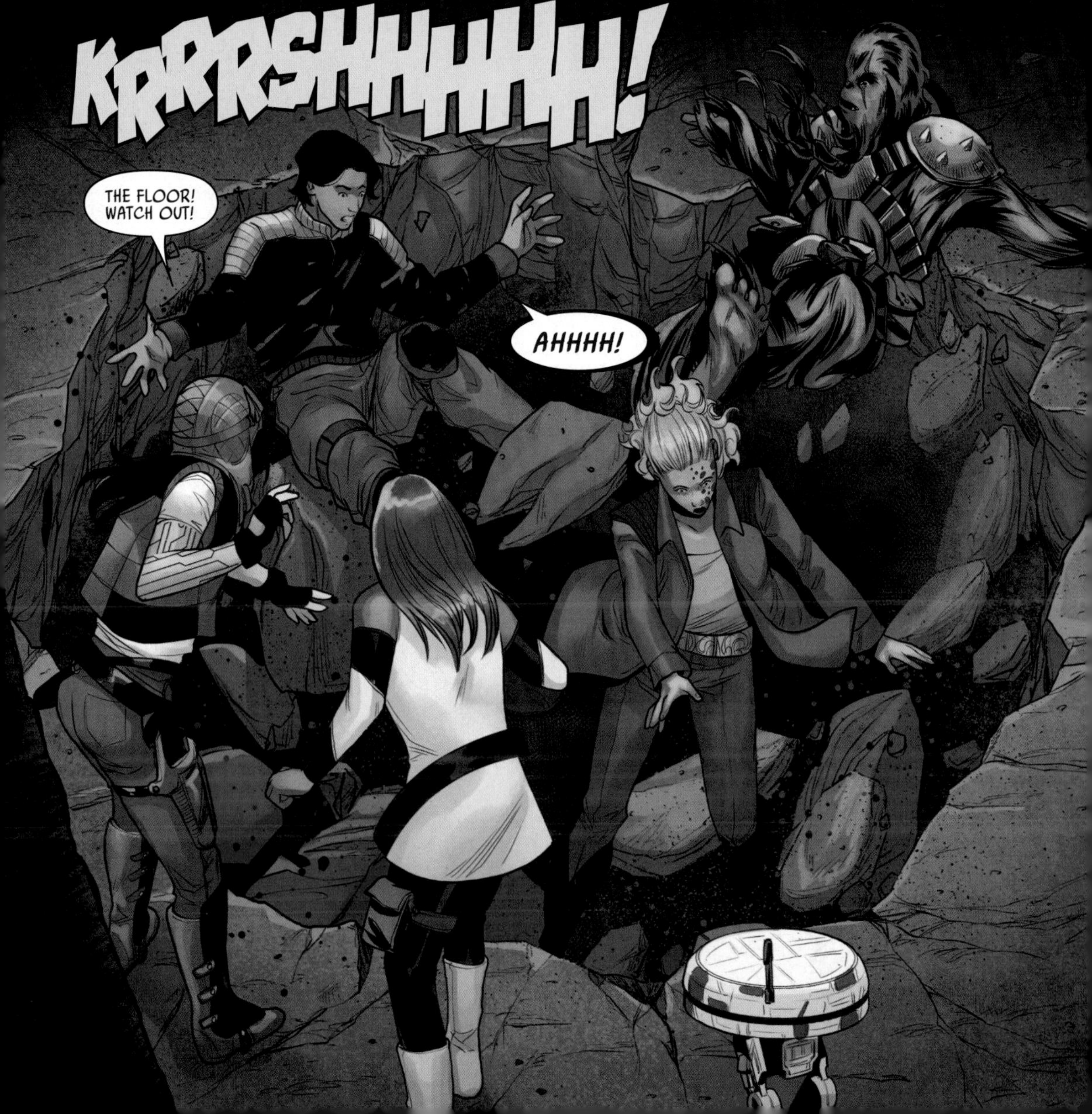
KRRRSHHHHHH!
THE FLOOR! WATCH OUT!
AHHHH!

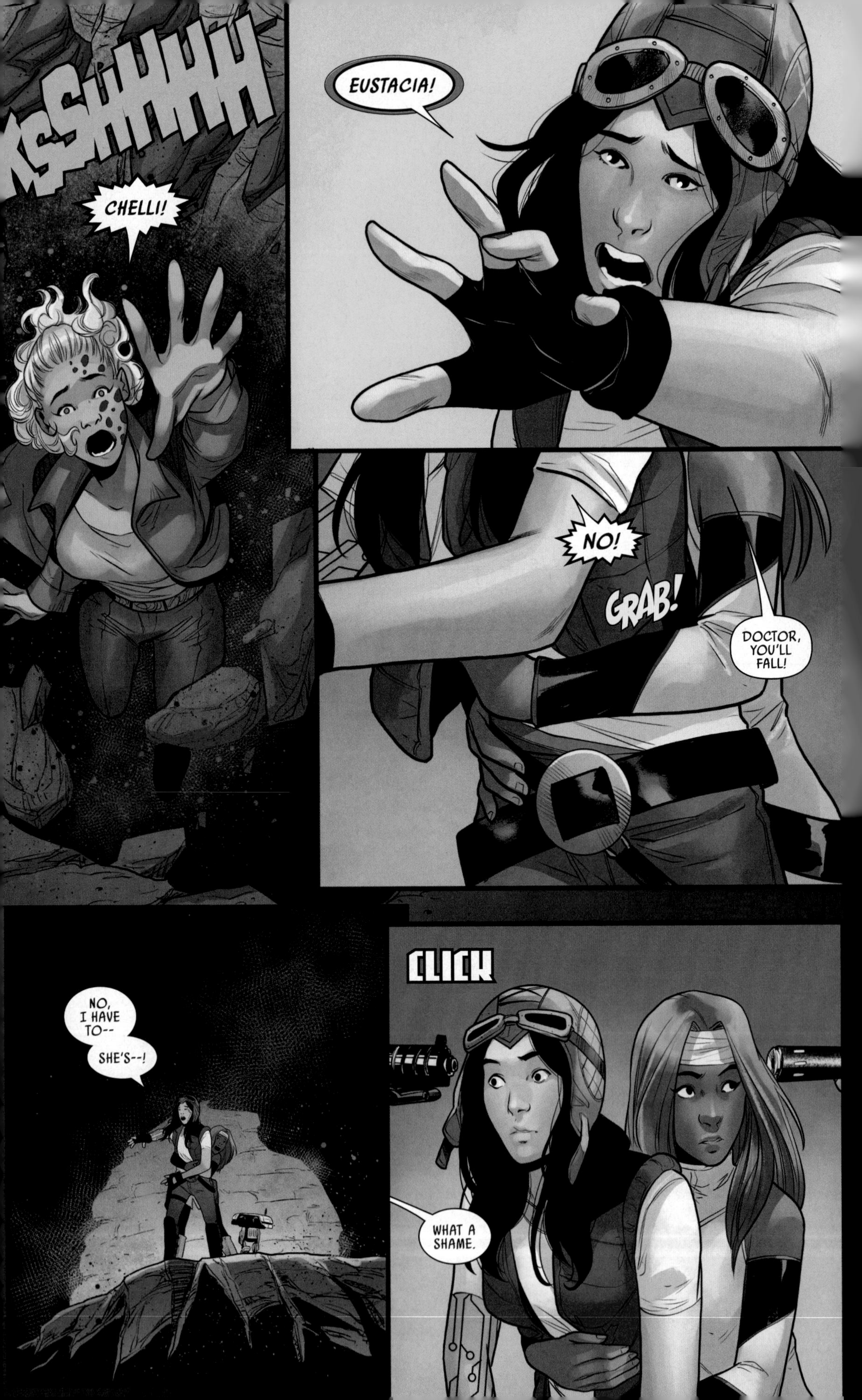
KSHHHHH
CHELLI!
EUSTACIA!
NO!
GRAB!
DOCTOR, YOU'LL FALL!
NO, I HAVE TO--
SHE'S--!
CLICK
WHAT A SHAME.

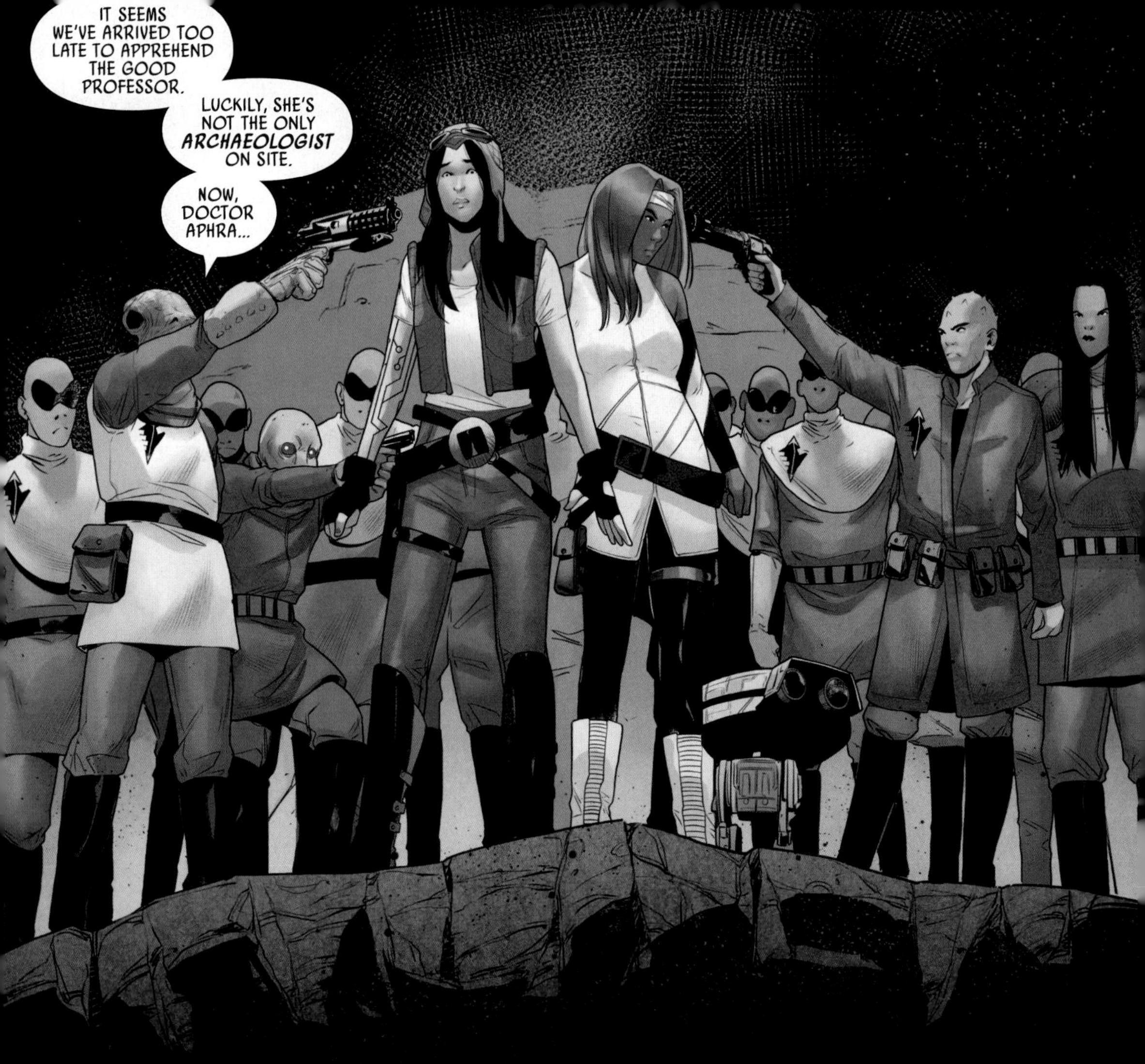
IT SEEMS WE'VE ARRIVED TOO LATE TO APPREHEND THE GOOD PROFESSOR.
LUCKILY, SHE'S NOT THE ONLY ARCHAEOLOGIST ON SITE.
NOW, DOCTOR APHRA...

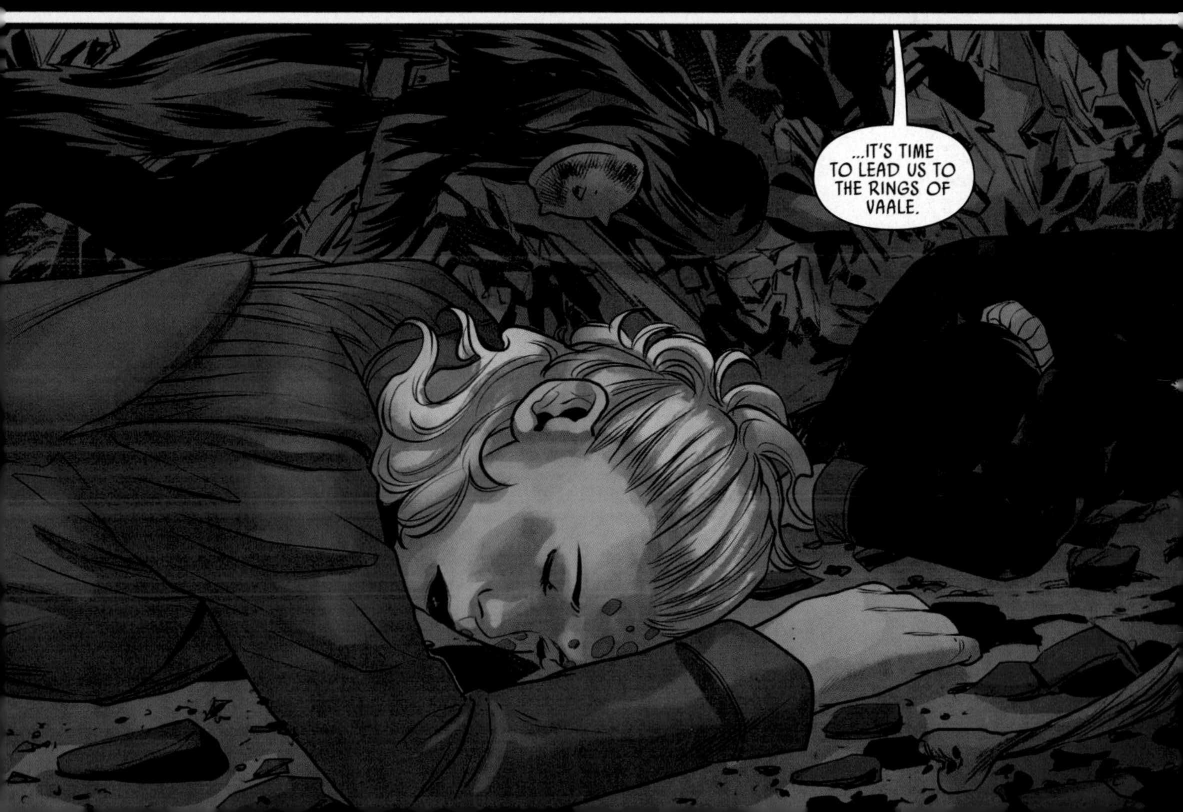
...IT'S TIME TO LEAD US TO THE RINGS OF VAALE.

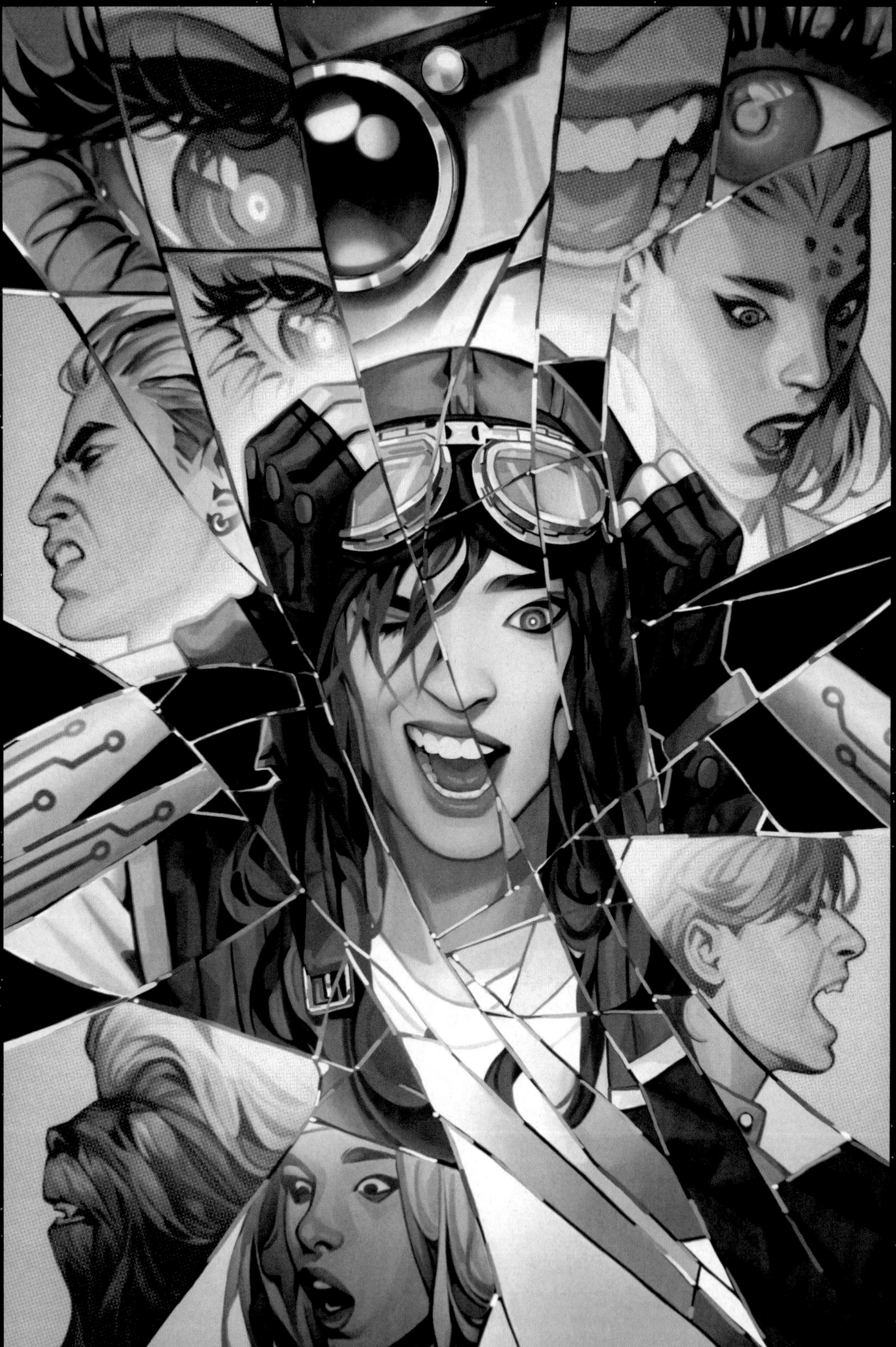

3 — TURNABOUT

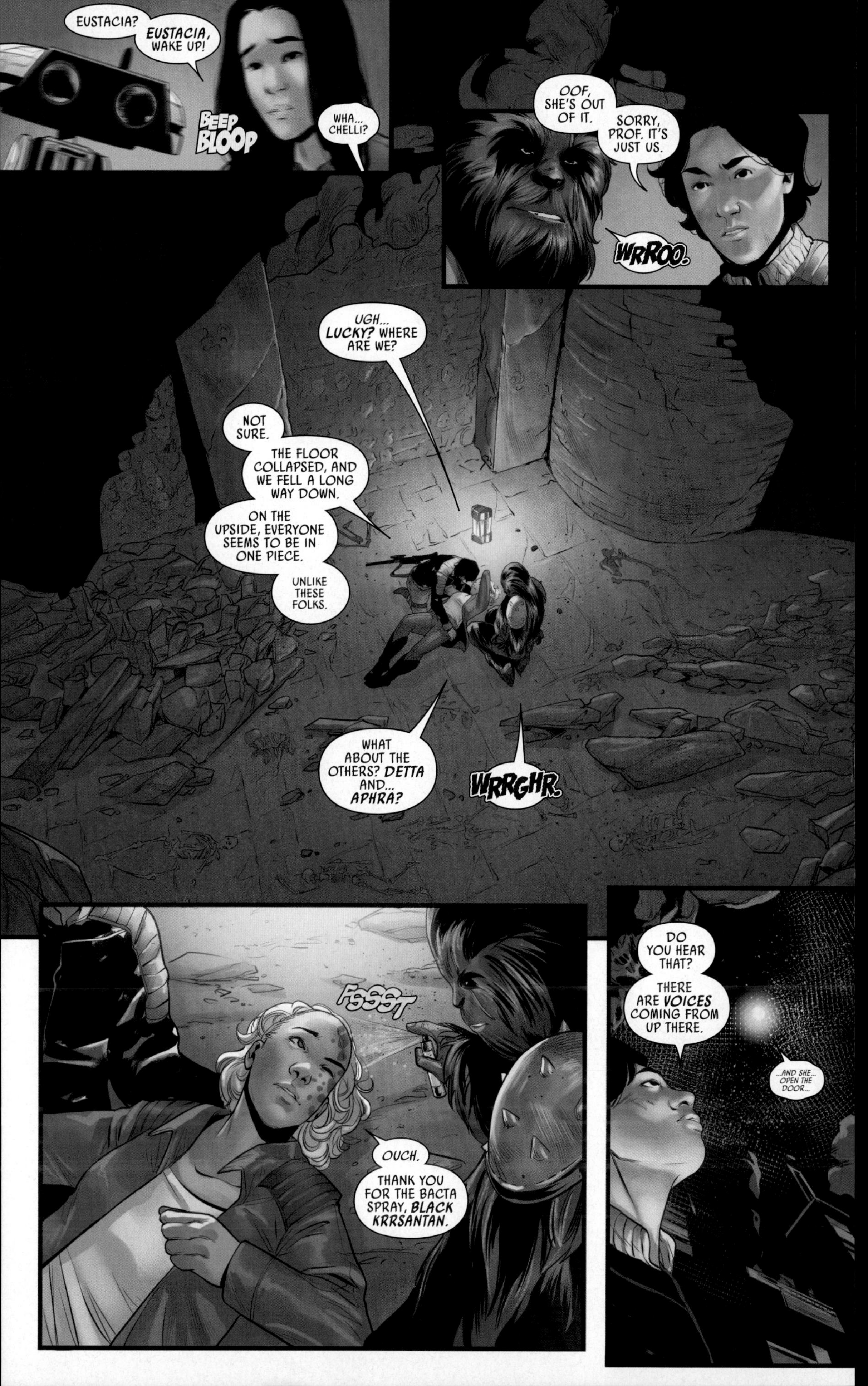

EUSTACIA?
EUSTACIA, WAKE UP!
BEEP BLOOP
WHA... CHELLI?
OOF, SHE'S OUT OF IT.
SORRY, PROF. IT'S JUST US.
WRROO.
UGH... LUCKY? WHERE ARE WE?
NOT SURE.
THE FLOOR COLLAPSED, AND WE FELL A LONG WAY DOWN.
ON THE UPSIDE, EVERYONE SEEMS TO BE IN ONE PIECE.
UNLIKE THESE FOLKS.
WHAT ABOUT THE OTHERS? DETTA AND... APHRA?
WRRGHR.
FSSST
OUCH.
THANK YOU FOR THE BACTA SPRAY, BLACK KRRSANTAN.
DO YOU HEAR THAT?
THERE ARE VOICES COMING FROM UP THERE.
...AND SHE... OPEN THE DOOR...

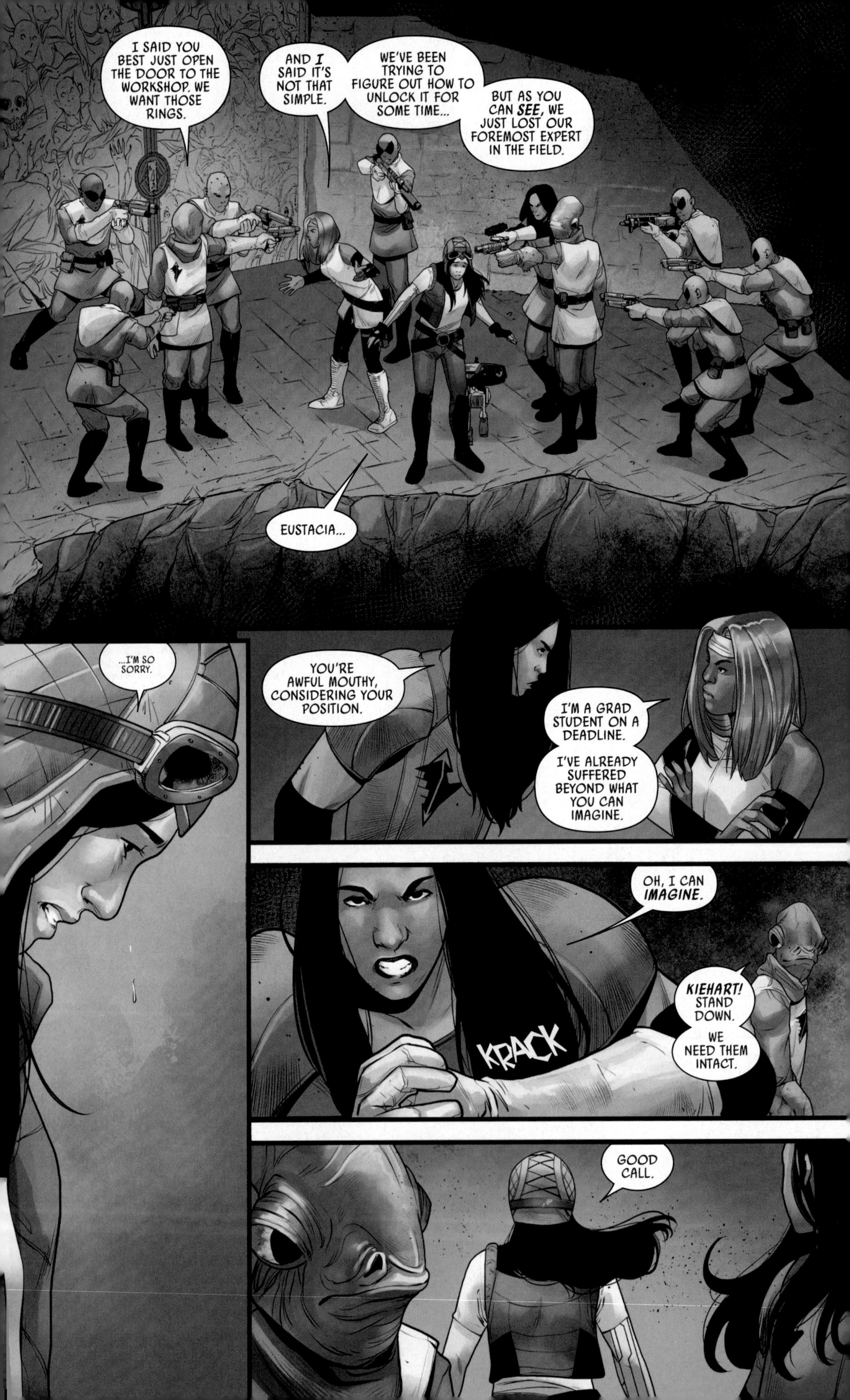
I SAID YOU BEST JUST OPEN THE DOOR TO THE WORKSHOP. WE WANT THOSE RINGS.
AND I SAID IT'S NOT THAT SIMPLE.
WE'VE BEEN TRYING TO FIGURE OUT HOW TO UNLOCK IT FOR SOME TIME...
BUT AS YOU CAN SEE, WE JUST LOST OUR FOREMOST EXPERT IN THE FIELD.
EUSTACIA...
...I'M SO SORRY.
YOU'RE AWFUL MOUTHY, CONSIDERING YOUR POSITION.
I'M A GRAD STUDENT ON A DEADLINE.
I'VE ALREADY SUFFERED BEYOND WHAT YOU CAN IMAGINE.
OH, I CAN IMAGINE.
KRACK
KIEHART! STAND DOWN.
WE NEED THEM INTACT.
GOOD CALL.

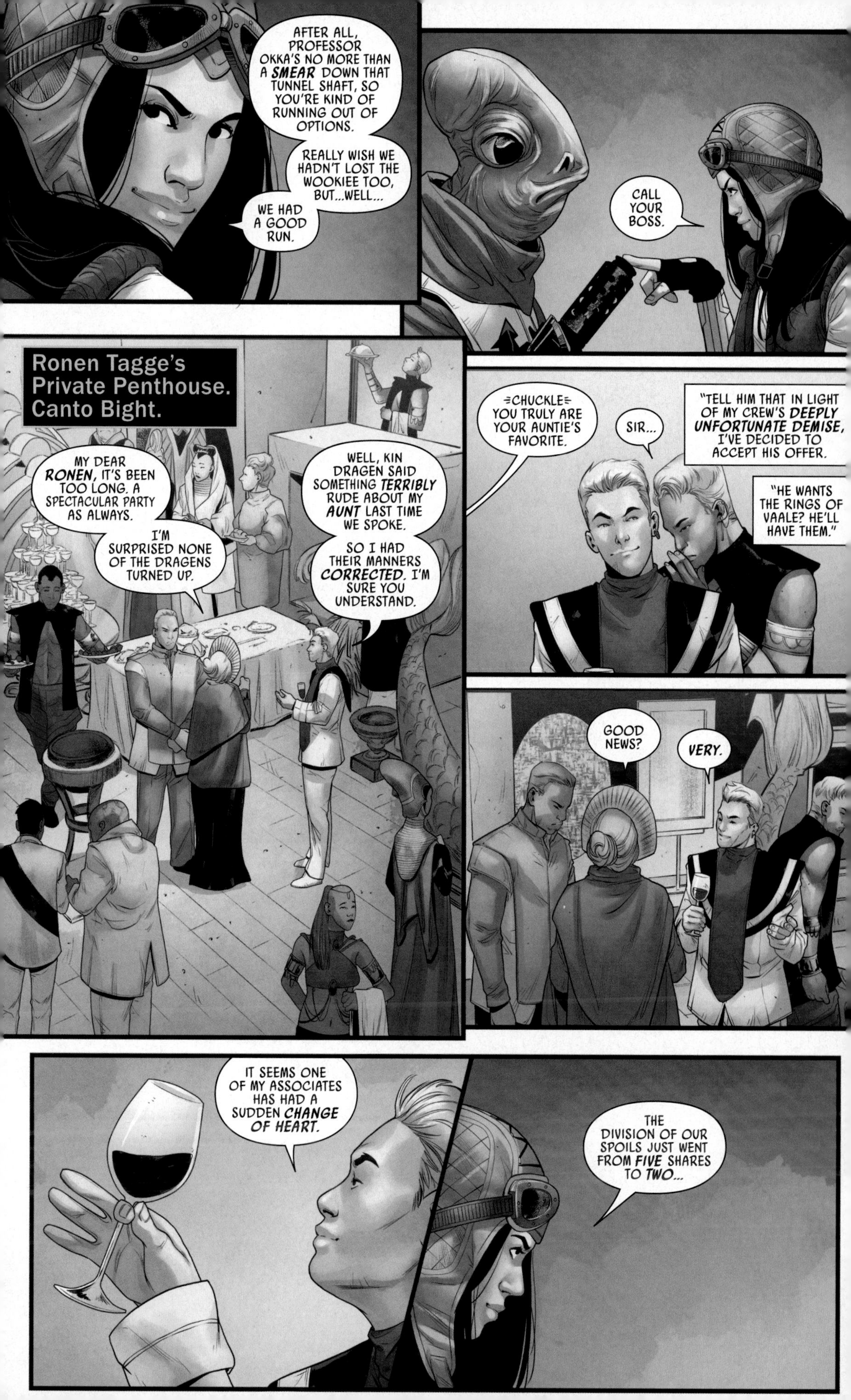
AFTER ALL, PROFESSOR OKKA'S NO MORE THAN A SMEAR DOWN THAT TUNNEL SHAFT, SO YOU'RE KIND OF RUNNING OUT OF OPTIONS.
REALLY WISH WE HADN'T LOST THE WOOKIEE TOO, BUT...WELL...
WE HAD A GOOD RUN.
CALL YOUR BOSS.
Ronen Tagge's Private Penthouse. Canto Bight.
MY DEAR RONEN, IT'S BEEN TOO LONG. A SPECTACULAR PARTY AS ALWAYS.
I'M SURPRISED NONE OF THE DRAGENS TURNED UP.
WELL, KIN DRAGEN SAID SOMETHING TERRIBLY RUDE ABOUT MY AUNT LAST TIME WE SPOKE.
SO I HAD THEIR MANNERS CORRECTED. I'M SURE YOU UNDERSTAND.
=CHUCKLE= YOU TRULY ARE YOUR AUNTIE'S FAVORITE.
SIR...
"TELL HIM THAT IN LIGHT OF MY CREW'S DEEPLY UNFORTUNATE DEMISE, I'VE DECIDED TO ACCEPT HIS OFFER.
"HE WANTS THE RINGS OF VAALE? HE'LL HAVE THEM."
GOOD NEWS?
VERY.
IT SEEMS ONE OF MY ASSOCIATES HAS HAD A SUDDEN CHANGE OF HEART.
THE DIVISION OF OUR SPOILS JUST WENT FROM FIVE SHARES TO TWO...

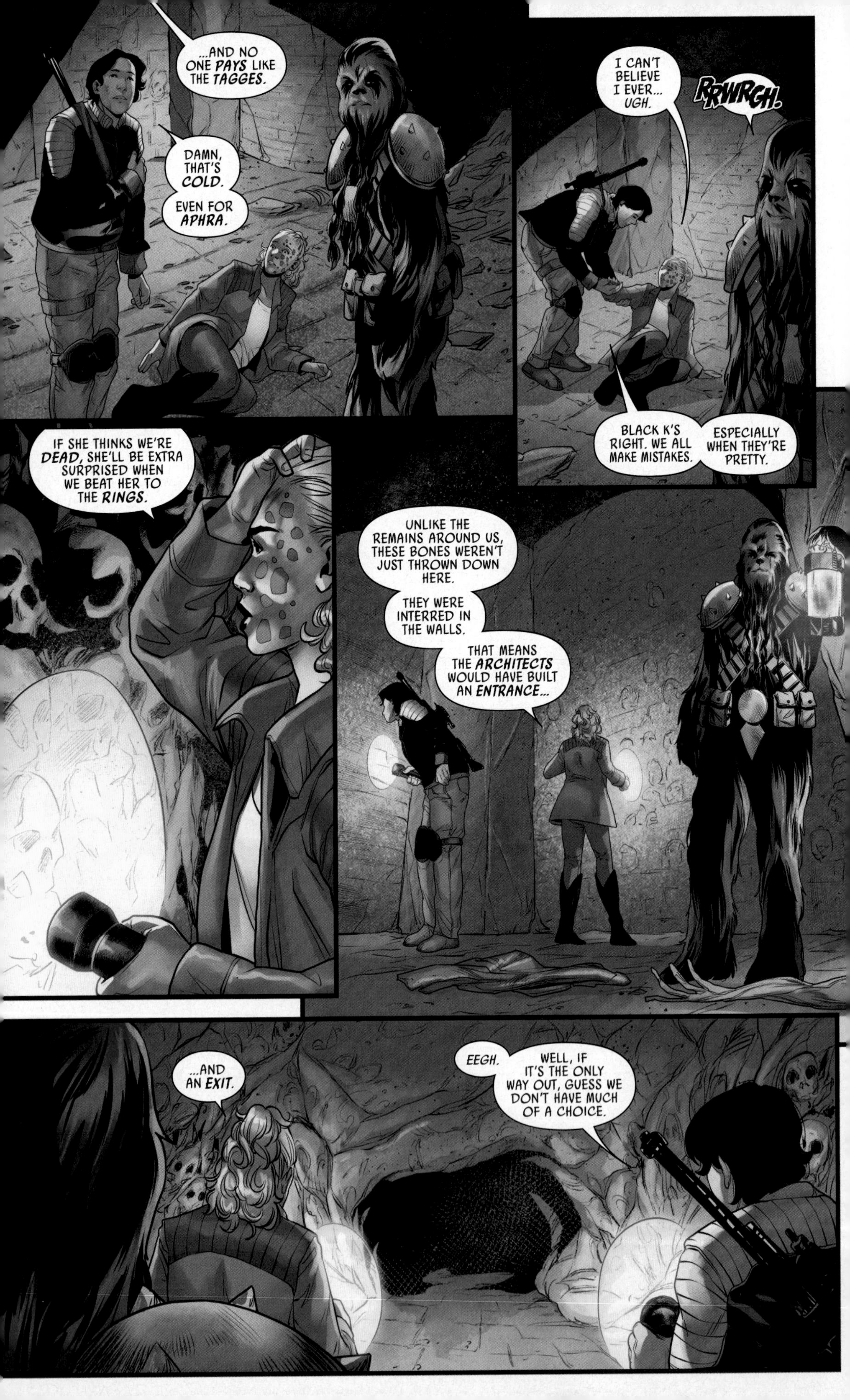
...AND NO ONE PAYS LIKE THE TAGGES.
DAMN, THAT'S COLD.
EVEN FOR APHRA.
I CAN'T BELIEVE I EVER... UGH.
RRWRGH.
BLACK K'S RIGHT. WE ALL MAKE MISTAKES.
ESPECIALLY WHEN THEY'RE PRETTY.
IF SHE THINKS WE'RE DEAD, SHE'LL BE EXTRA SURPRISED WHEN WE BEAT HER TO THE RINGS.
UNLIKE THE REMAINS AROUND US, THESE BONES WEREN'T JUST THROWN DOWN HERE.
THEY WERE INTERRED IN THE WALLS.
THAT MEANS THE ARCHITECTS WOULD HAVE BUILT AN ENTRANCE...
...AND AN EXIT.
EEGH.
WELL, IF IT'S THE ONLY WAY OUT, GUESS WE DON'T HAVE MUCH OF A CHOICE.

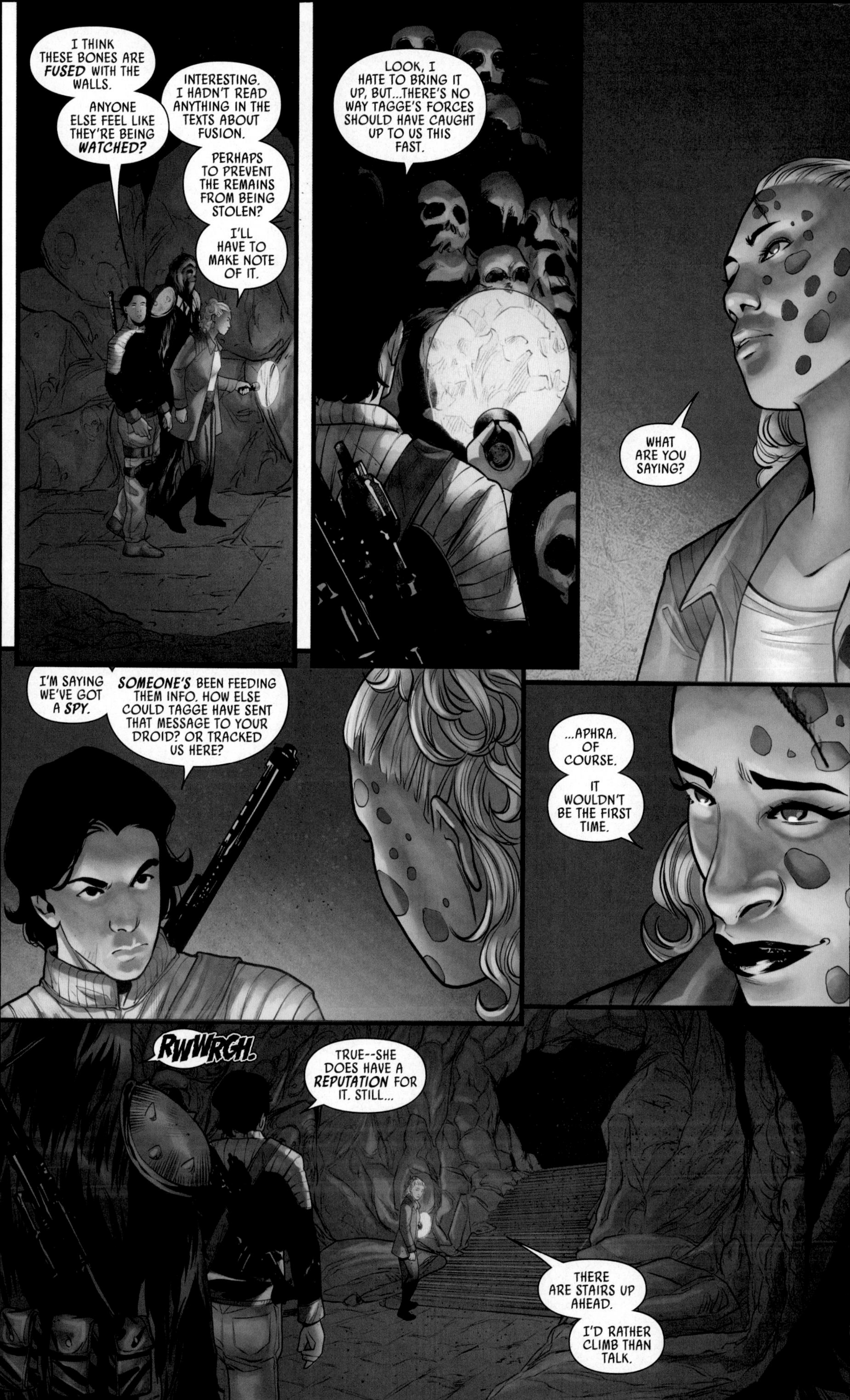

I THINK THESE BONES ARE FUSED WITH THE WALLS.
ANYONE ELSE FEEL LIKE THEY'RE BEING WATCHED?
INTERESTING. I HADN'T READ ANYTHING IN THE TEXTS ABOUT FUSION.
PERHAPS TO PREVENT THE REMAINS FROM BEING STOLEN?
I'LL HAVE TO MAKE NOTE OF IT.
LOOK, I HATE TO BRING IT UP, BUT...THERE'S NO WAY TAGGE'S FORCES SHOULD HAVE CAUGHT UP TO US THIS FAST.
WHAT ARE YOU SAYING?
I'M SAYING WE'VE GOT A SPY.
SOMEONE'S BEEN FEEDING THEM INFO. HOW ELSE COULD TAGGE HAVE SENT THAT MESSAGE TO YOUR DROID? OR TRACKED US HERE?
...APHRA. OF COURSE.
IT WOULDN'T BE THE FIRST TIME.
RWWRGH.
TRUE--SHE DOES HAVE A REPUTATION FOR IT. STILL...
THERE ARE STAIRS UP AHEAD.
I'D RATHER CLIMB THAN TALK.

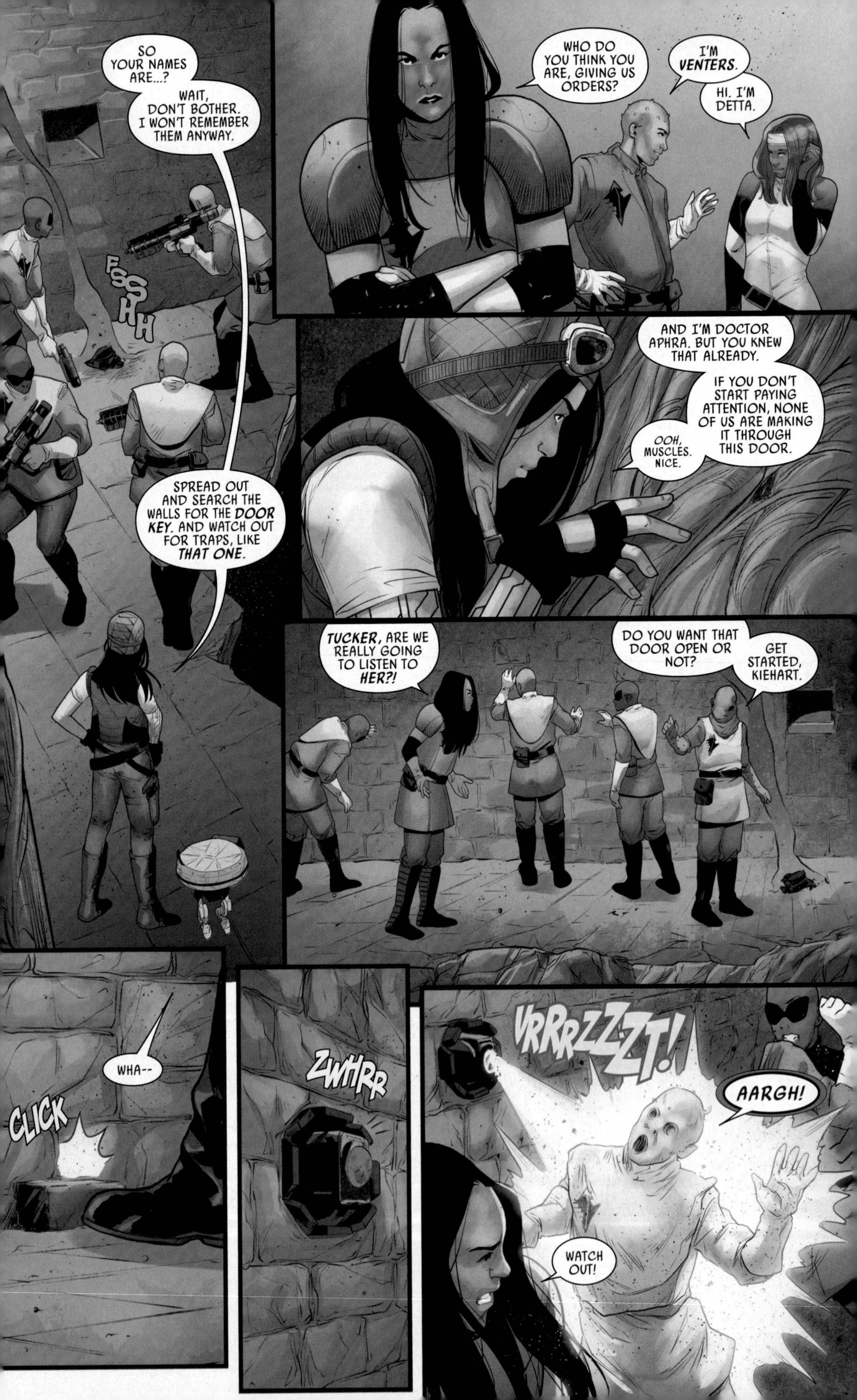
SO YOUR NAMES ARE...?
WAIT, DON'T BOTHER. I WON'T REMEMBER THEM ANYWAY.
FSSHH
SPREAD OUT AND SEARCH THE WALLS FOR THE DOOR KEY. AND WATCH OUT FOR TRAPS, LIKE THAT ONE.
WHO DO YOU THINK YOU ARE, GIVING US ORDERS?
I'M VENTERS.
HI. I'M DETTA.
AND I'M DOCTOR APHRA. BUT YOU KNEW THAT ALREADY.
IF YOU DON'T START PAYING ATTENTION, NONE OF US ARE MAKING IT THROUGH THIS DOOR.
OOH, MUSCLES. NICE.
TUCKER, ARE WE REALLY GOING TO LISTEN TO HER?!
DO YOU WANT THAT DOOR OPEN OR NOT?
GET STARTED, KIEHART.
CLICK
WHA--
ZWHRR
VRRRZZZT!
AARGH!
WATCH OUT!

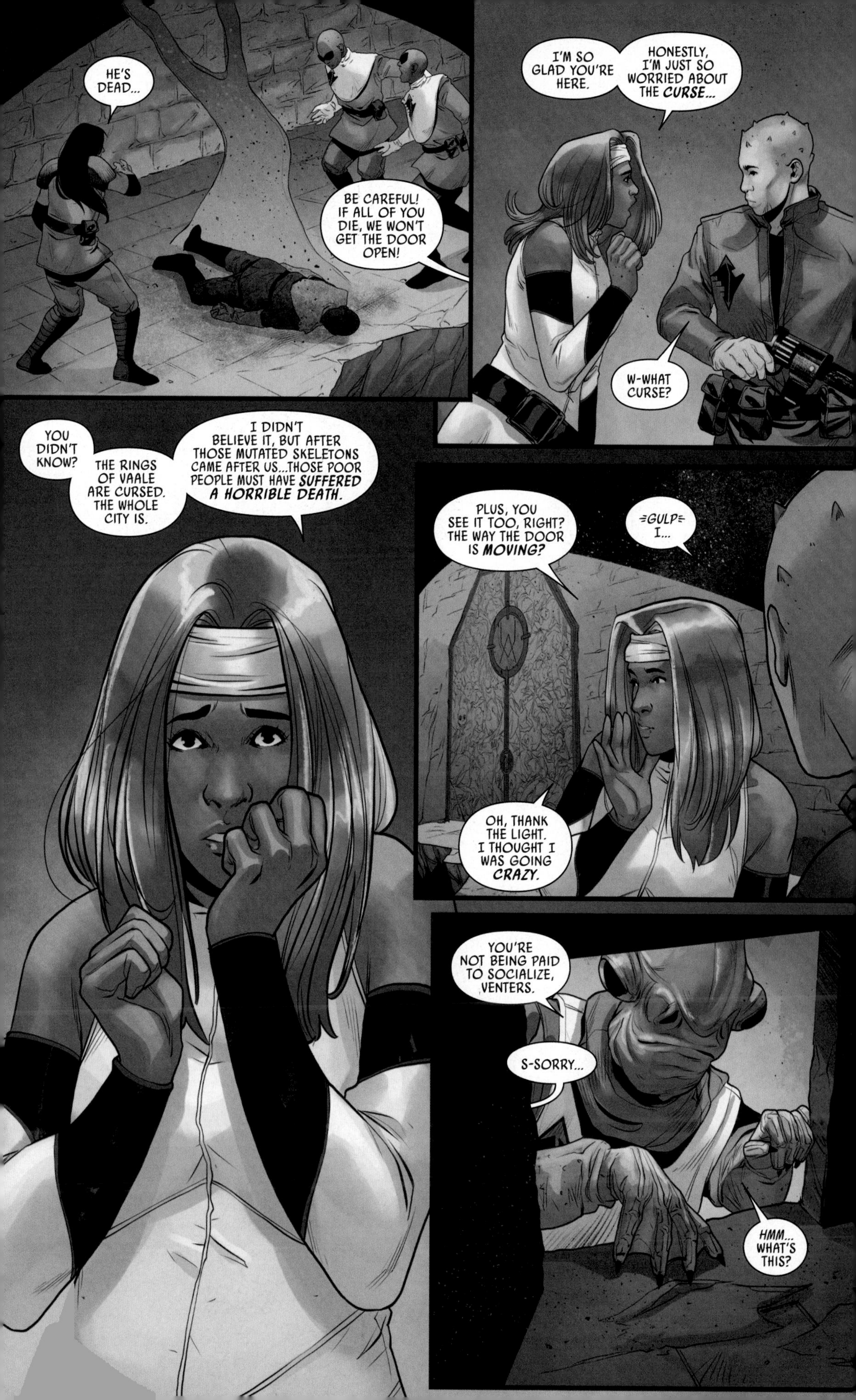
HE'S DEAD...
BE CAREFUL! IF ALL OF YOU DIE, WE WON'T GET THE DOOR OPEN!
I'M SO GLAD YOU'RE HERE.
HONESTLY, I'M JUST SO WORRIED ABOUT THE CURSE...
W-WHAT CURSE?
YOU DIDN'T KNOW?
THE RINGS OF VAALE ARE CURSED. THE WHOLE CITY IS.
I DIDN'T BELIEVE IT, BUT AFTER THOSE MUTATED SKELETONS CAME AFTER US...THOSE POOR PEOPLE MUST HAVE SUFFERED A HORRIBLE DEATH.
PLUS, YOU SEE IT TOO, RIGHT? THE WAY THE DOOR IS MOVING?
GULP I...
OH, THANK THE LIGHT. I THOUGHT I WAS GOING CRAZY.
YOU'RE NOT BEING PAID TO SOCIALIZE, VENTERS.
S-SORRY...
HMM... WHAT'S THIS?

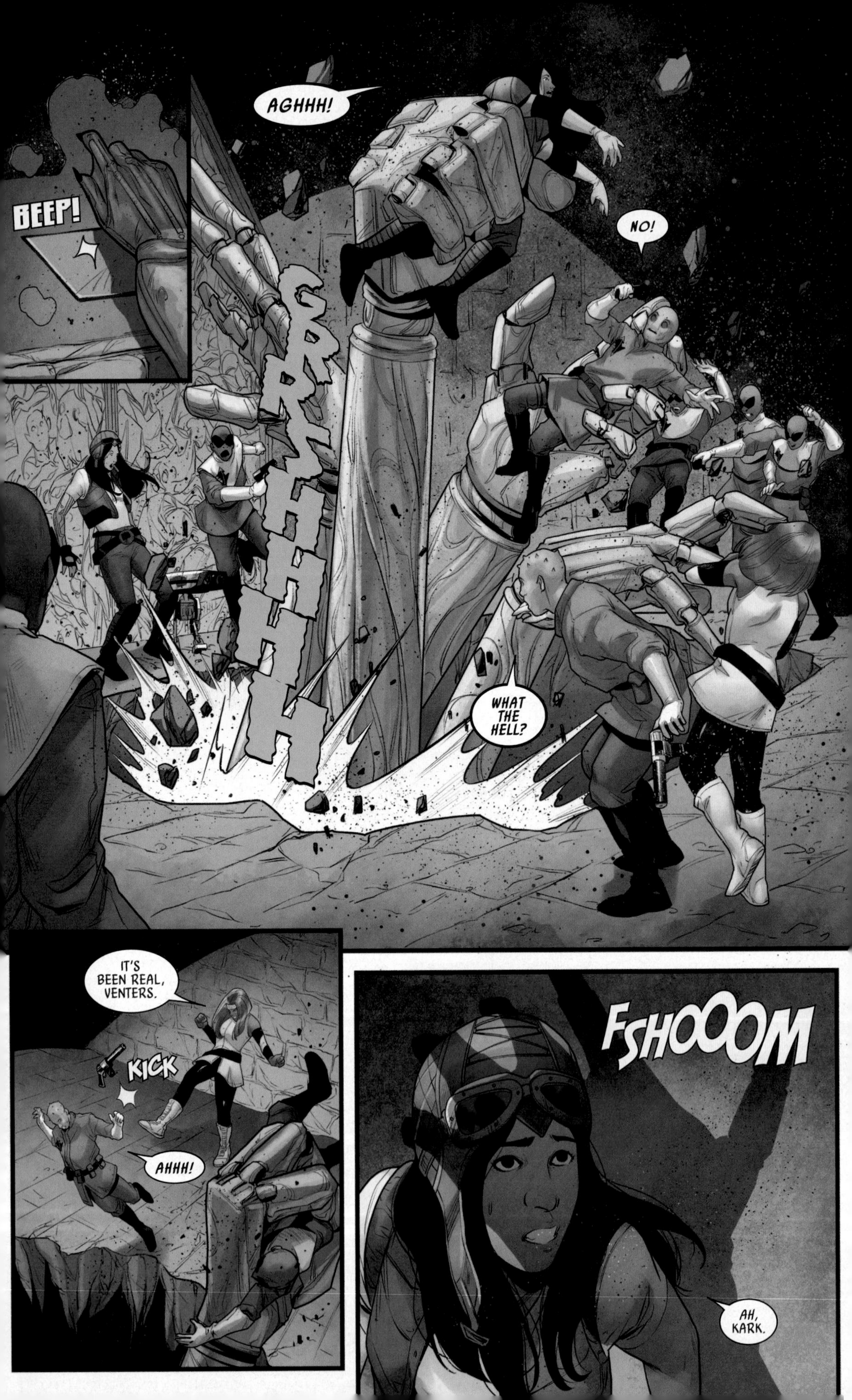
BEEP!
AGHHH!
NO!
GRASHHHHH
WHAT THE HELL?
IT'S BEEN REAL, VENTERS.
KICK
AHHH!
FSHOOOM
AH, KARK.

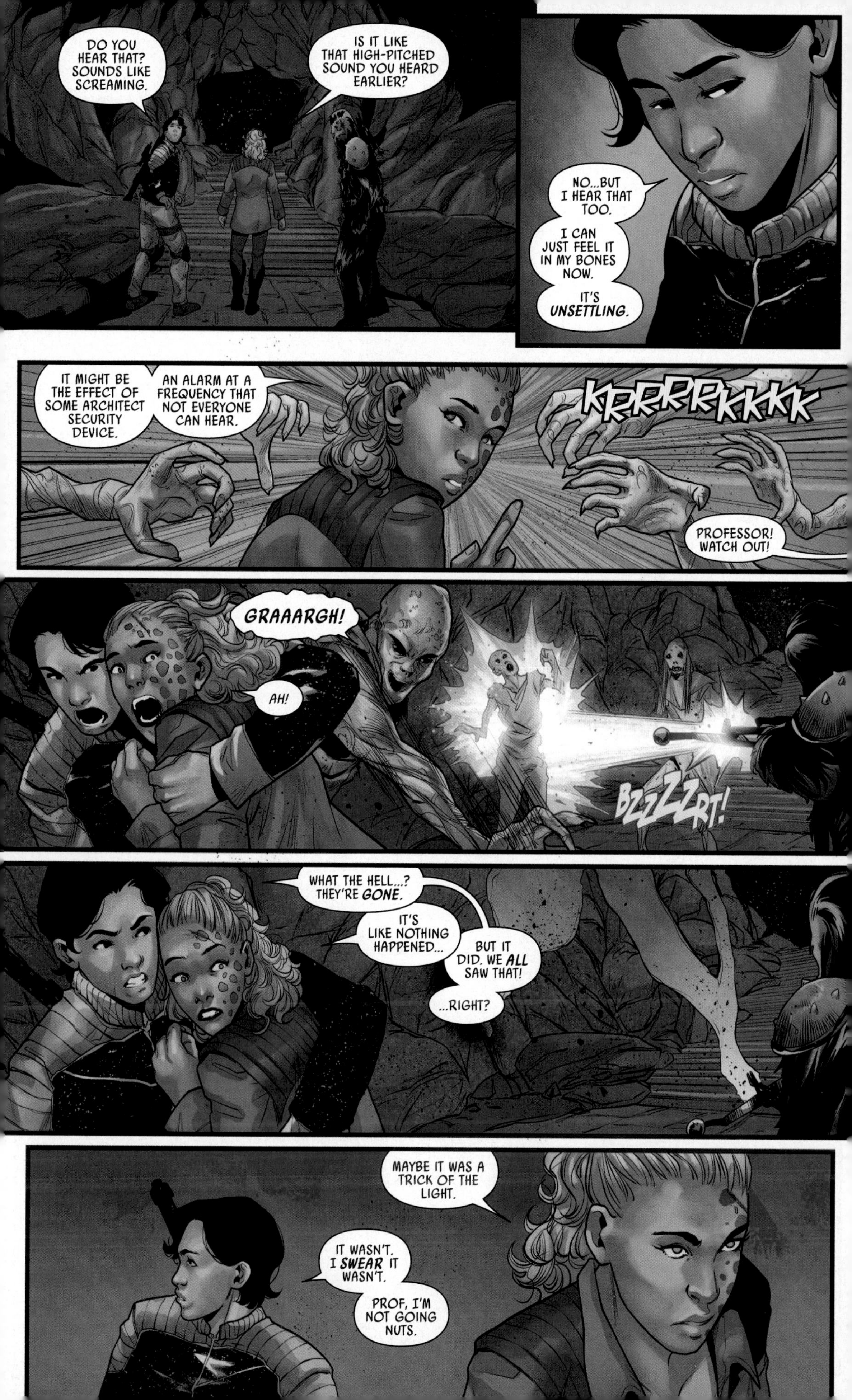
DO YOU HEAR THAT? SOUNDS LIKE SCREAMING.
IS IT LIKE THAT HIGH-PITCHED SOUND YOU HEARD EARLIER?
NO...BUT I HEAR THAT TOO.
I CAN JUST FEEL IT IN MY BONES NOW.
IT'S *UNSETTLING.*
IT MIGHT BE THE EFFECT OF SOME ARCHITECT SECURITY DEVICE.
AN ALARM AT A FREQUENCY THAT NOT EVERYONE CAN HEAR.
KRRRRKKKK
PROFESSOR! WATCH OUT!
GRAAARGH!
AH!
BZZZZRT!
WHAT THE HELL...? THEY'RE *GONE.*
IT'S LIKE NOTHING HAPPENED...
BUT IT DID. WE *ALL* SAW THAT!
...RIGHT?
MAYBE IT WAS A TRICK OF THE LIGHT.
IT WASN'T. I *SWEAR* IT WASN'T.
PROF, I'M NOT GOING NUTS.

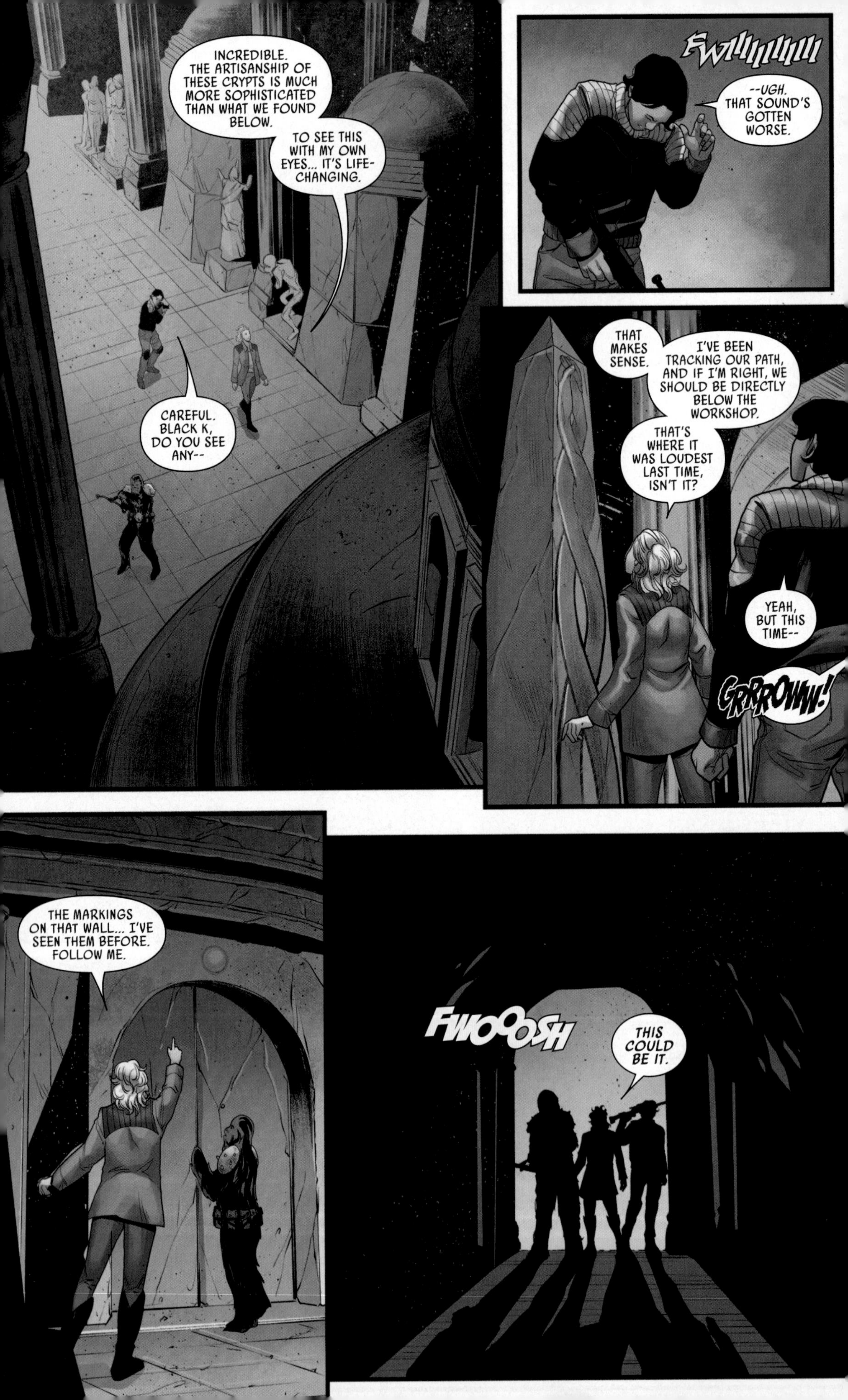
INCREDIBLE. THE ARTISANSHIP OF THESE CRYPTS IS MUCH MORE SOPHISTICATED THAN WHAT WE FOUND BELOW.
TO SEE THIS WITH MY OWN EYES... IT'S LIFE-CHANGING.
CAREFUL. BLACK K, DO YOU SEE ANY--
FWIIIIIIIIII
--UGH. THAT SOUND'S GOTTEN WORSE.
THAT MAKES SENSE.
I'VE BEEN TRACKING OUR PATH, AND IF I'M RIGHT, WE SHOULD BE DIRECTLY BELOW THE WORKSHOP.
THAT'S WHERE IT WAS LOUDEST LAST TIME, ISN'T IT?
YEAH, BUT THIS TIME--
GRRROWW!
THE MARKINGS ON THAT WALL... I'VE SEEN THEM BEFORE. FOLLOW ME.
FWOOOSH
THIS COULD BE IT.

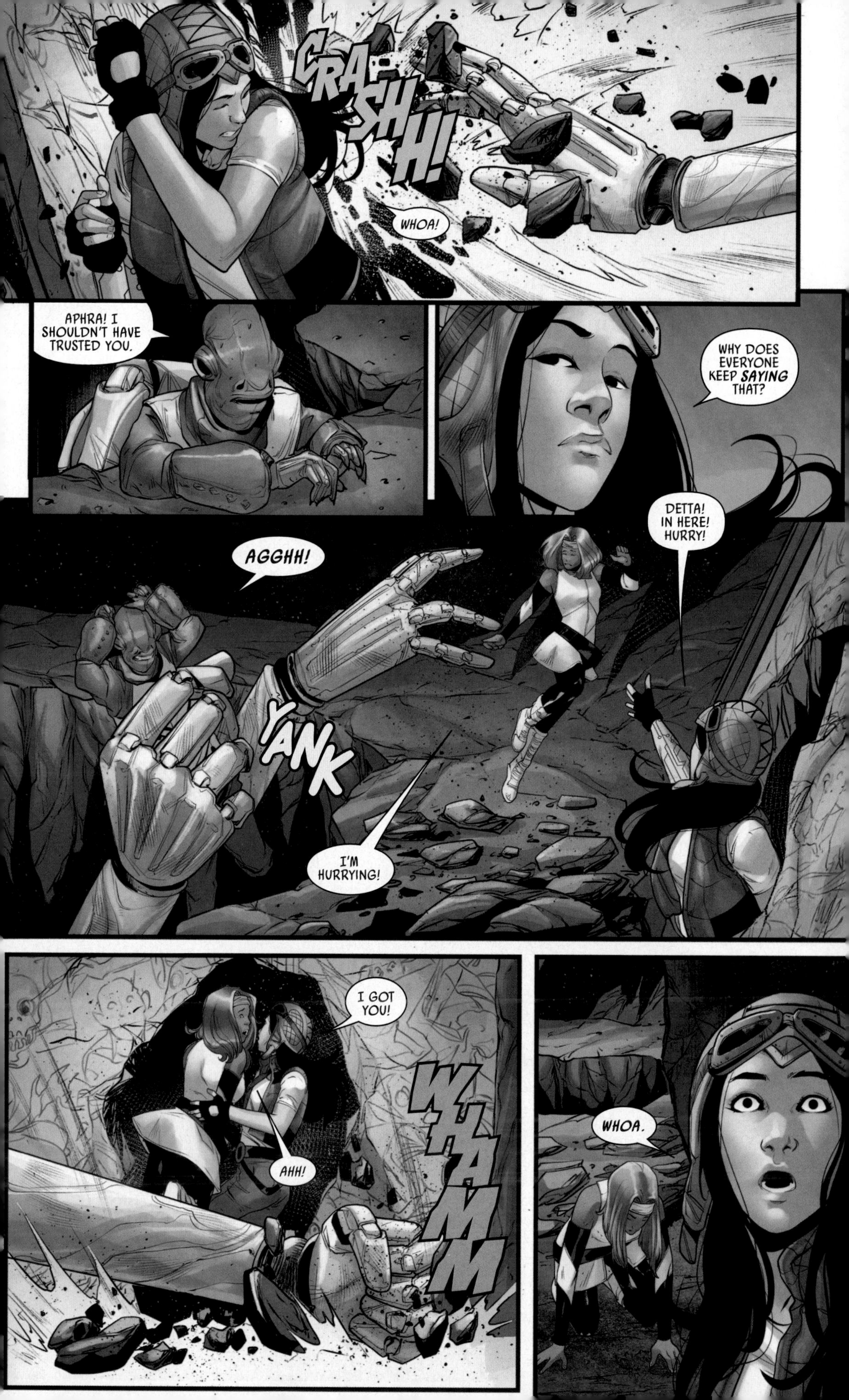
CRASHHH!
WHOA!
APHRA! I SHOULDN'T HAVE TRUSTED YOU.
WHY DOES EVERYONE KEEP SAYING THAT?
AGGHH!
DETTA! IN HERE! HURRY!
YANK
I'M HURRYING!
I GOT YOU!
AHH!
WHAMM
WHOA.

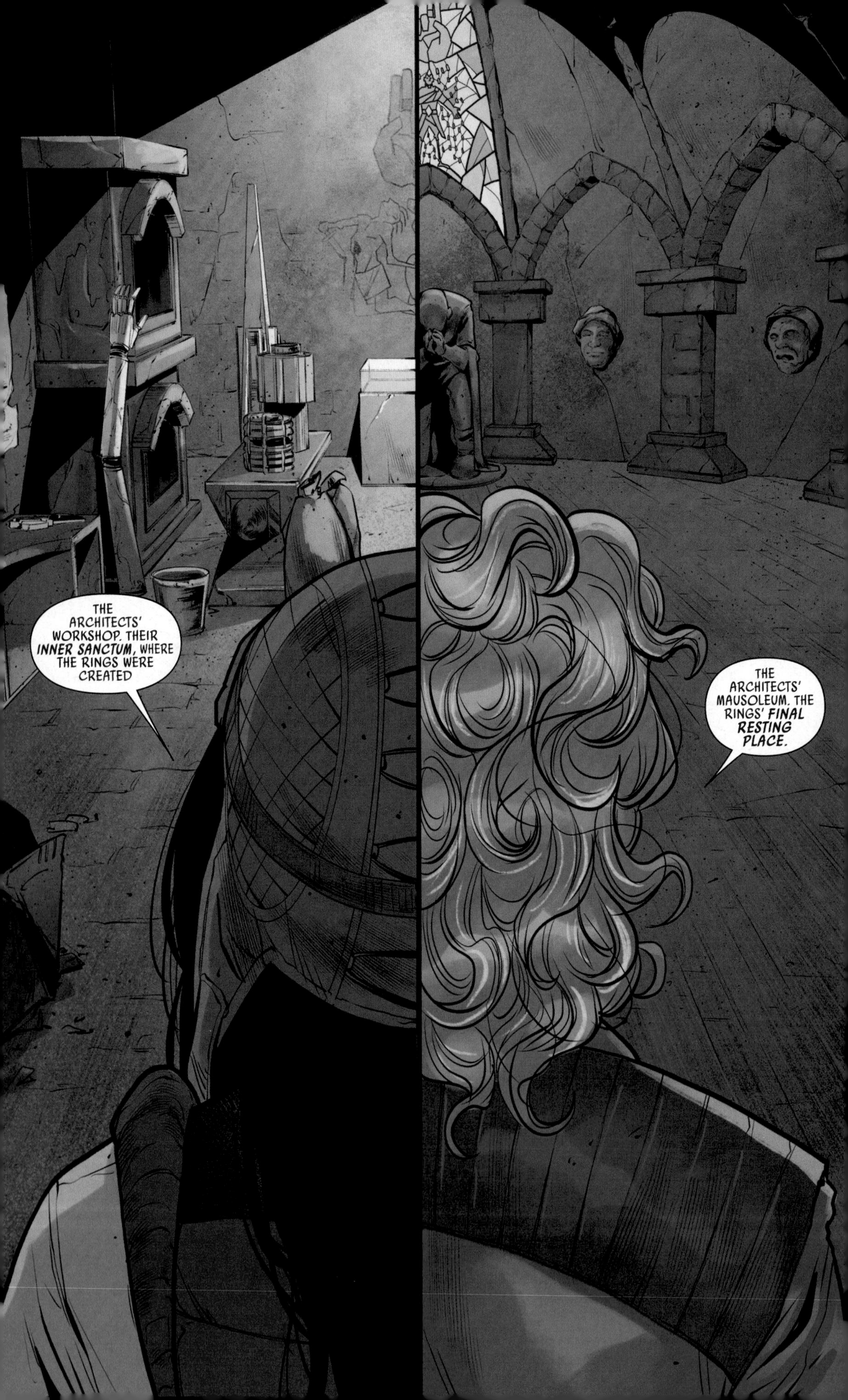
THE ARCHITECTS' WORKSHOP. THEIR INNER SANCTUM, WHERE THE RINGS WERE CREATED
THE ARCHITECTS' MAUSOLEUM. THE RINGS' FINAL RESTING PLACE.

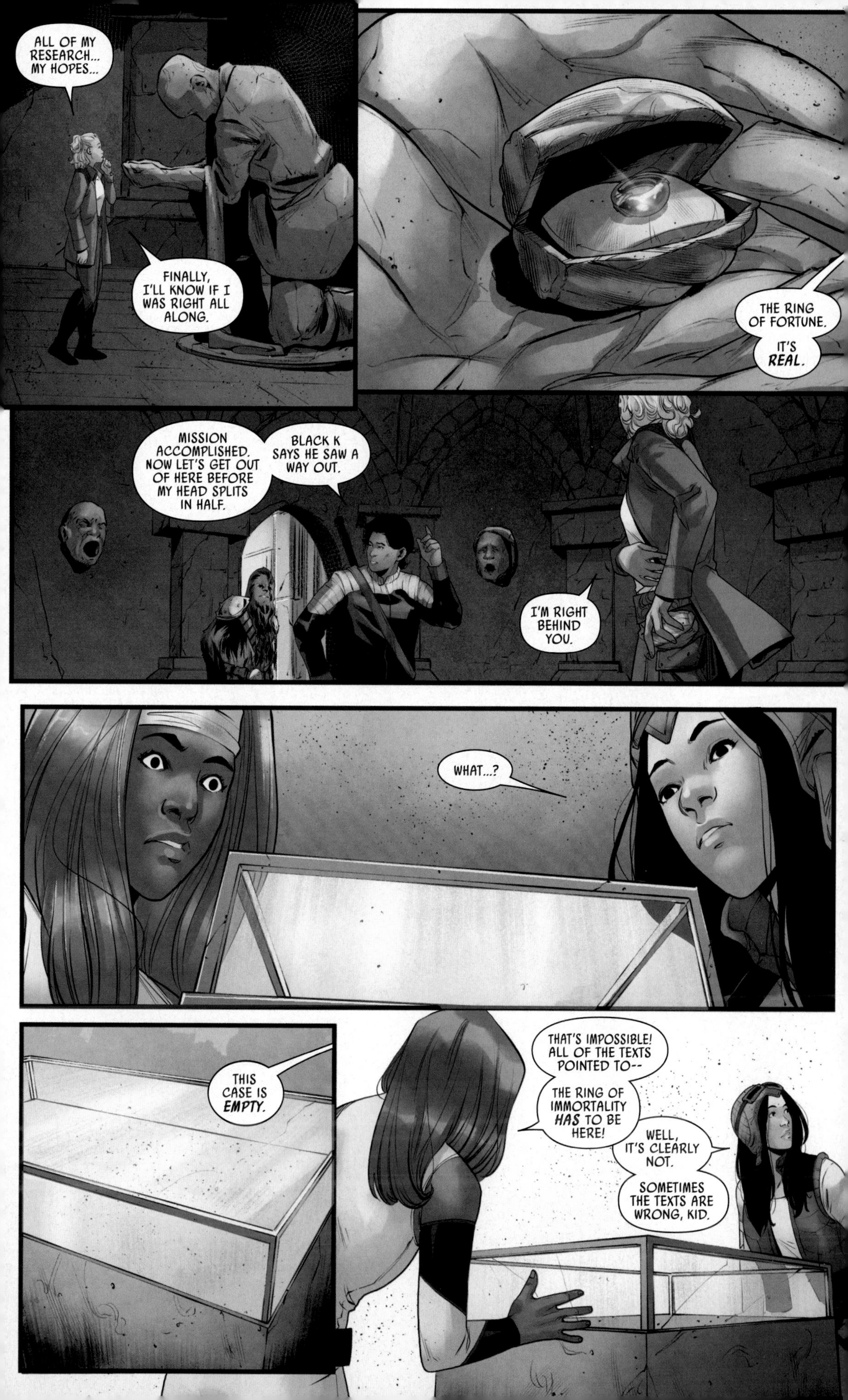
ALL OF MY RESEARCH... MY HOPES...
FINALLY, I'LL KNOW IF I WAS RIGHT ALL ALONG.
THE RING OF FORTUNE.
IT'S **REAL**.
MISSION ACCOMPLISHED. NOW LET'S GET OUT OF HERE BEFORE MY HEAD SPLITS IN HALF.
BLACK K SAYS HE SAW A WAY OUT.
I'M RIGHT BEHIND YOU.
WHAT...?
THIS CASE IS **EMPTY**.
THAT'S IMPOSSIBLE! ALL OF THE TEXTS POINTED TO--
THE RING OF IMMORTALITY **HAS** TO BE HERE!
WELL, IT'S CLEARLY NOT.
SOMETIMES THE TEXTS ARE WRONG, KID.

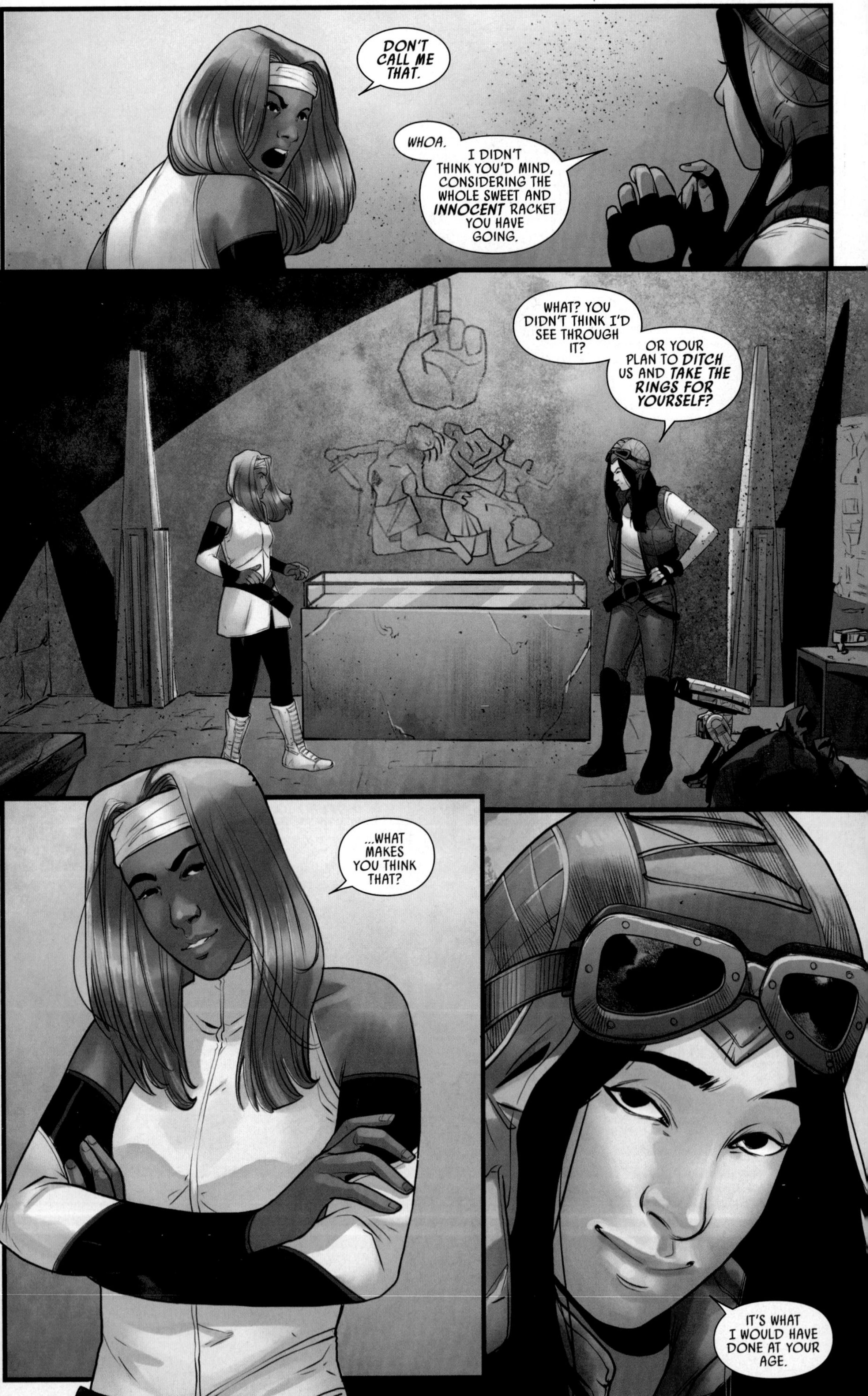
DON'T CALL ME THAT.
WHOA.
I DIDN'T THINK YOU'D MIND, CONSIDERING THE WHOLE SWEET AND INNOCENT RACKET YOU HAVE GOING.
WHAT? YOU DIDN'T THINK I'D SEE THROUGH IT?
OR YOUR PLAN TO DITCH US AND TAKE THE RINGS FOR YOURSELF?
...WHAT MAKES YOU THINK THAT?
IT'S WHAT I WOULD HAVE DONE AT YOUR AGE.

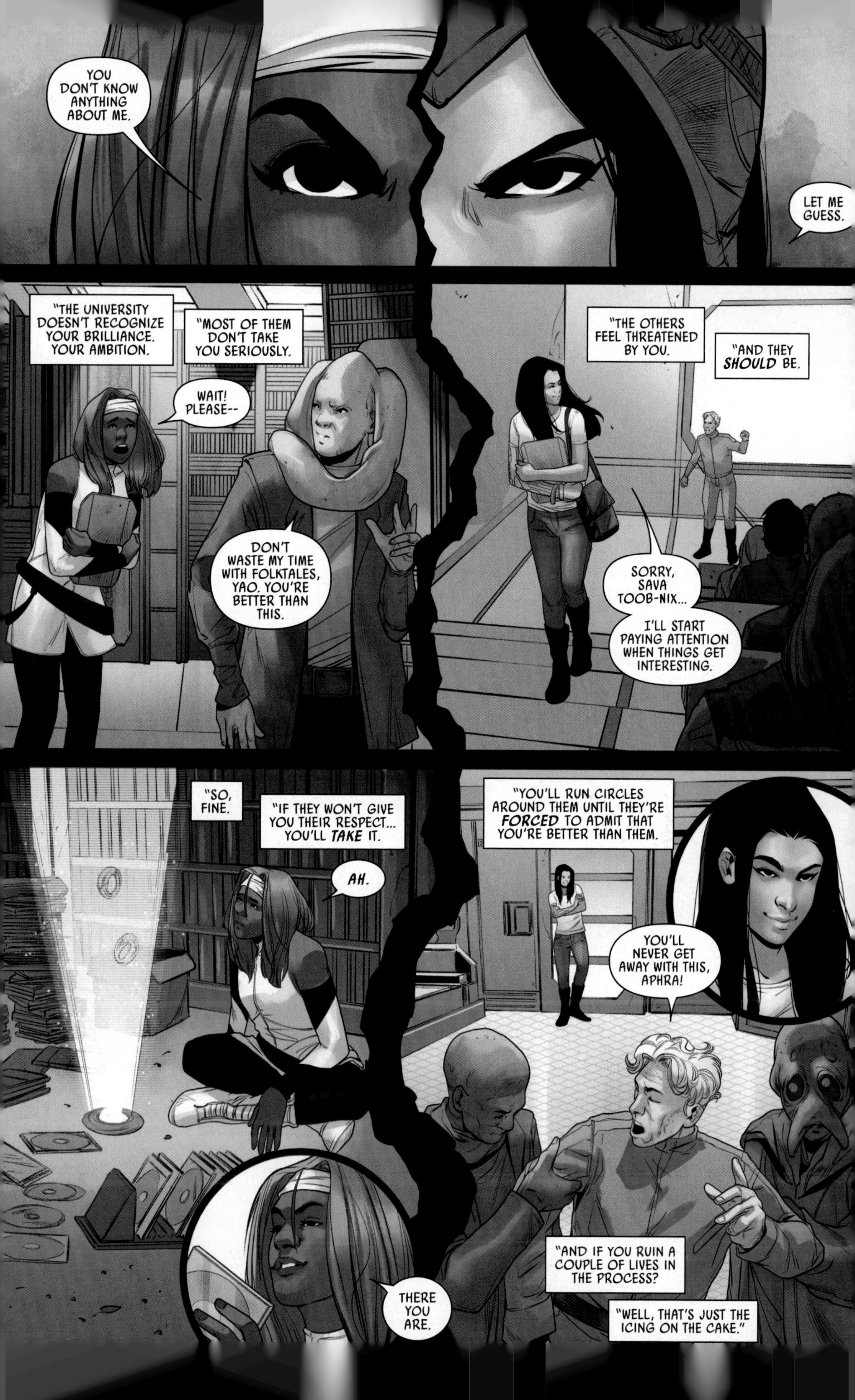

YOU DON'T KNOW ANYTHING ABOUT ME.
LET ME GUESS.
"THE UNIVERSITY DOESN'T RECOGNIZE YOUR BRILLIANCE. YOUR AMBITION.
"MOST OF THEM DON'T TAKE YOU SERIOUSLY.
WAIT! PLEASE--
DON'T WASTE MY TIME WITH FOLKTALES, YAO. YOU'RE BETTER THAN THIS.
"THE OTHERS FEEL THREATENED BY YOU.
"AND THEY SHOULD BE.
SORRY, SAVA TOOB-NIX...
I'LL START PAYING ATTENTION WHEN THINGS GET INTERESTING.
"SO, FINE.
"IF THEY WON'T GIVE YOU THEIR RESPECT... YOU'LL TAKE IT.
AH.
"YOU'LL RUN CIRCLES AROUND THEM UNTIL THEY'RE FORCED TO ADMIT THAT YOU'RE BETTER THAN THEM.
YOU'LL NEVER GET AWAY WITH THIS, APHRA!
THERE YOU ARE.
"AND IF YOU RUIN A COUPLE OF LIVES IN THE PROCESS?
"WELL, THAT'S JUST THE ICING ON THE CAKE."

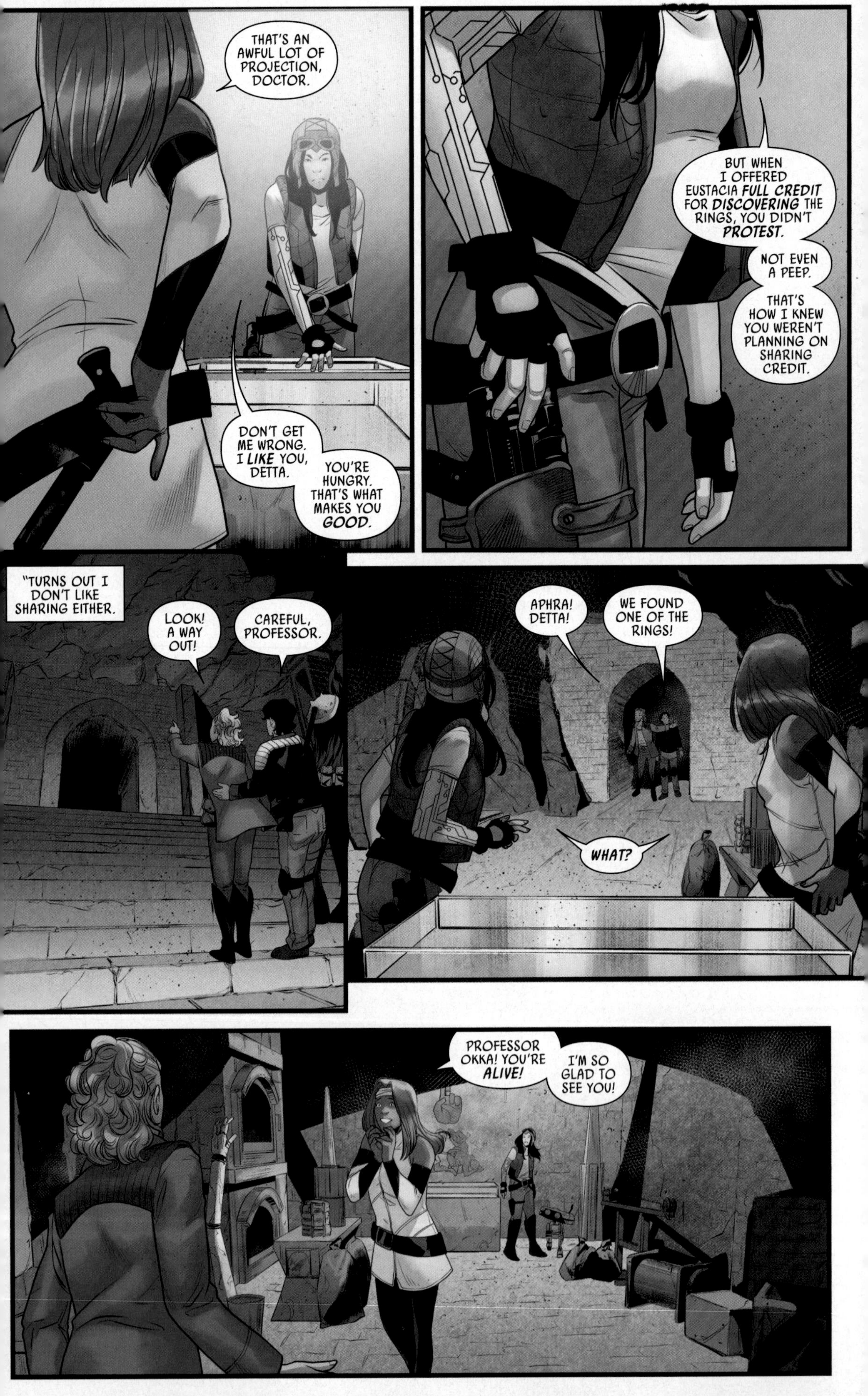
THAT'S AN AWFUL LOT OF PROJECTION, DOCTOR.
DON'T GET ME WRONG. I LIKE YOU, DETTA.
YOU'RE HUNGRY. THAT'S WHAT MAKES YOU GOOD.
BUT WHEN I OFFERED EUSTACIA FULL CREDIT FOR DISCOVERING THE RINGS, YOU DIDN'T PROTEST.
NOT EVEN A PEEP.
THAT'S HOW I KNEW YOU WEREN'T PLANNING ON SHARING CREDIT.
"TURNS OUT I DON'T LIKE SHARING EITHER.
LOOK! A WAY OUT!
CAREFUL, PROFESSOR.
APHRA! DETTA!
WE FOUND ONE OF THE RINGS!
WHAT?
PROFESSOR OKKA! YOU'RE ALIVE!
I'M SO GLAD TO SEE YOU!

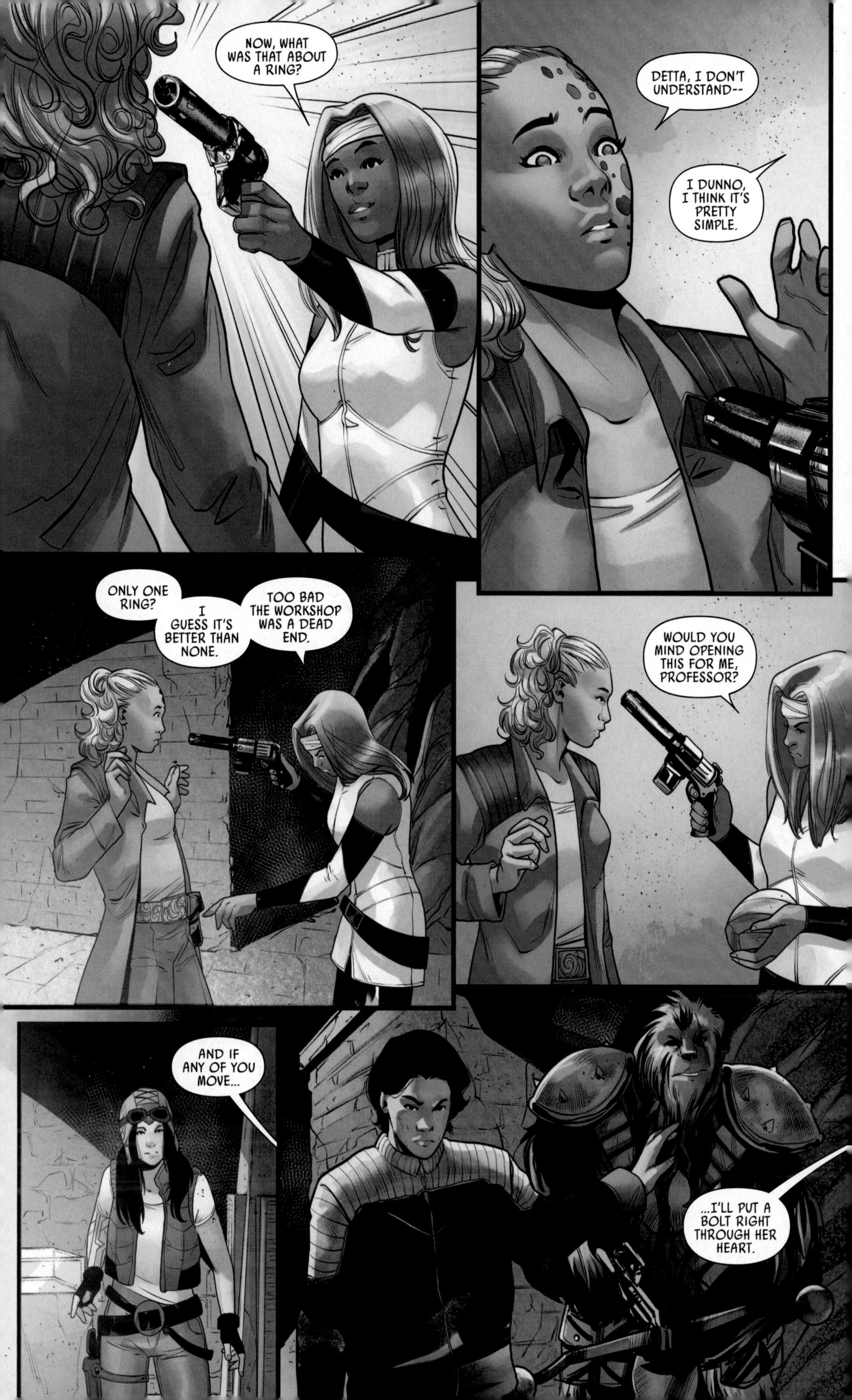
NOW, WHAT WAS THAT ABOUT A RING?
DETTA, I DON'T UNDERSTAND--
I DUNNO, I THINK IT'S PRETTY SIMPLE.
ONLY ONE RING?
I GUESS IT'S BETTER THAN NONE.
TOO BAD THE WORKSHOP WAS A DEAD END.
WOULD YOU MIND OPENING THIS FOR ME, PROFESSOR?
AND IF ANY OF YOU MOVE...
...I'LL PUT A BOLT RIGHT THROUGH HER HEART.

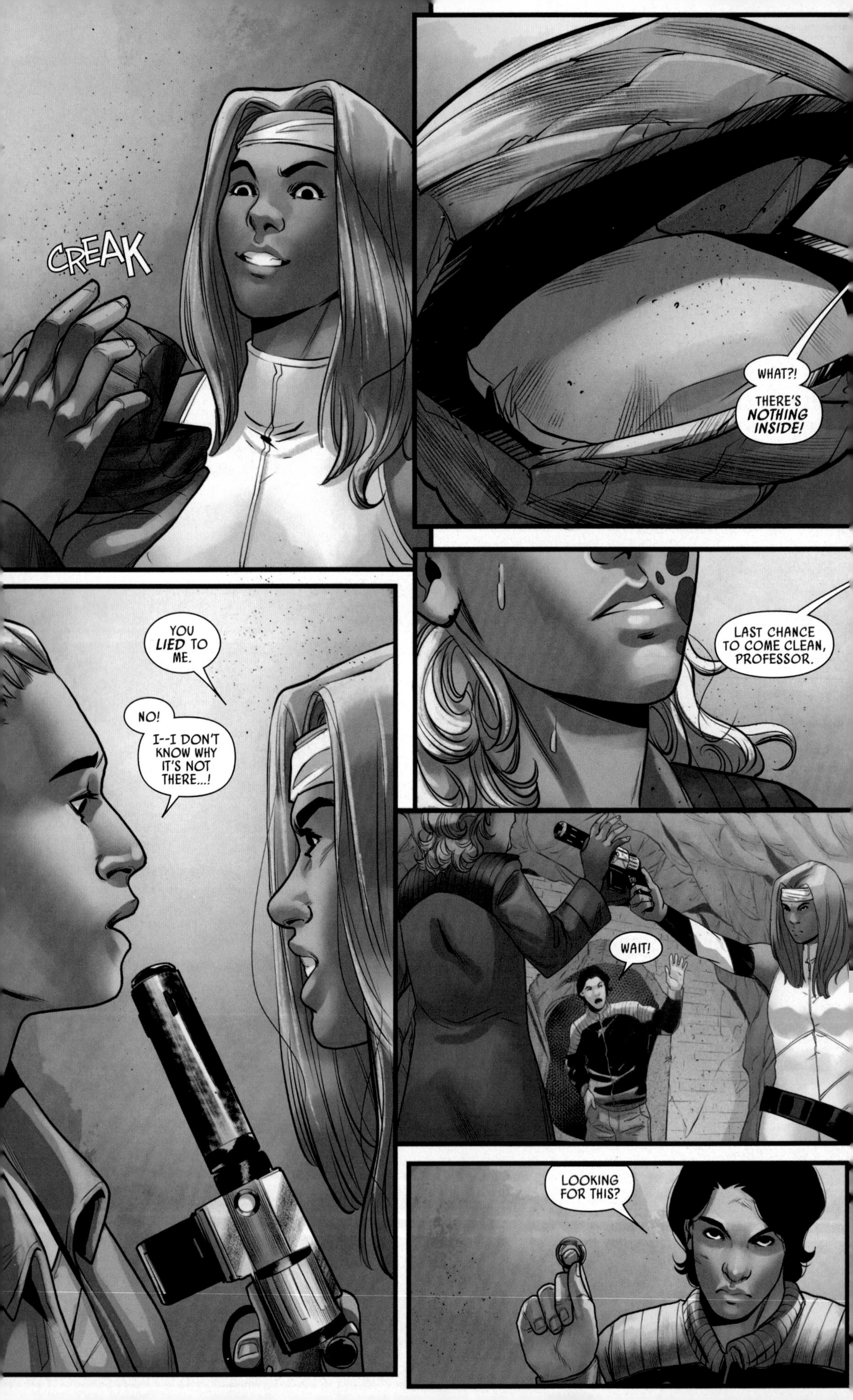
CREAK
WHAT?!
THERE'S NOTHING INSIDE!
YOU LIED TO ME.
NO!
I--I DON'T KNOW WHY IT'S NOT THERE...!
LAST CHANCE TO COME CLEAN, PROFESSOR.
WAIT!
LOOKING FOR THIS?

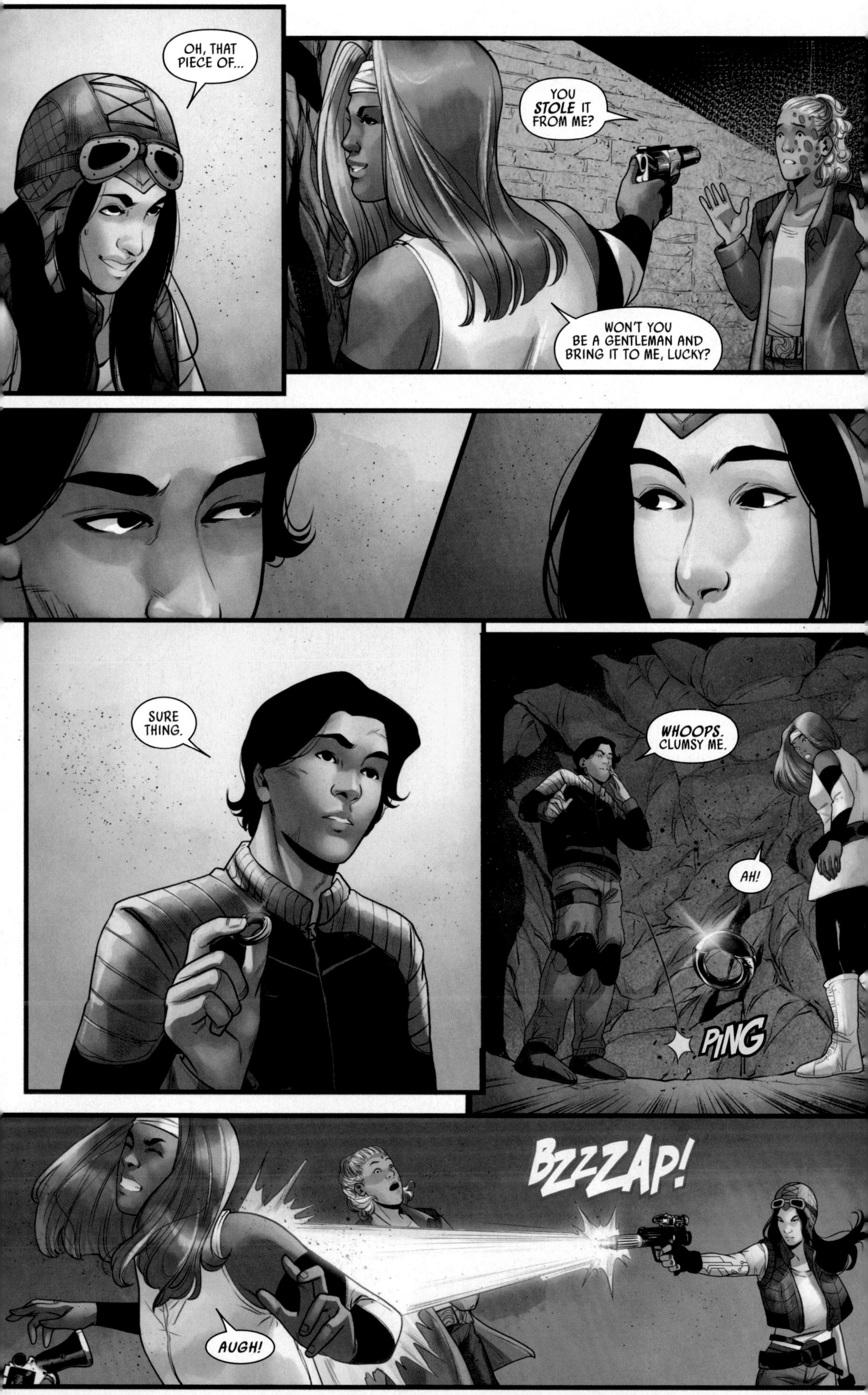

OH, THAT PIECE OF...
YOU STOLE IT FROM ME?
WON'T YOU BE A GENTLEMAN AND BRING IT TO ME, LUCKY?
SURE THING.
WHOOPS. CLUMSY ME.
AH!
PING
BZZZAP!
AUGH!

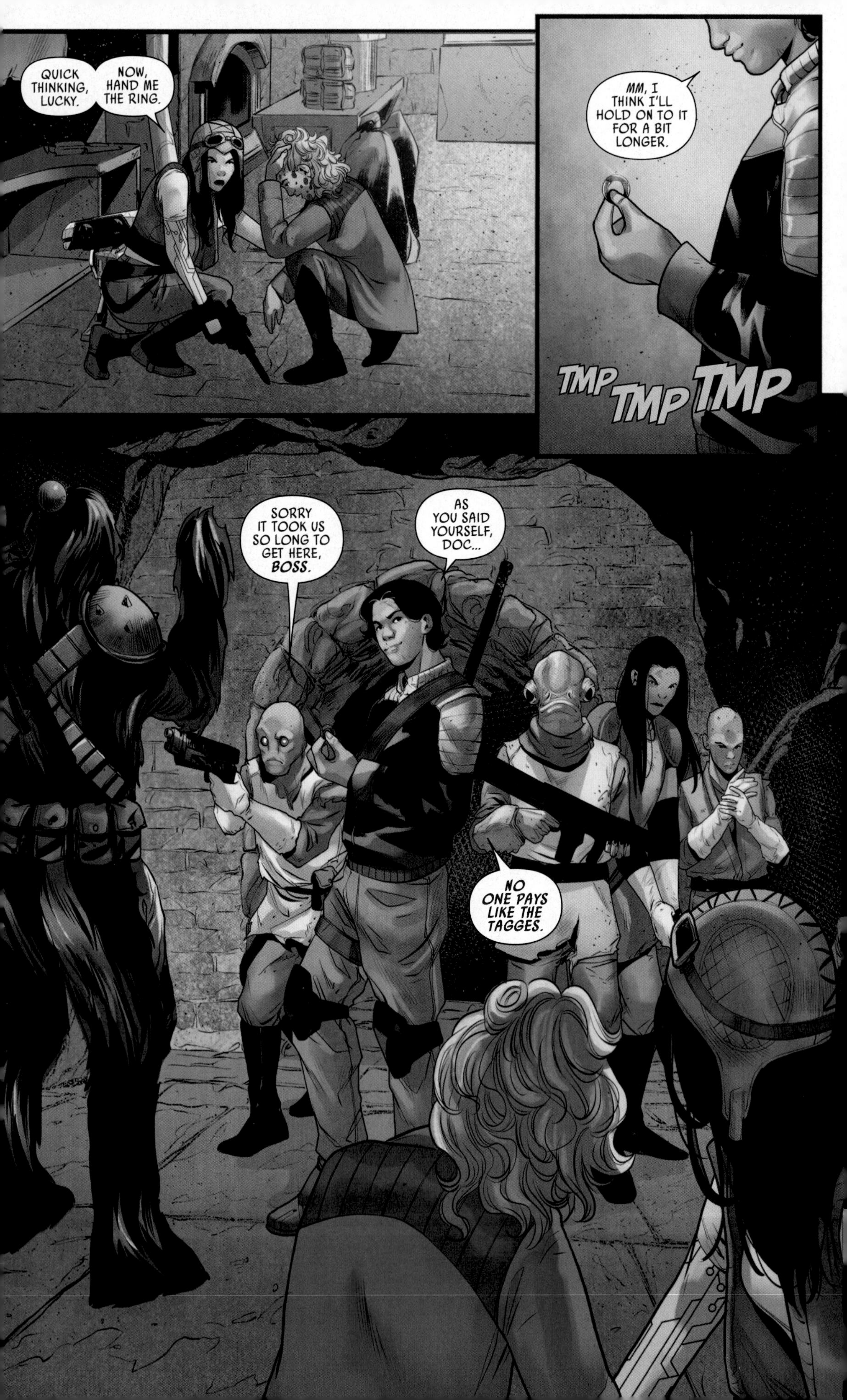
QUICK THINKING, LUCKY.
NOW, HAND ME THE RING.
MM, I THINK I'LL HOLD ON TO IT FOR A BIT LONGER.
TMP TMP TMP
SORRY IT TOOK US SO LONG TO GET HERE, BOSS.
AS YOU SAID YOURSELF, DOC...
NO ONE PAYS LIKE THE TAGGES.

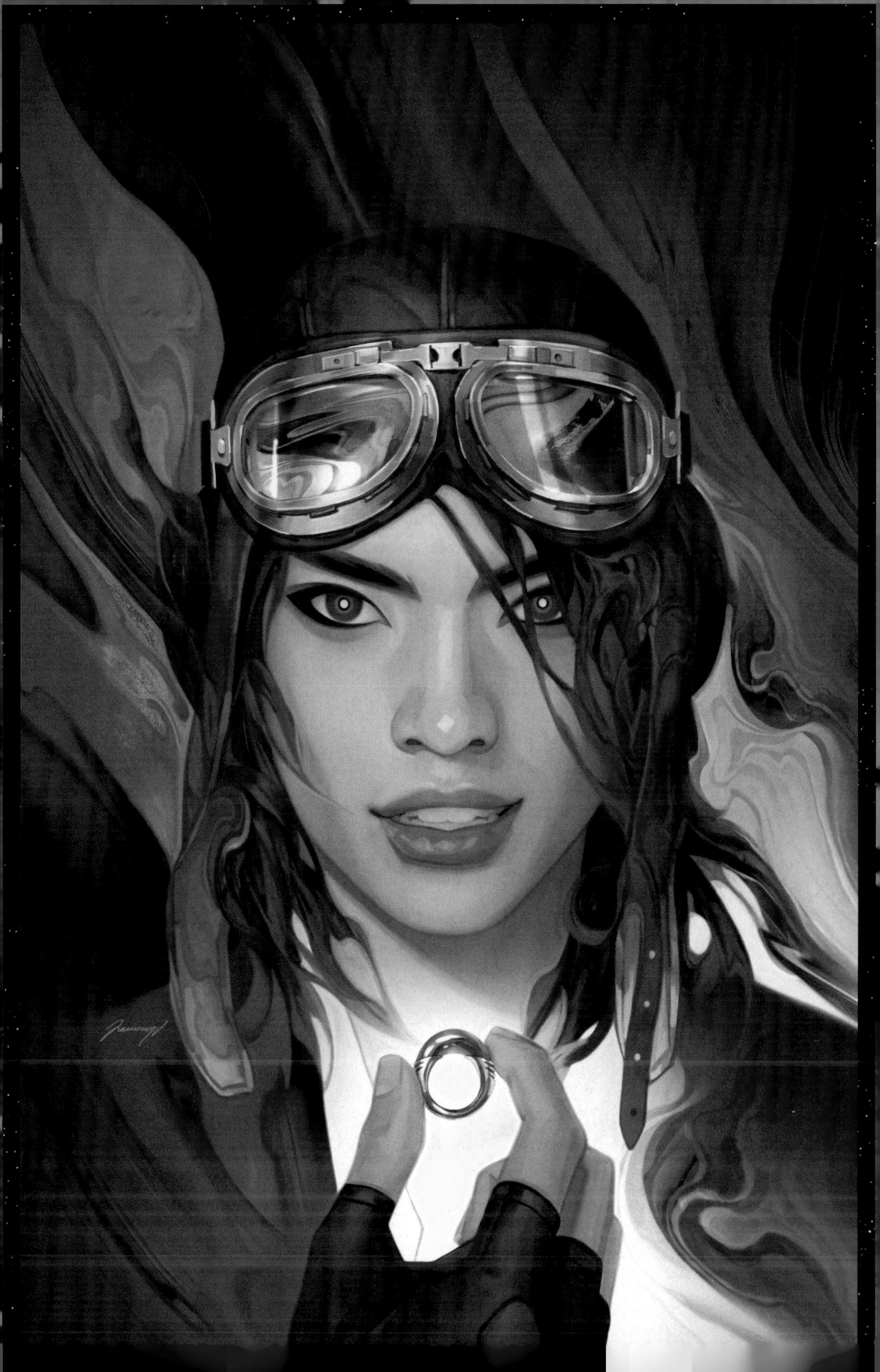

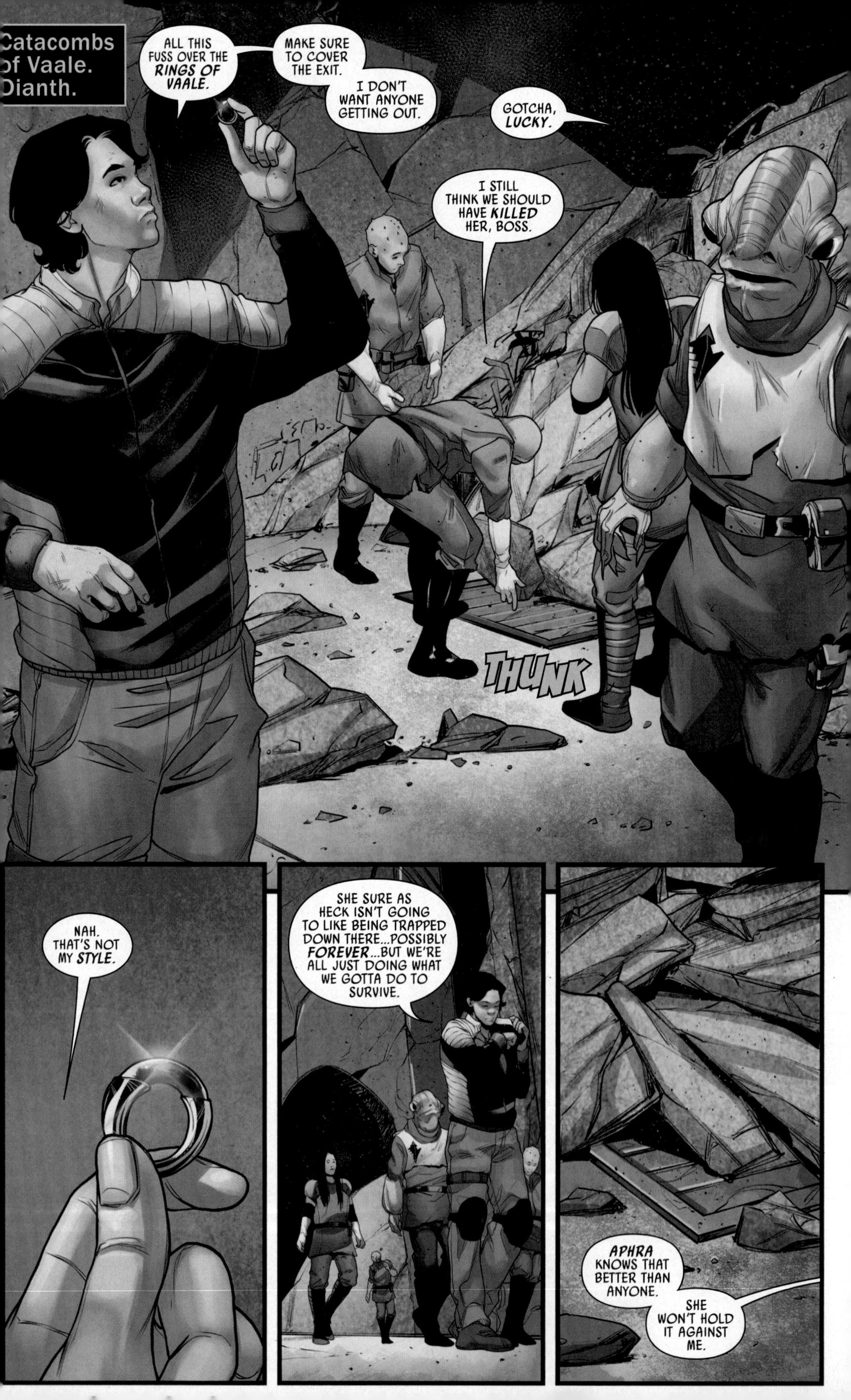

Catacombs of Vaale. Dianth.
ALL THIS FUSS OVER THE RINGS OF VAALE.
MAKE SURE TO COVER THE EXIT.
I DON'T WANT ANYONE GETTING OUT.
GOTCHA, LUCKY.
I STILL THINK WE SHOULD HAVE KILLED HER, BOSS.
THUNK
NAH. THAT'S NOT MY STYLE.
SHE SURE AS HECK ISN'T GOING TO LIKE BEING TRAPPED DOWN THERE...POSSIBLY FOREVER...BUT WE'RE ALL JUST DOING WHAT WE GOTTA DO TO SURVIVE.
APHRA KNOWS THAT BETTER THAN ANYONE.
SHE WON'T HOLD IT AGAINST ME.

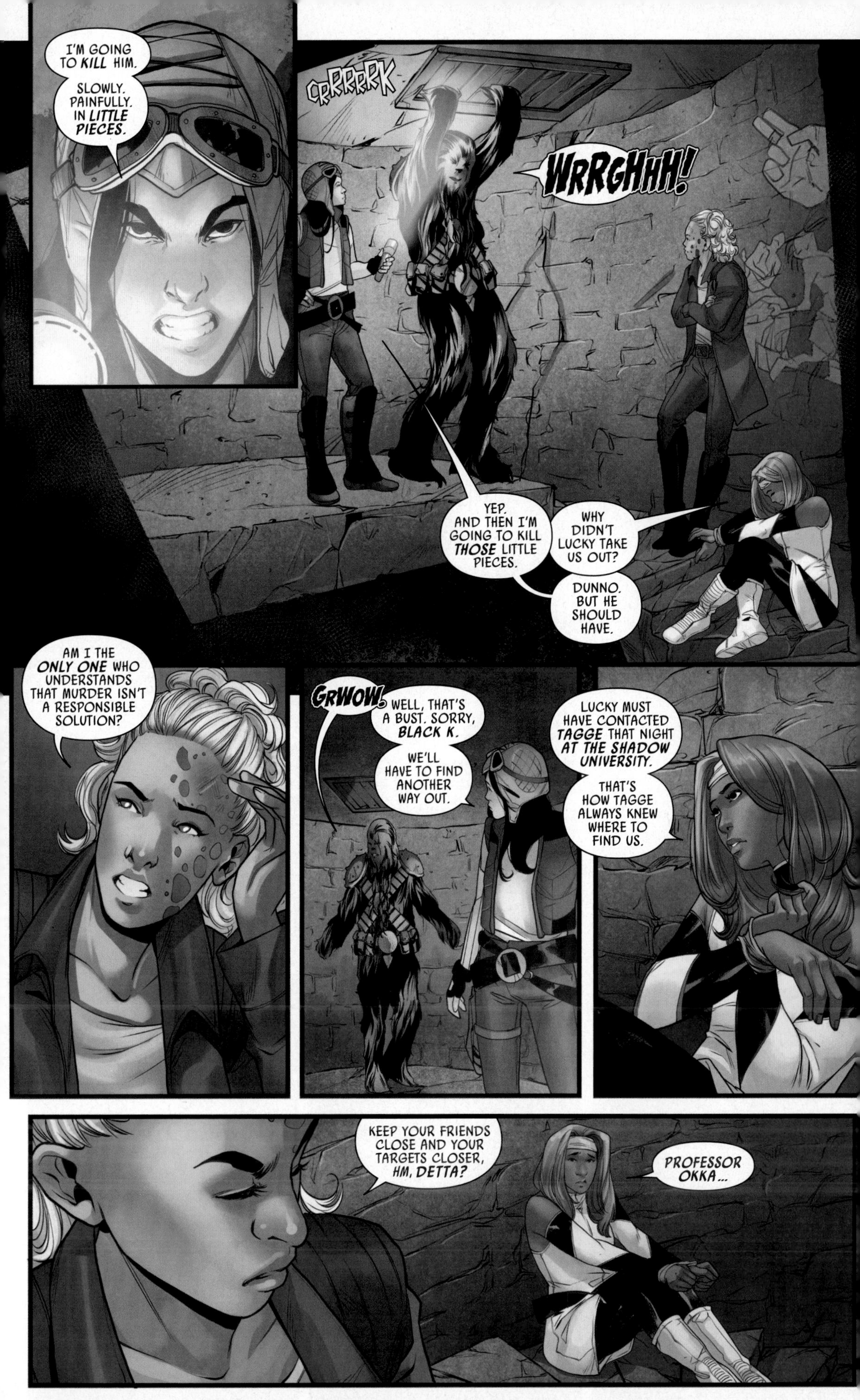
I'M GOING TO KILL HIM.
SLOWLY. PAINFULLY. IN LITTLE PIECES.
CRRRRRK
WRRGHHH!
YEP. AND THEN I'M GOING TO KILL THOSE LITTLE PIECES.
WHY DIDN'T LUCKY TAKE US OUT?
DUNNO. BUT HE SHOULD HAVE.
AM I THE ONLY ONE WHO UNDERSTANDS THAT MURDER ISN'T A RESPONSIBLE SOLUTION?
GRWOW.
WELL, THAT'S A BUST. SORRY, BLACK K.
WE'LL HAVE TO FIND ANOTHER WAY OUT.
LUCKY MUST HAVE CONTACTED TAGGE THAT NIGHT AT THE SHADOW UNIVERSITY.
THAT'S HOW TAGGE ALWAYS KNEW WHERE TO FIND US.
KEEP YOUR FRIENDS CLOSE AND YOUR TARGETS CLOSER, HM, DETTA?
PROFESSOR OKKA...

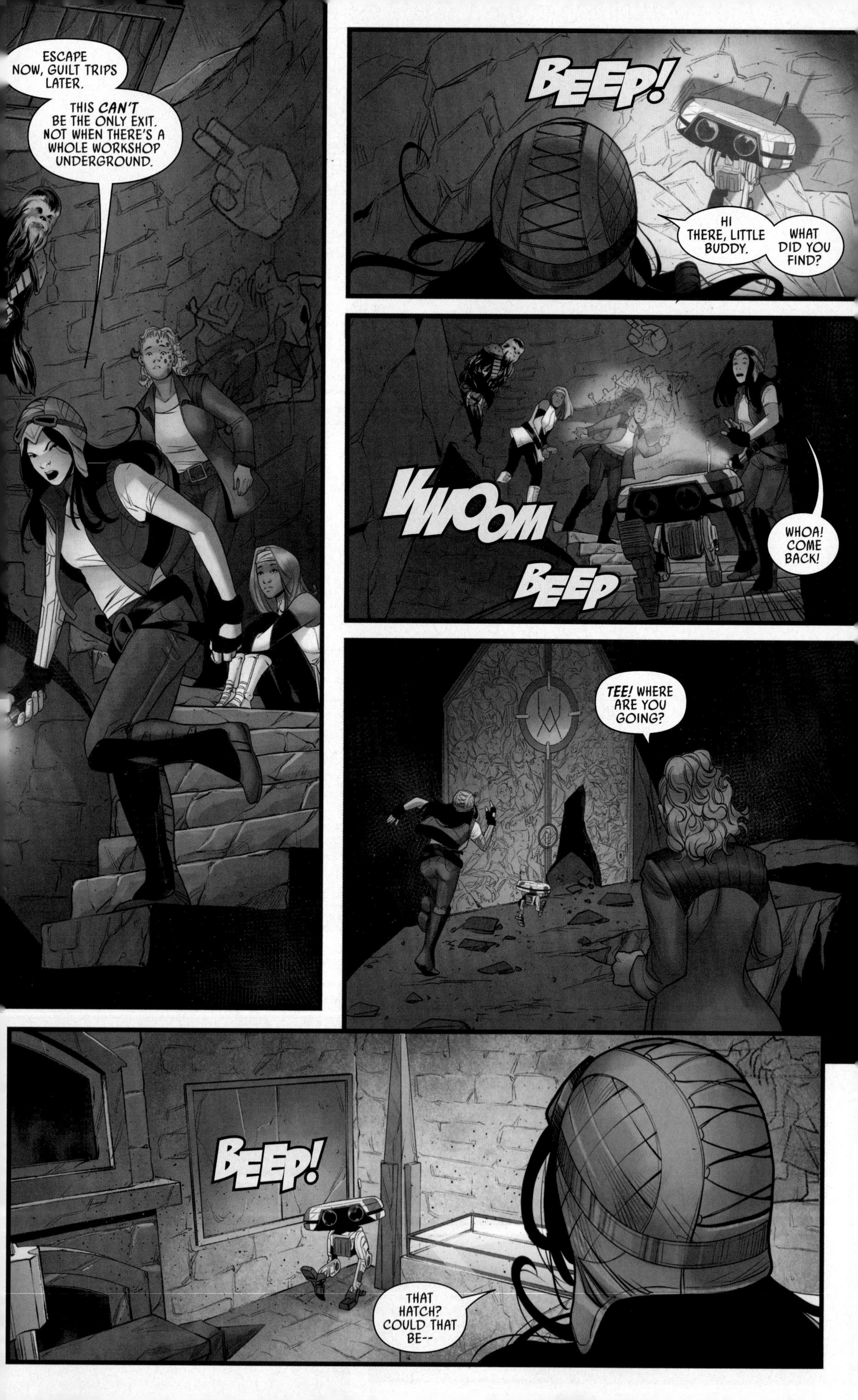
ESCAPE NOW, GUILT TRIPS LATER.
THIS CAN'T BE THE ONLY EXIT. NOT WHEN THERE'S A WHOLE WORKSHOP UNDERGROUND.
BEEP!
HI THERE, LITTLE BUDDY.
WHAT DID YOU FIND?
VWOOM
BEEP
WHOA! COME BACK!
TEE! WHERE ARE YOU GOING?
BEEP!
THAT HATCH? COULD THAT BE--

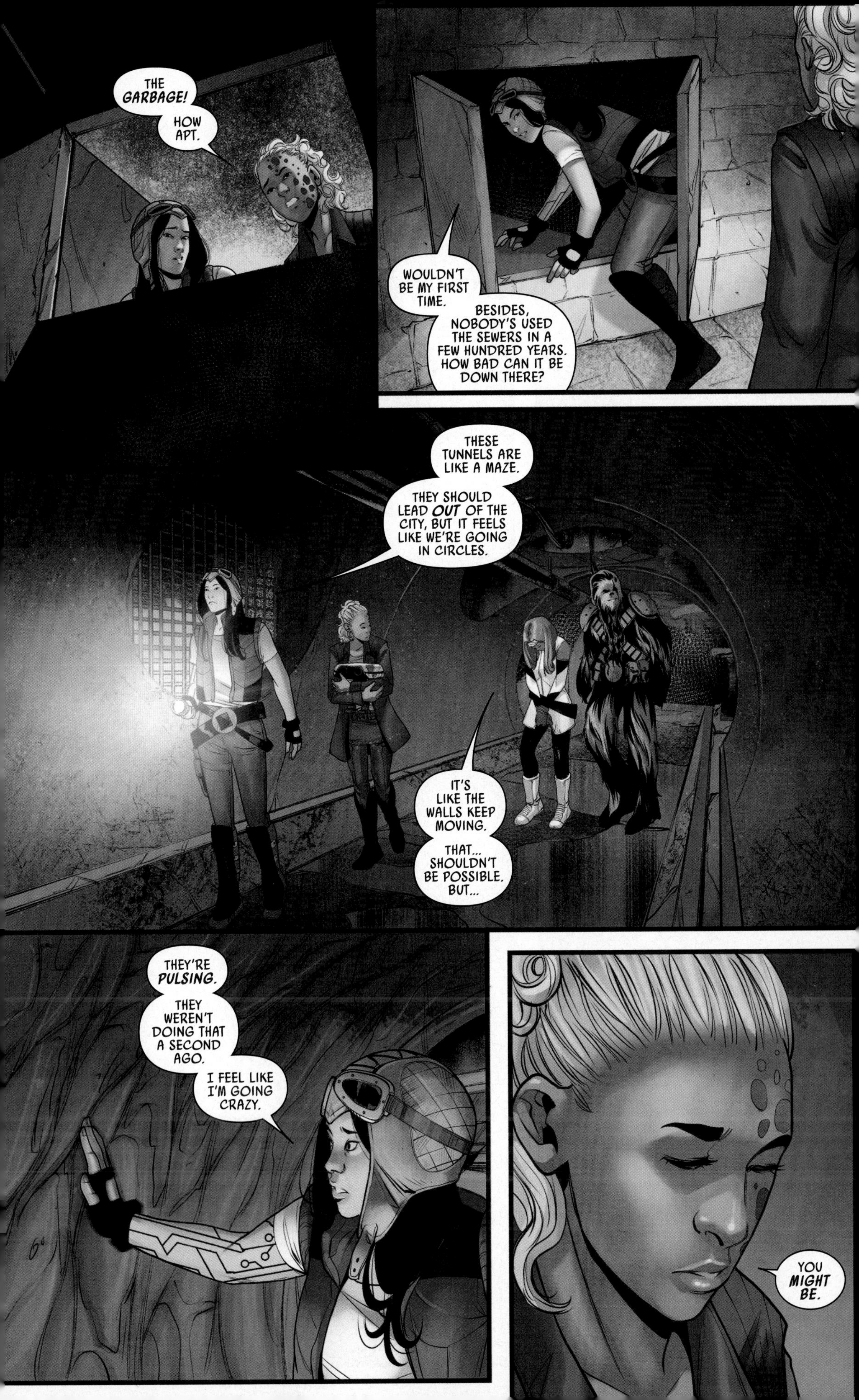
THE GARBAGE!
HOW APT.
WOULDN'T BE MY FIRST TIME.
BESIDES, NOBODY'S USED THE SEWERS IN A FEW HUNDRED YEARS. HOW BAD CAN IT BE DOWN THERE?
THESE TUNNELS ARE LIKE A MAZE.
THEY SHOULD LEAD OUT OF THE CITY, BUT IT FEELS LIKE WE'RE GOING IN CIRCLES.
IT'S LIKE THE WALLS KEEP MOVING.
THAT... SHOULDN'T BE POSSIBLE, BUT...
THEY'RE PULSING.
THEY WEREN'T DOING THAT A SECOND AGO.
I FEEL LIKE I'M GOING CRAZY.
YOU MIGHT BE.

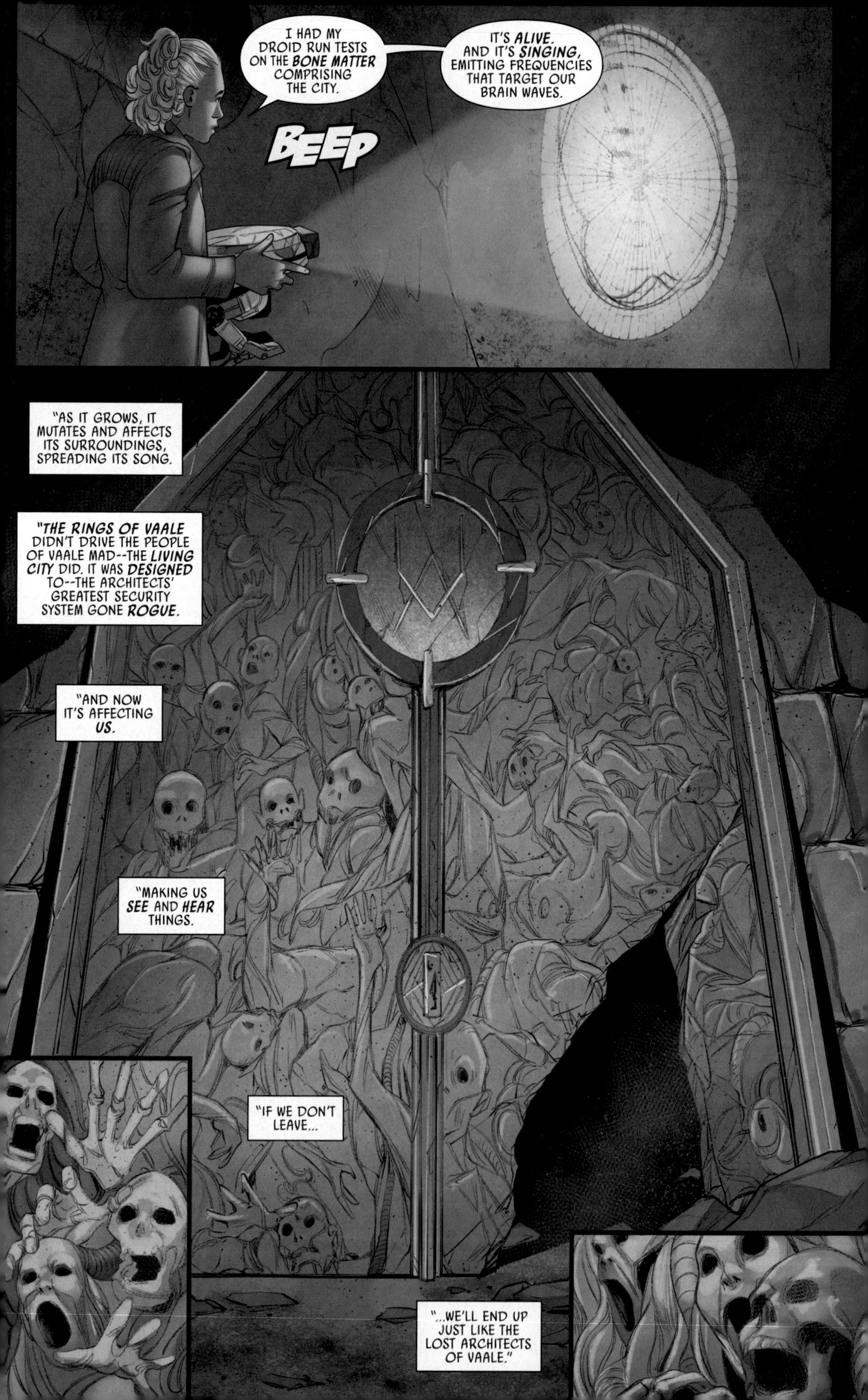
I HAD MY DROID RUN TESTS ON THE BONE MATTER COMPRISING THE CITY.
IT'S ALIVE. AND IT'S SINGING, EMITTING FREQUENCIES THAT TARGET OUR BRAIN WAVES.
BEEP
"AS IT GROWS, IT MUTATES AND AFFECTS ITS SURROUNDINGS, SPREADING ITS SONG.
"THE RINGS OF VAALE DIDN'T DRIVE THE PEOPLE OF VAALE MAD--THE LIVING CITY DID. IT WAS DESIGNED TO--THE ARCHITECTS' GREATEST SECURITY SYSTEM GONE ROGUE.
"AND NOW IT'S AFFECTING US.
"MAKING US SEE AND HEAR THINGS.
"IF WE DON'T LEAVE...
"...WE'LL END UP JUST LIKE THE LOST ARCHITECTS OF VAALE."

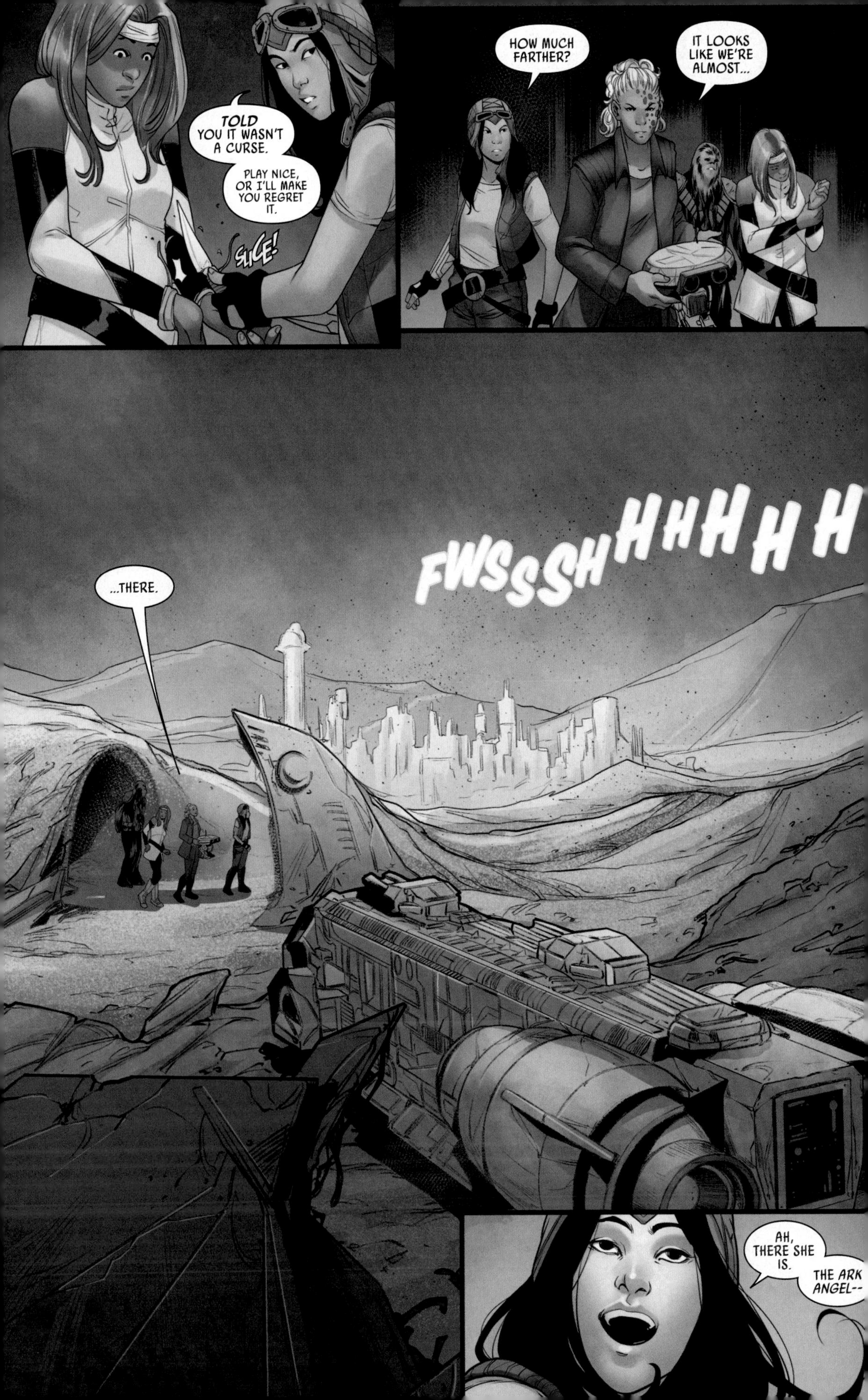
TOLD YOU IT WASN'T A CURSE.
PLAY NICE, OR I'LL MAKE YOU REGRET IT.
SLICE!
HOW MUCH FARTHER?
IT LOOKS LIKE WE'RE ALMOST...
...THERE.
FWSSSHHHHHHH
AH, THERE SHE IS.
THE ARK ANGEL--

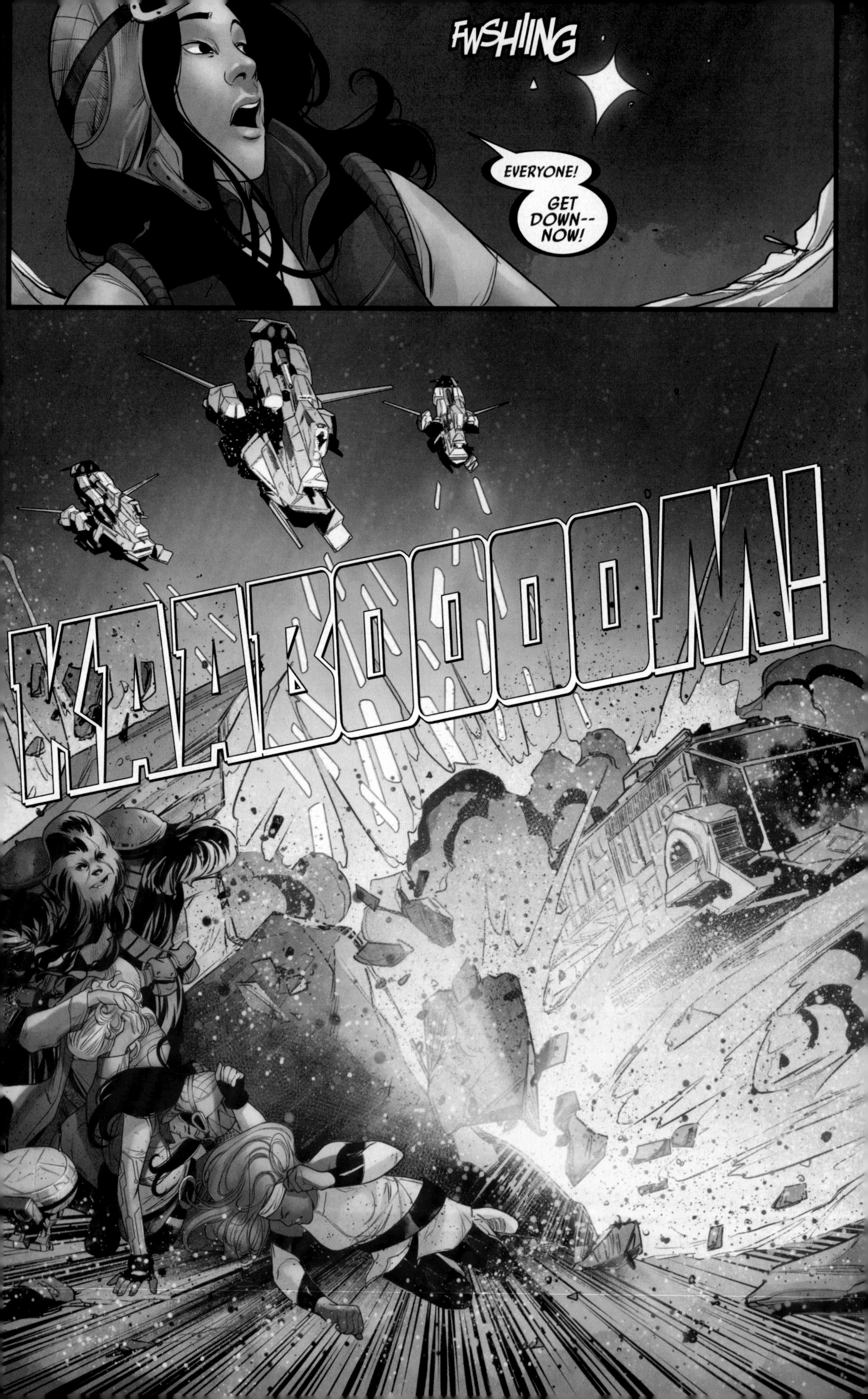
FWSHIING
EVERYONE!
GET DOWN-- NOW!
KAABOOOOM!

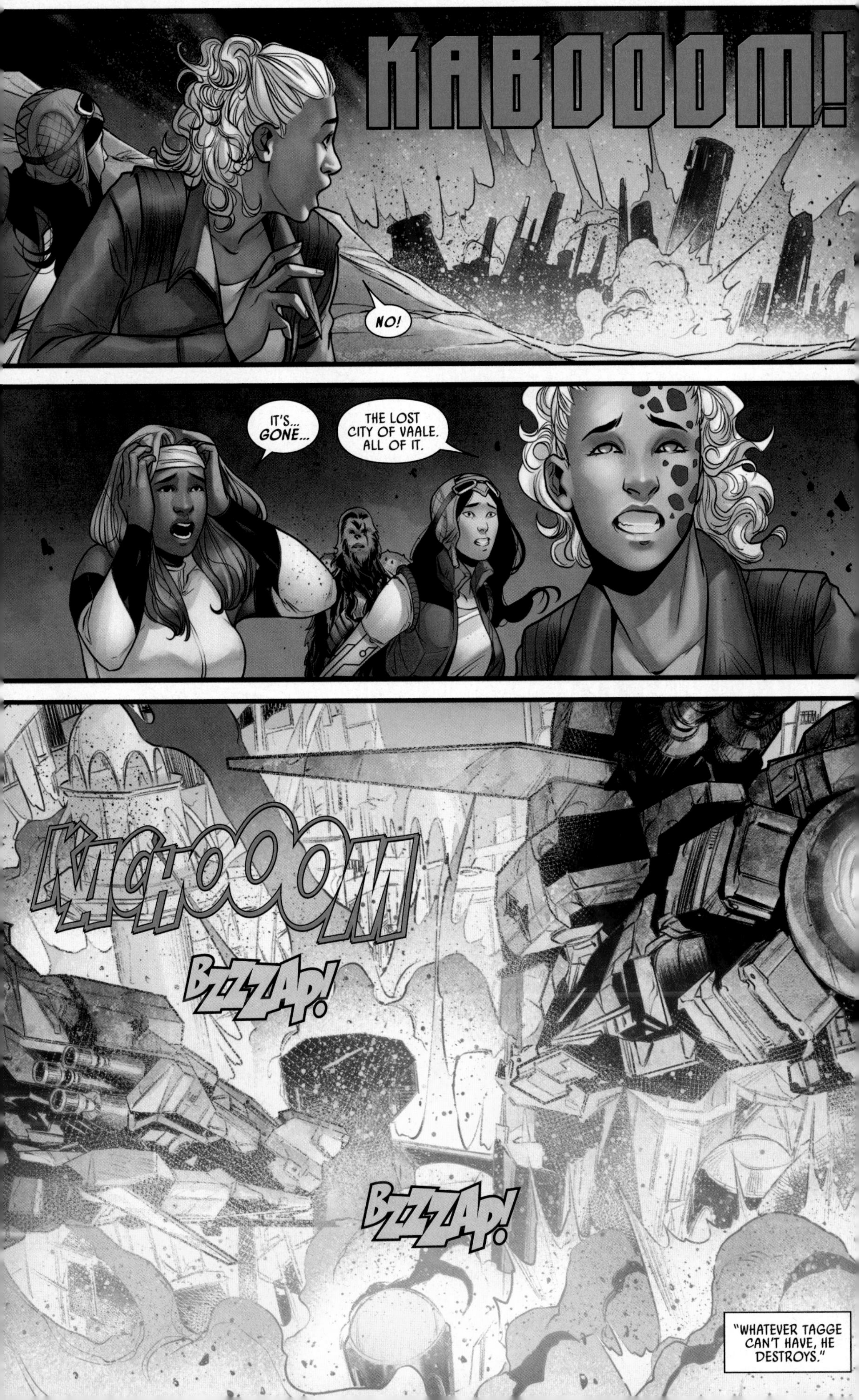
KABOOOM!
NO!
IT'S... GONE...
THE LOST CITY OF VAALE. ALL OF IT.
BZZZAP!
BZZZAP!
"WHATEVER TAGGE CAN'T HAVE, HE DESTROYS."

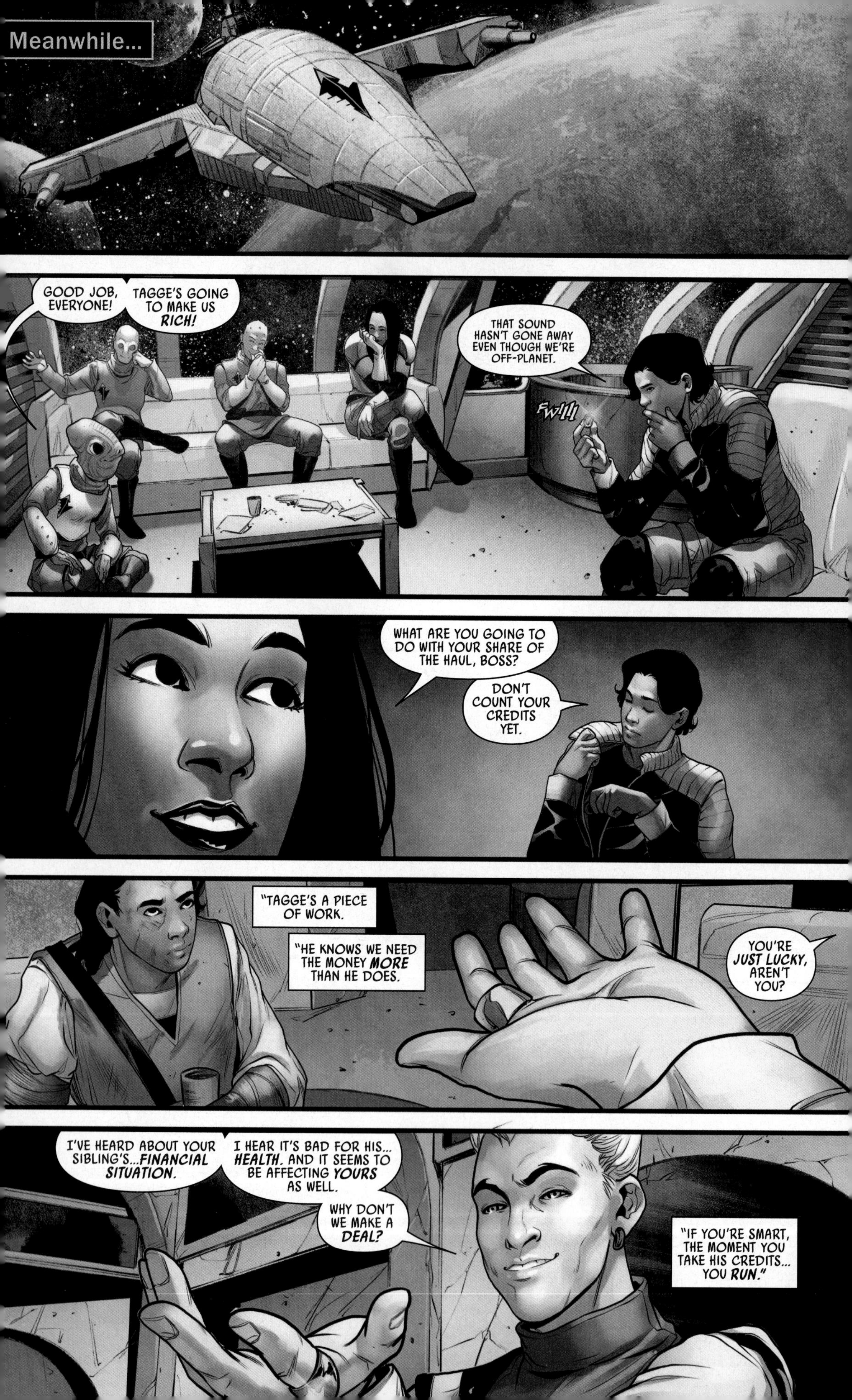
Meanwhile...
GOOD JOB, EVERYONE!
TAGGE'S GOING TO MAKE US RICH!
THAT SOUND HASN'T GONE AWAY EVEN THOUGH WE'RE OFF-PLANET.
FWIII
WHAT ARE YOU GOING TO DO WITH YOUR SHARE OF THE HAUL, BOSS?
DON'T COUNT YOUR CREDITS YET.
"TAGGE'S A PIECE OF WORK.
"HE KNOWS WE NEED THE MONEY MORE THAN HE DOES.
YOU'RE JUST LUCKY, AREN'T YOU?
I'VE HEARD ABOUT YOUR SIBLING'S...FINANCIAL SITUATION.
I HEAR IT'S BAD FOR HIS... HEALTH. AND IT SEEMS TO BE AFFECTING YOURS AS WELL.
WHY DON'T WE MAKE A DEAL?
"IF YOU'RE SMART, THE MOMENT YOU TAKE HIS CREDITS... YOU RUN."

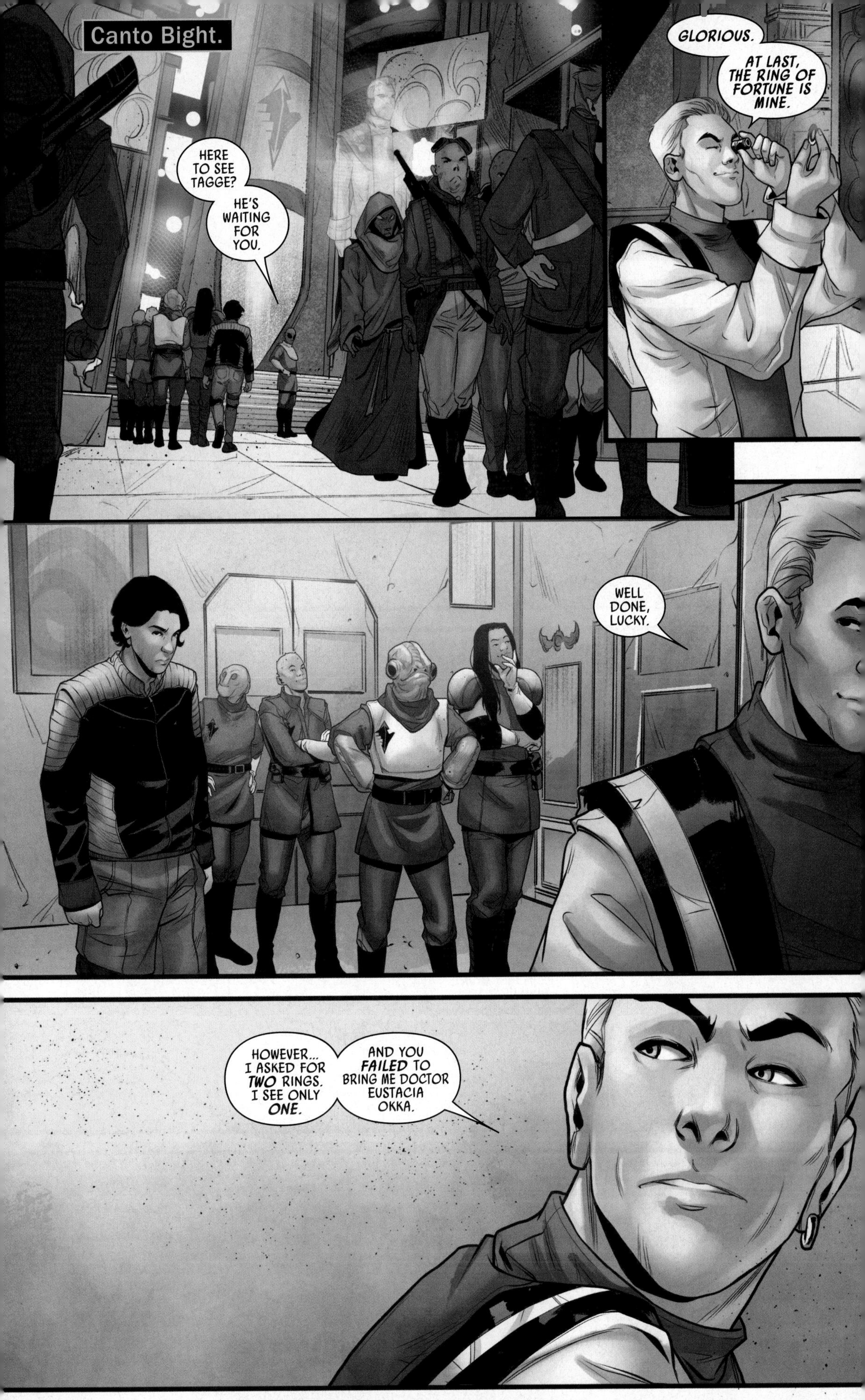
Canto Bight.
HERE TO SEE TAGGE?
HE'S WAITING FOR YOU.
GLORIOUS.
AT LAST, THE RING OF FORTUNE IS MINE.
WELL DONE, LUCKY.
HOWEVER... I ASKED FOR TWO RINGS. I SEE ONLY ONE.
AND YOU FAILED TO BRING ME DOCTOR EUSTACIA OKKA.

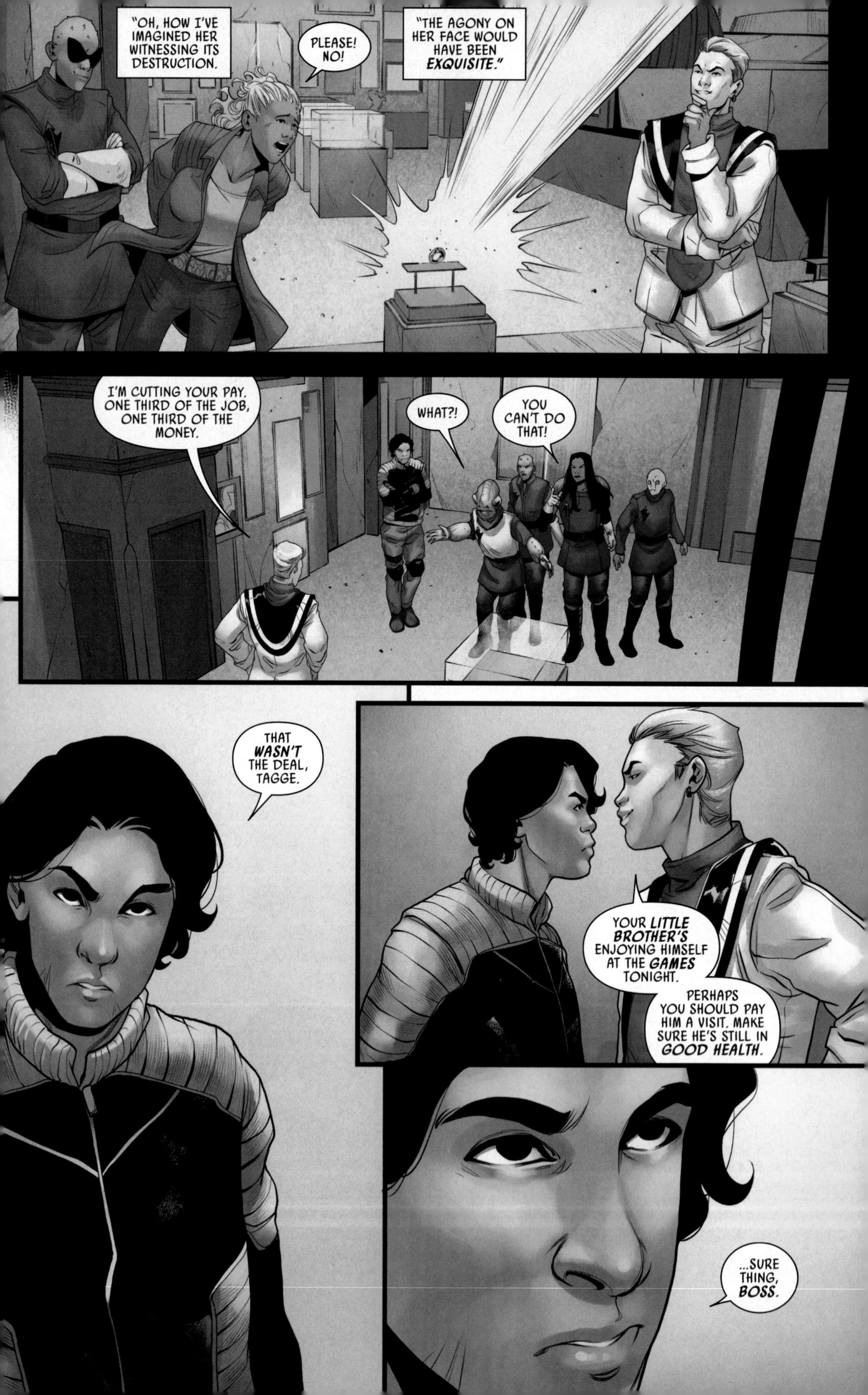
"OH, HOW I'VE IMAGINED HER WITNESSING ITS DESTRUCTION.
PLEASE! NO!
"THE AGONY ON HER FACE WOULD HAVE BEEN EXQUISITE."
I'M CUTTING YOUR PAY. ONE THIRD OF THE JOB, ONE THIRD OF THE MONEY.
WHAT?!
YOU CAN'T DO THAT!
THAT WASN'T THE DEAL, TAGGE.
YOUR LITTLE BROTHER'S ENJOYING HIMSELF AT THE GAMES TONIGHT.
PERHAPS YOU SHOULD PAY HIM A VISIT. MAKE SURE HE'S STILL IN GOOD HEALTH.
...SURE THING, BOSS.

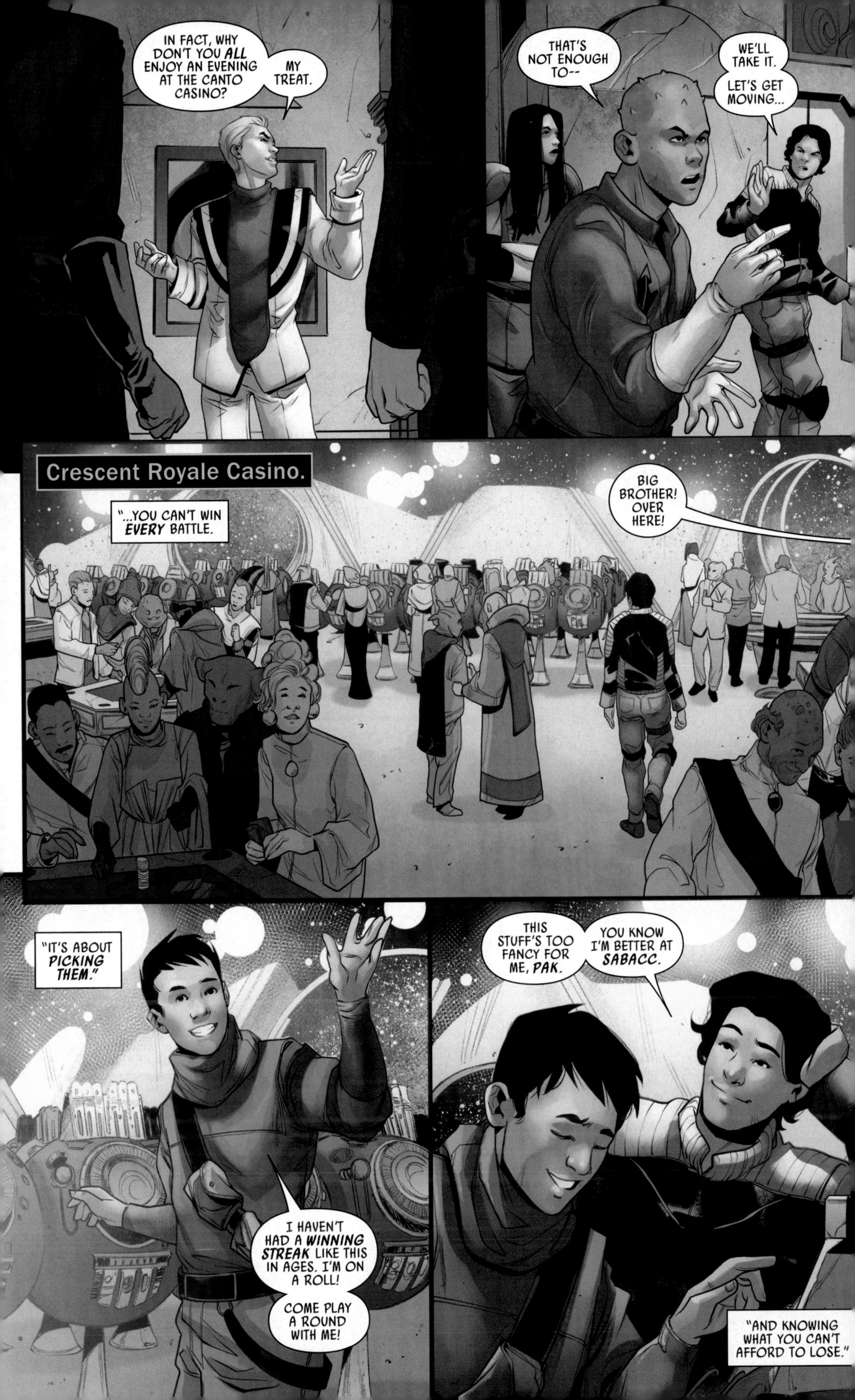
IN FACT, WHY DON'T YOU ALL ENJOY AN EVENING AT THE CANTO CASINO?
MY TREAT.
THAT'S NOT ENOUGH TO--
WE'LL TAKE IT.
LET'S GET MOVING...
Crescent Royale Casino.
"...YOU CAN'T WIN EVERY BATTLE.
BIG BROTHER! OVER HERE!
"IT'S ABOUT PICKING THEM."
I HAVEN'T HAD A WINNING STREAK LIKE THIS IN AGES. I'M ON A ROLL!
COME PLAY A ROUND WITH ME!
THIS STUFF'S TOO FANCY FOR ME, PAK.
YOU KNOW I'M BETTER AT SABACC.
"AND KNOWING WHAT YOU CAN'T AFFORD TO LOSE."

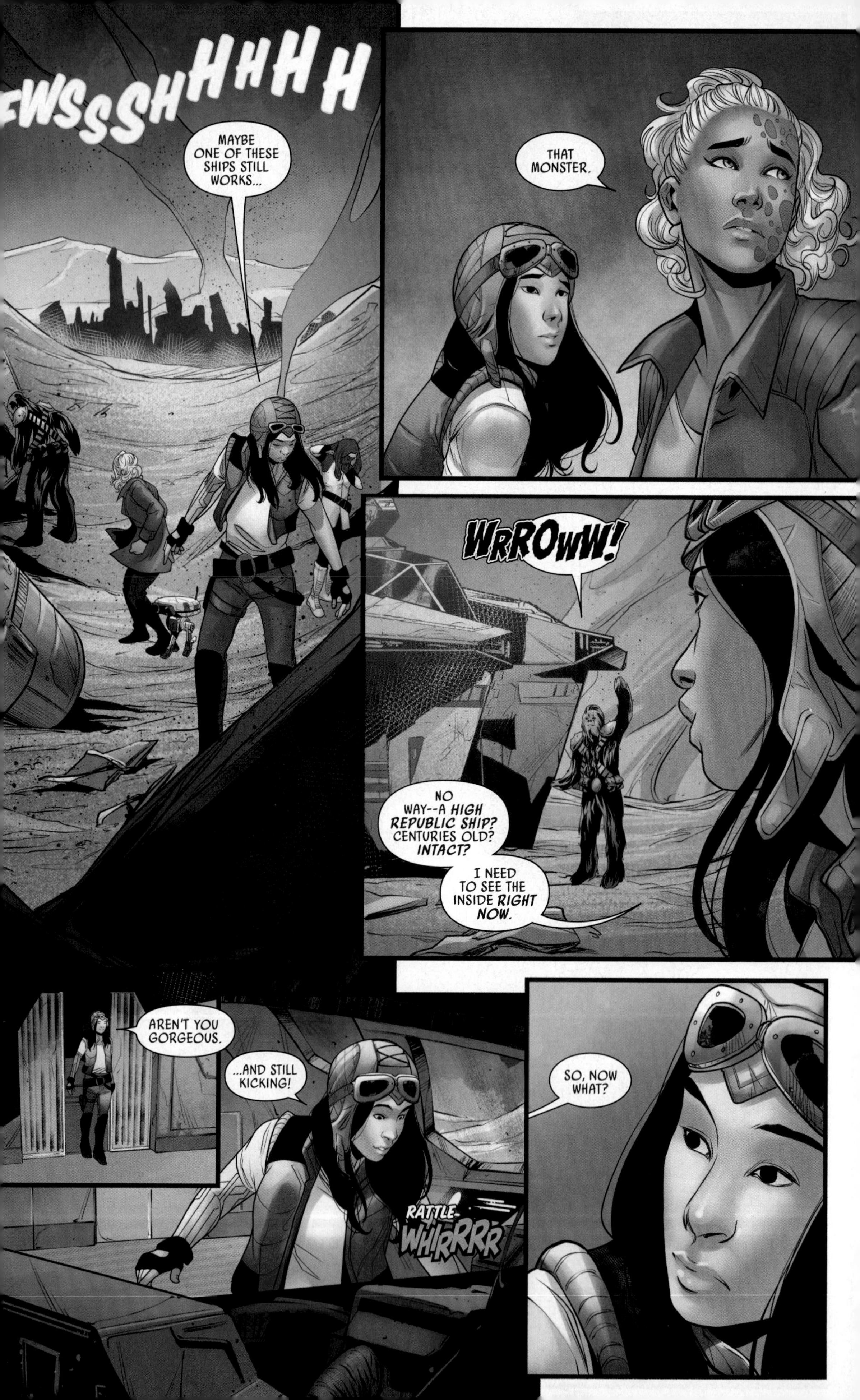
FWSSSHHHHH
MAYBE ONE OF THESE SHIPS STILL WORKS...
THAT MONSTER.
WRROWW!
NO WAY--A HIGH REPUBLIC SHIP? CENTURIES OLD? INTACT?
I NEED TO SEE THE INSIDE RIGHT NOW.
AREN'T YOU GORGEOUS.
...AND STILL KICKING!
RATTLE
WHIRRRR
SO, NOW WHAT?

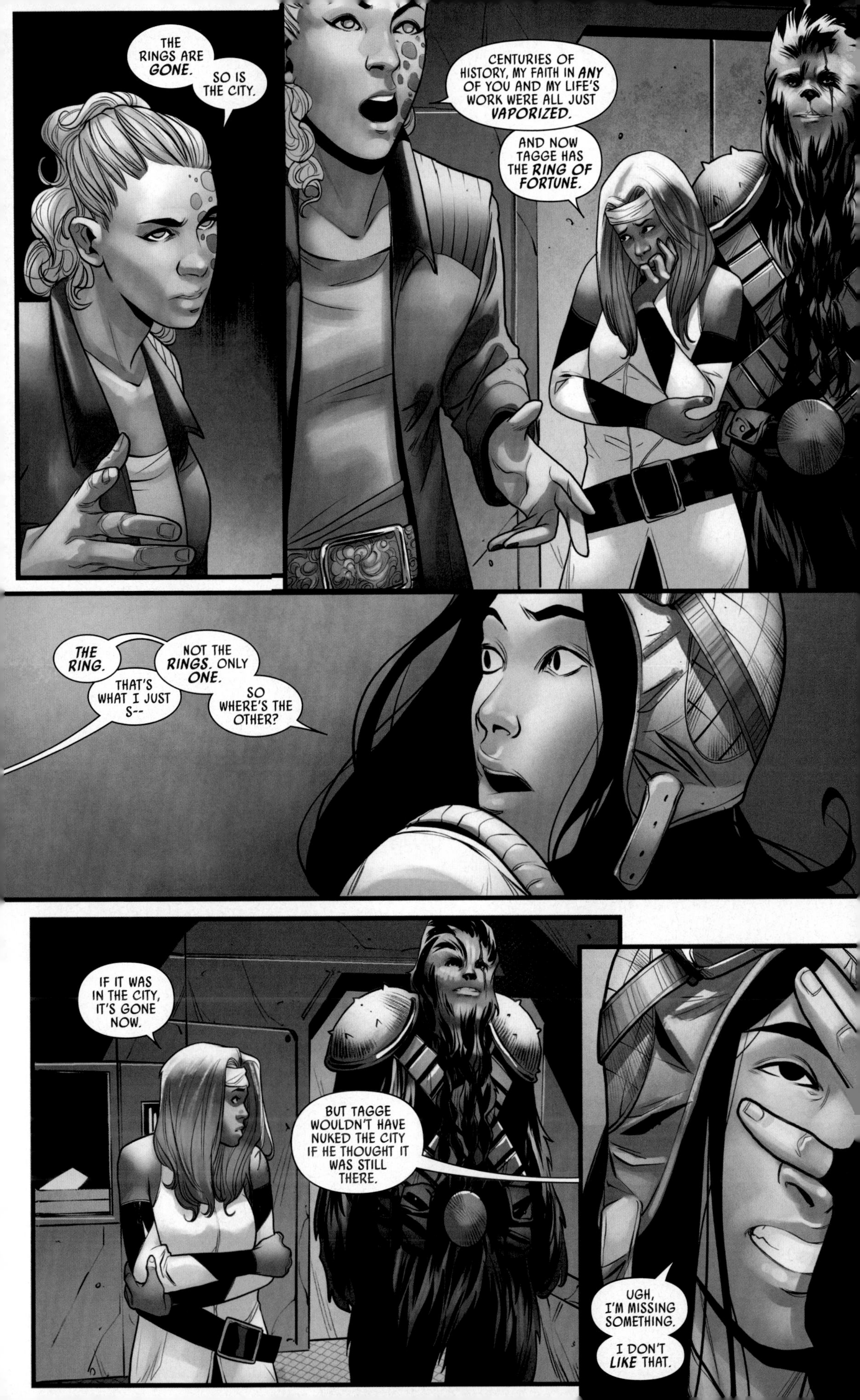
THE RINGS ARE GONE.
SO IS THE CITY.
CENTURIES OF HISTORY, MY FAITH IN ANY OF YOU AND MY LIFE'S WORK WERE ALL JUST VAPORIZED.
AND NOW TAGGE HAS THE RING OF FORTUNE.
THE RING.
NOT THE RINGS. ONLY ONE.
THAT'S WHAT I JUST S--
SO WHERE'S THE OTHER?
IF IT WAS IN THE CITY, IT'S GONE NOW.
BUT TAGGE WOULDN'T HAVE NUKED THE CITY IF HE THOUGHT IT WAS STILL THERE.
UGH, I'M MISSING SOMETHING.
I DON'T LIKE THAT.

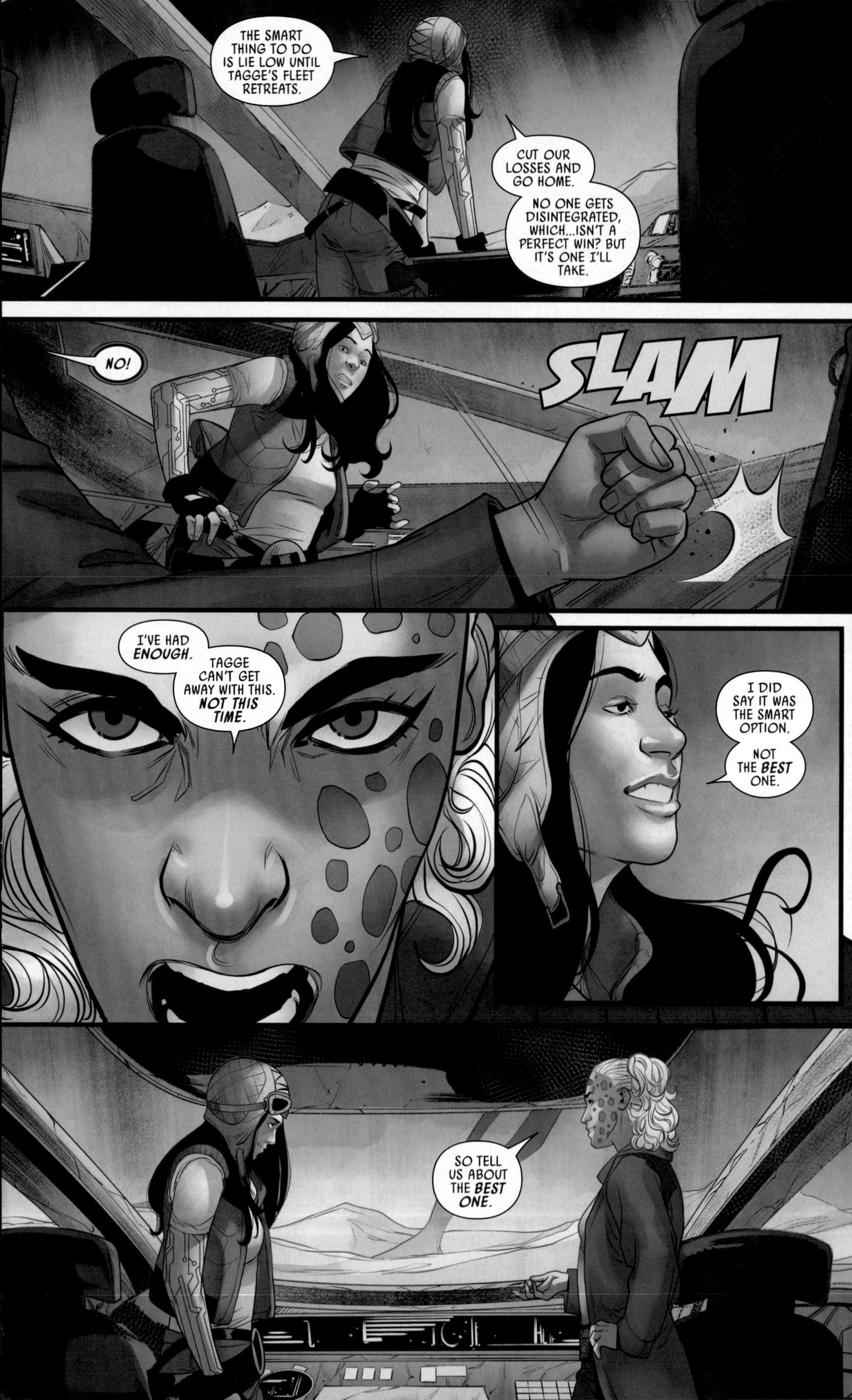
THE SMART THING TO DO IS LIE LOW UNTIL TAGGE'S FLEET RETREATS.
CUT OUR LOSSES AND GO HOME.
NO ONE GETS DISINTEGRATED, WHICH...ISN'T A PERFECT WIN? BUT IT'S ONE I'LL TAKE.
NO!
SLAM
I'VE HAD ENOUGH.
TAGGE CAN'T GET AWAY WITH THIS. NOT THIS TIME.
I DID SAY IT WAS THE SMART OPTION.
NOT THE BEST ONE.
SO TELL US ABOUT THE BEST ONE.

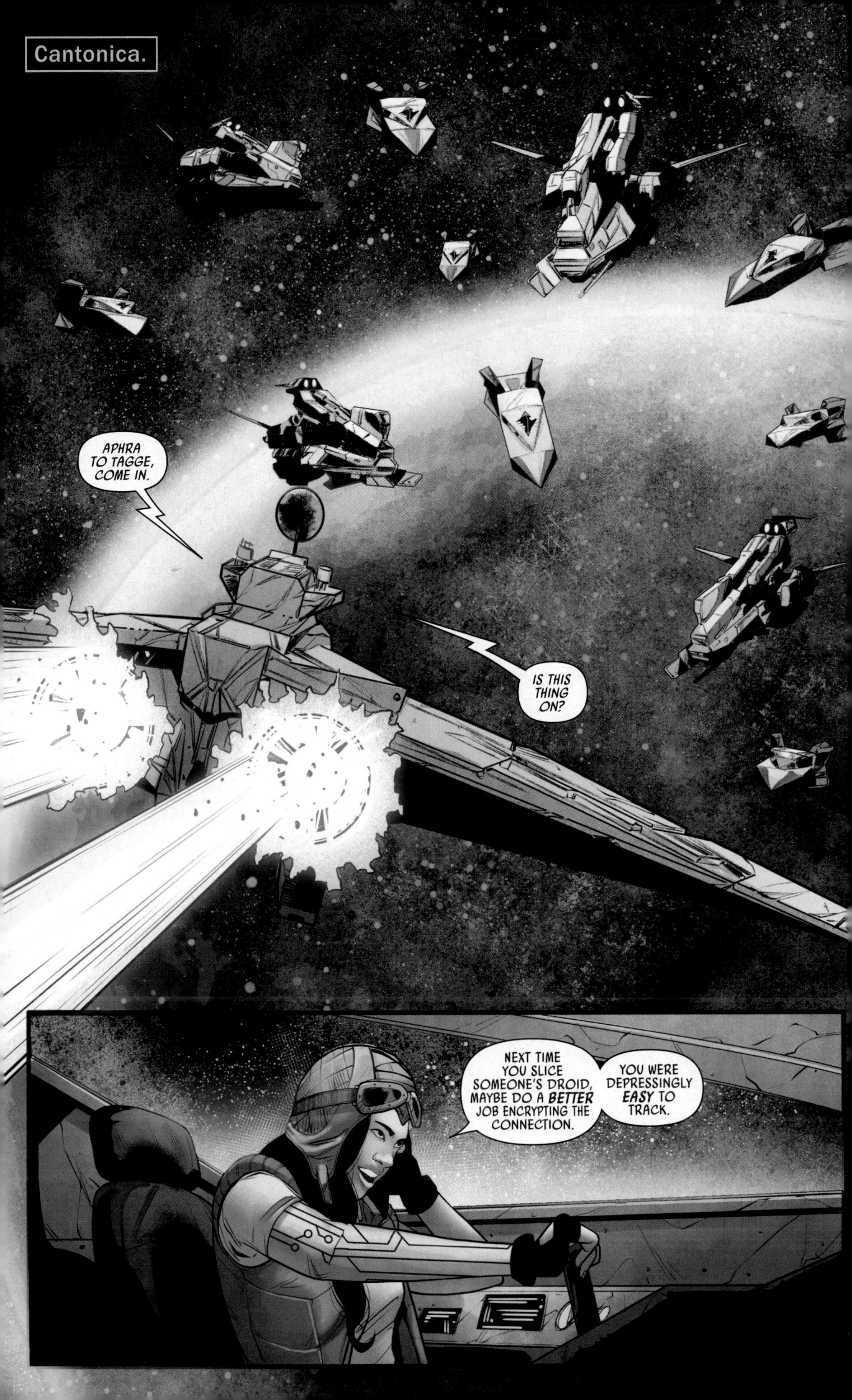
Cantonica.
APHRA TO TAGGE, COME IN.
IS THIS THING ON?
NEXT TIME YOU SLICE SOMEONE'S DROID, MAYBE DO A BETTER JOB ENCRYPTING THE CONNECTION.
YOU WERE DEPRESSINGLY EASY TO TRACK.

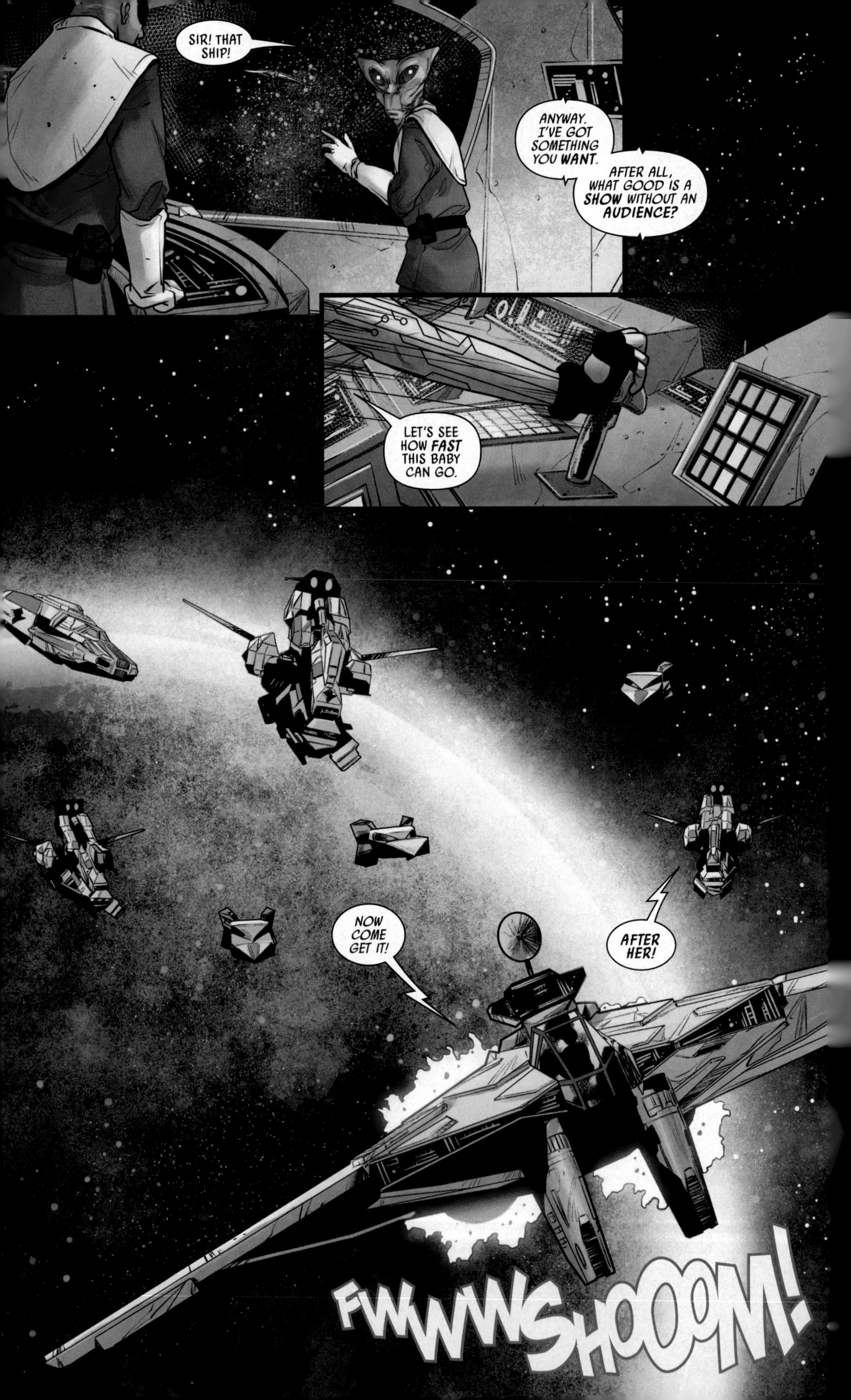

SIR! THAT SHIP!
ANYWAY. I'VE GOT SOMETHING YOU WANT.
AFTER ALL, WHAT GOOD IS A SHOW WITHOUT AN AUDIENCE?
LET'S SEE HOW FAST THIS BABY CAN GO.
NOW COME GET IT!
AFTER HER!
FWWWSHOOOM!

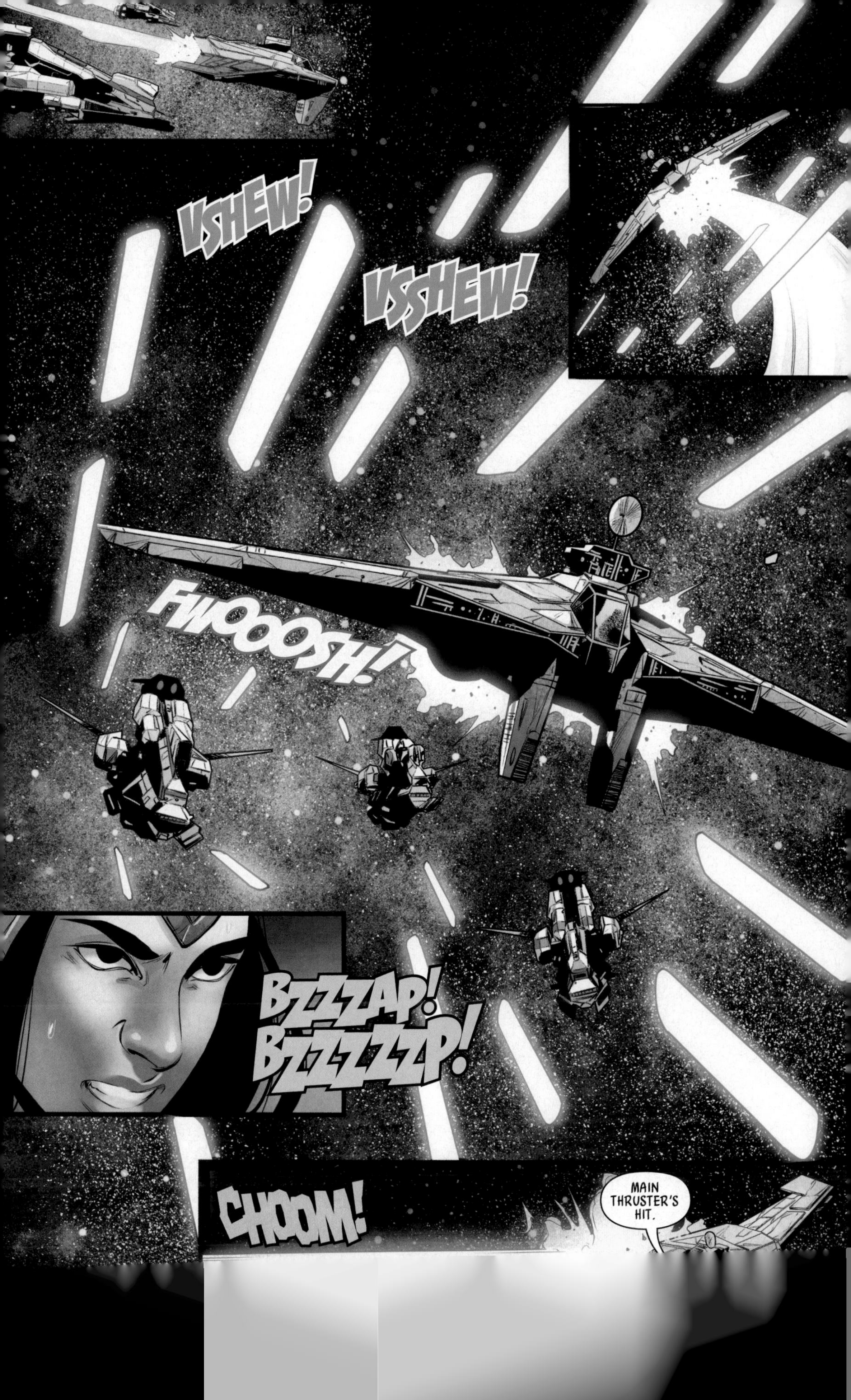
VSHEW!
VSSHEW!
FWOOOSH!
BZZZAP!
BZZZZZP!
CHOOM!
MAIN THRUSTER'S HIT.

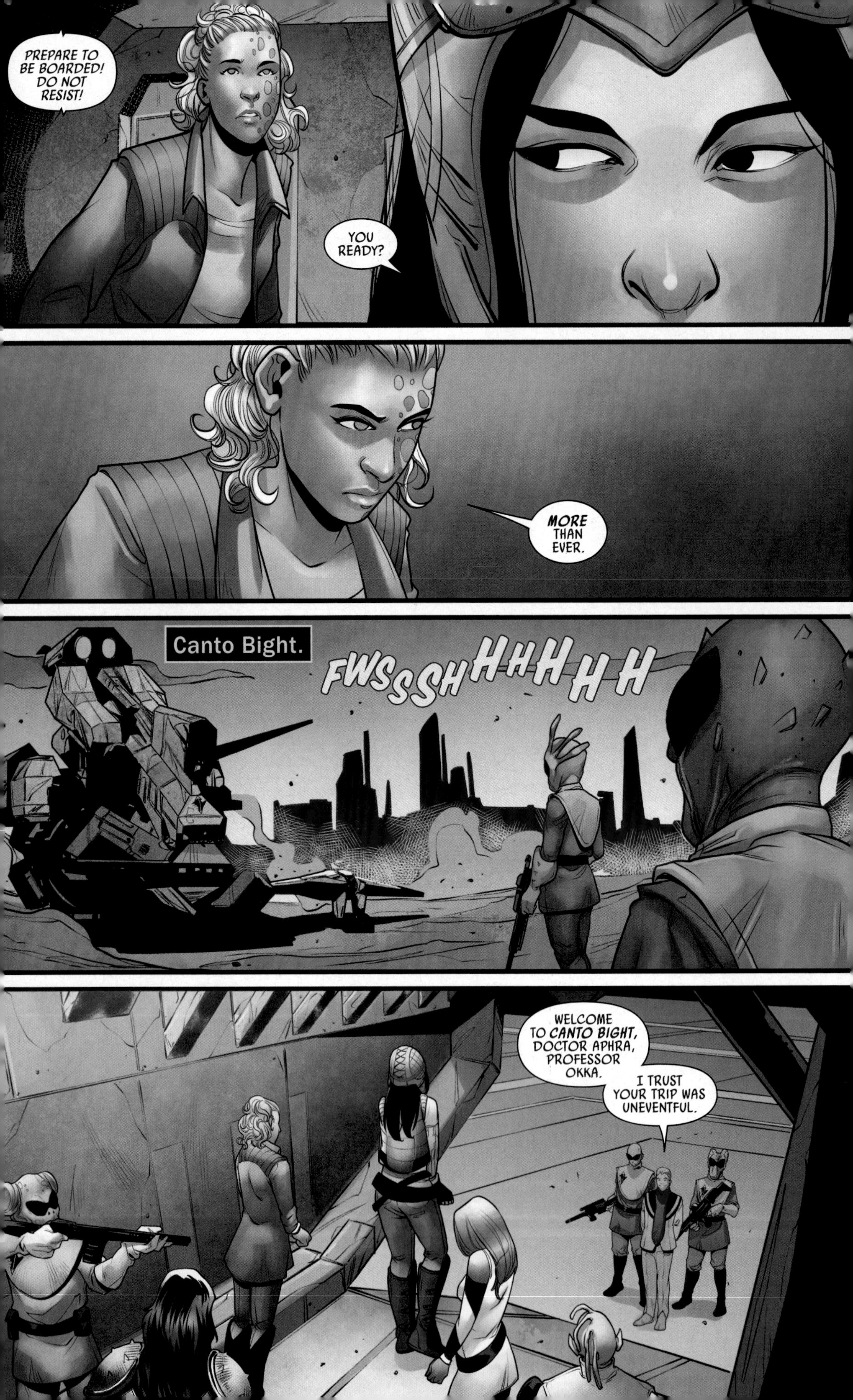
PREPARE TO BE BOARDED! DO NOT RESIST!
YOU READY?
MORE THAN EVER.
Canto Bight.
FWSSSHHHHHHH
WELCOME TO CANTO BIGHT, DOCTOR APHRA, PROFESSOR OKKA.
I TRUST YOUR TRIP WAS UNEVENTFUL.

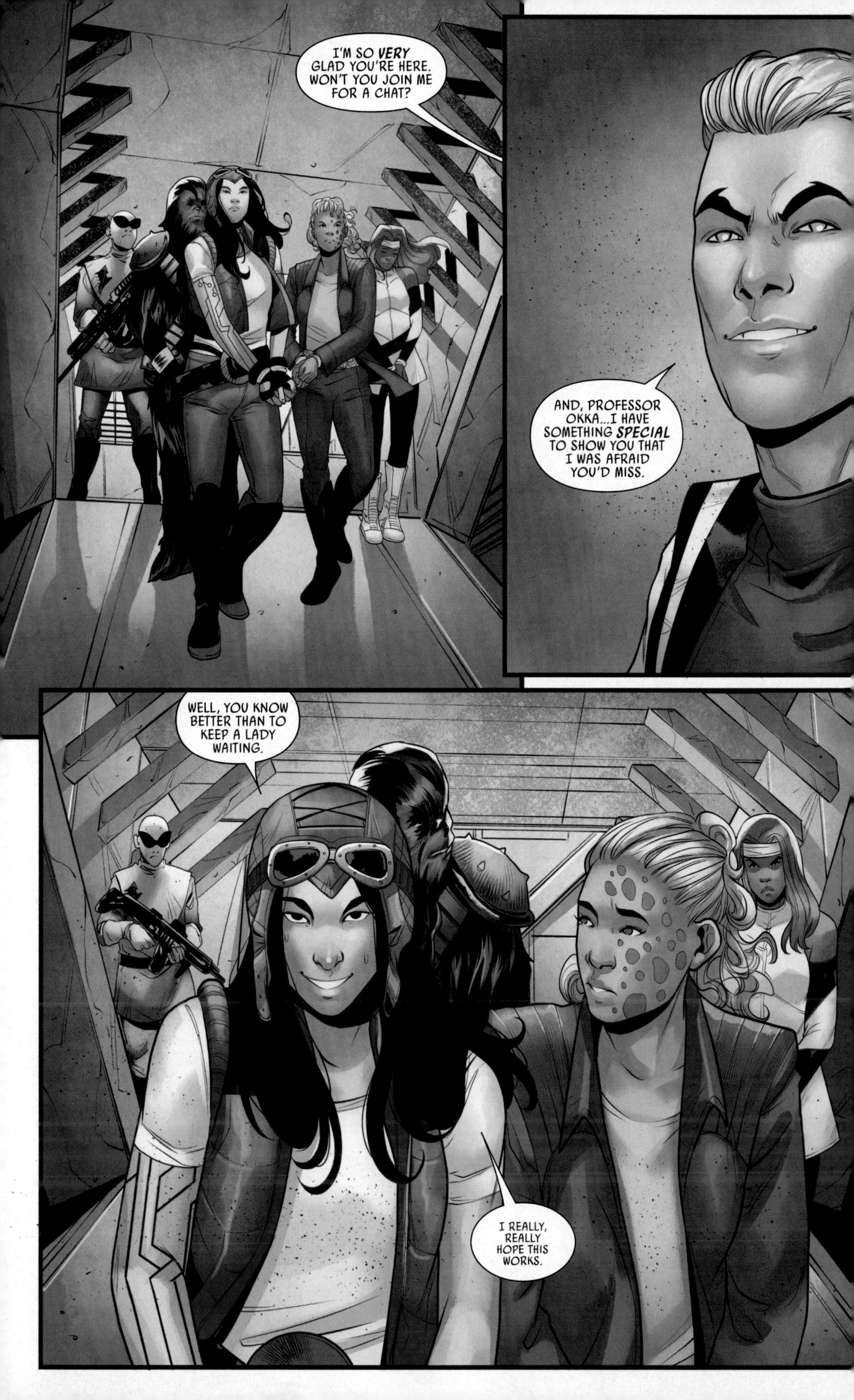
I'M SO VERY GLAD YOU'RE HERE. WON'T YOU JOIN ME FOR A CHAT?
AND, PROFESSOR OKKA...I HAVE SOMETHING SPECIAL TO SHOW YOU THAT I WAS AFRAID YOU'D MISS.
WELL, YOU KNOW BETTER THAN TO KEEP A LADY WAITING.
I REALLY, REALLY HOPE THIS WORKS.

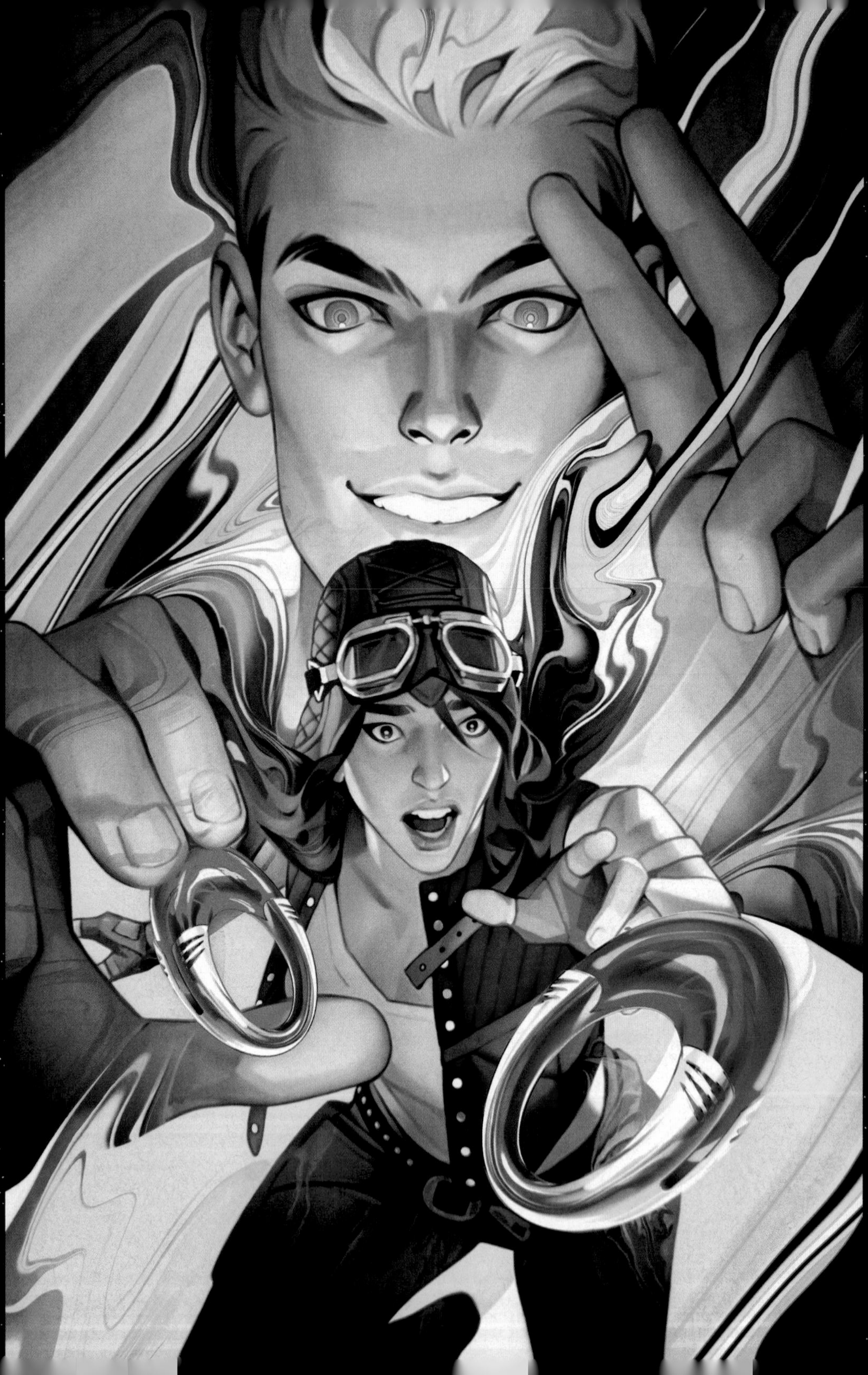

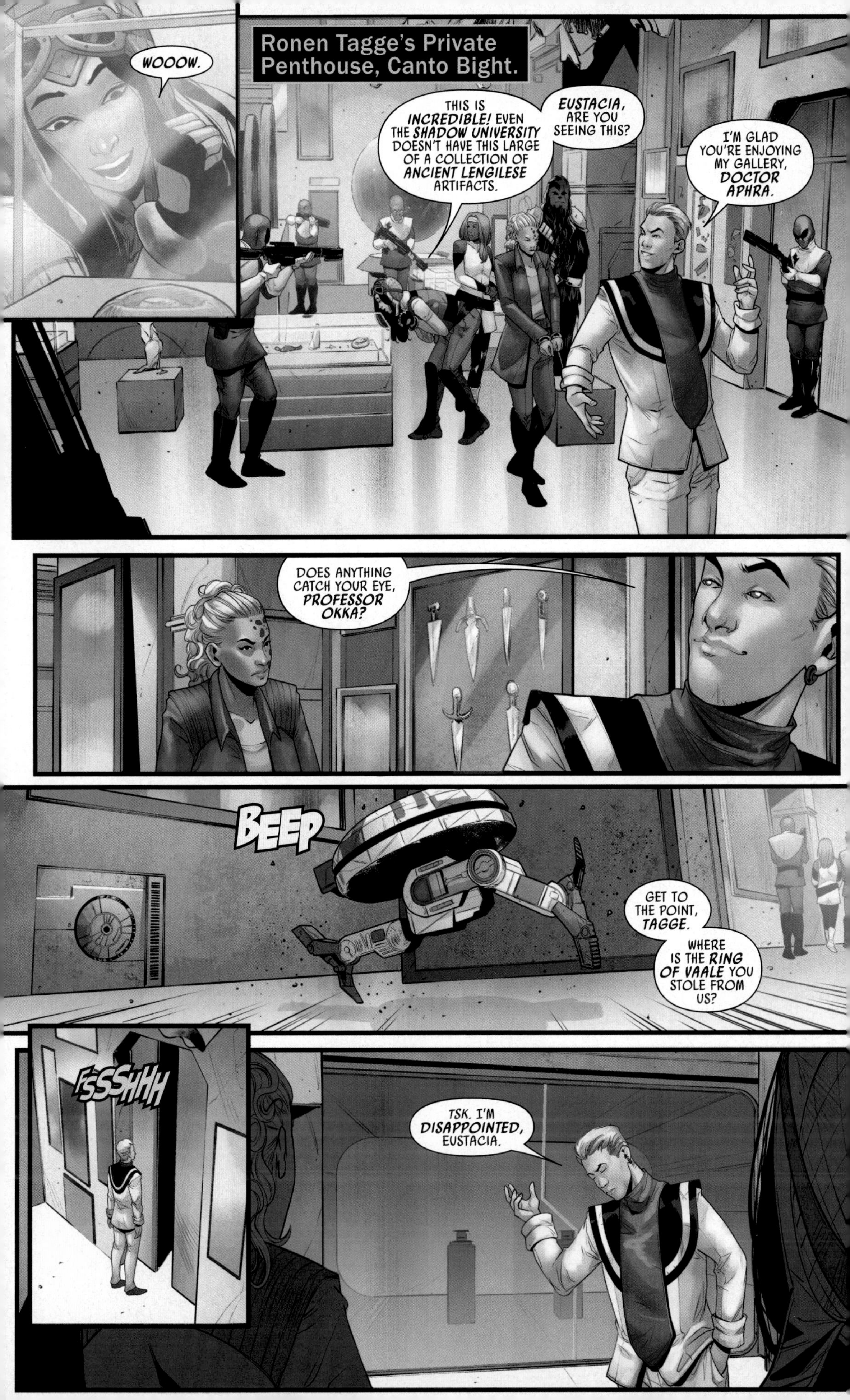

WOOOW.
Ronen Tagge's Private Penthouse, Canto Bight.
THIS IS INCREDIBLE! EVEN THE SHADOW UNIVERSITY DOESN'T HAVE THIS LARGE OF A COLLECTION OF ANCIENT LENGILESE ARTIFACTS.
EUSTACIA, ARE YOU SEEING THIS?
I'M GLAD YOU'RE ENJOYING MY GALLERY, DOCTOR APHRA.
DOES ANYTHING CATCH YOUR EYE, PROFESSOR OKKA?
BEEP
GET TO THE POINT, TAGGE.
WHERE IS THE RING OF VAALE YOU STOLE FROM US?
FSSSHHH
TSK. I'M DISAPPOINTED, EUSTACIA.

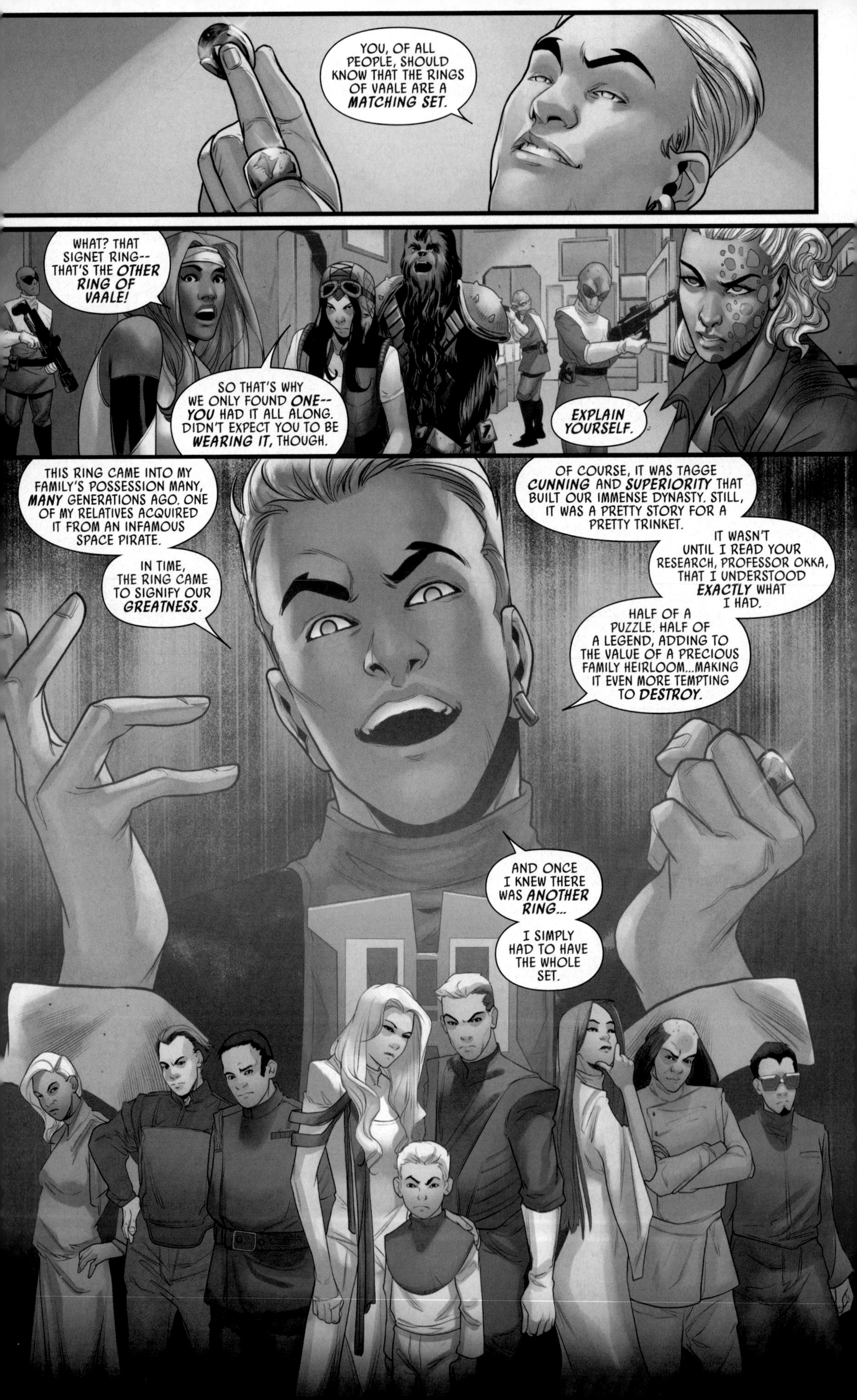
YOU, OF ALL PEOPLE, SHOULD KNOW THAT THE RINGS OF VAALE ARE A MATCHING SET.
WHAT? THAT SIGNET RING-- THAT'S THE OTHER RING OF VAALE!
SO THAT'S WHY WE ONLY FOUND ONE-- YOU HAD IT ALL ALONG. DIDN'T EXPECT YOU TO BE WEARING IT, THOUGH.
EXPLAIN YOURSELF.
THIS RING CAME INTO MY FAMILY'S POSSESSION MANY, MANY GENERATIONS AGO. ONE OF MY RELATIVES ACQUIRED IT FROM AN INFAMOUS SPACE PIRATE.
IN TIME, THE RING CAME TO SIGNIFY OUR GREATNESS.
OF COURSE, IT WAS TAGGE CUNNING AND SUPERIORITY THAT BUILT OUR IMMENSE DYNASTY. STILL, IT WAS A PRETTY STORY FOR A PRETTY TRINKET.
IT WASN'T UNTIL I READ YOUR RESEARCH, PROFESSOR OKKA, THAT I UNDERSTOOD EXACTLY WHAT I HAD.
HALF OF A PUZZLE. HALF OF A LEGEND, ADDING TO THE VALUE OF A PRECIOUS FAMILY HEIRLOOM...MAKING IT EVEN MORE TEMPTING TO DESTROY.
AND ONCE I KNEW THERE WAS ANOTHER RING...
I SIMPLY HAD TO HAVE THE WHOLE SET.

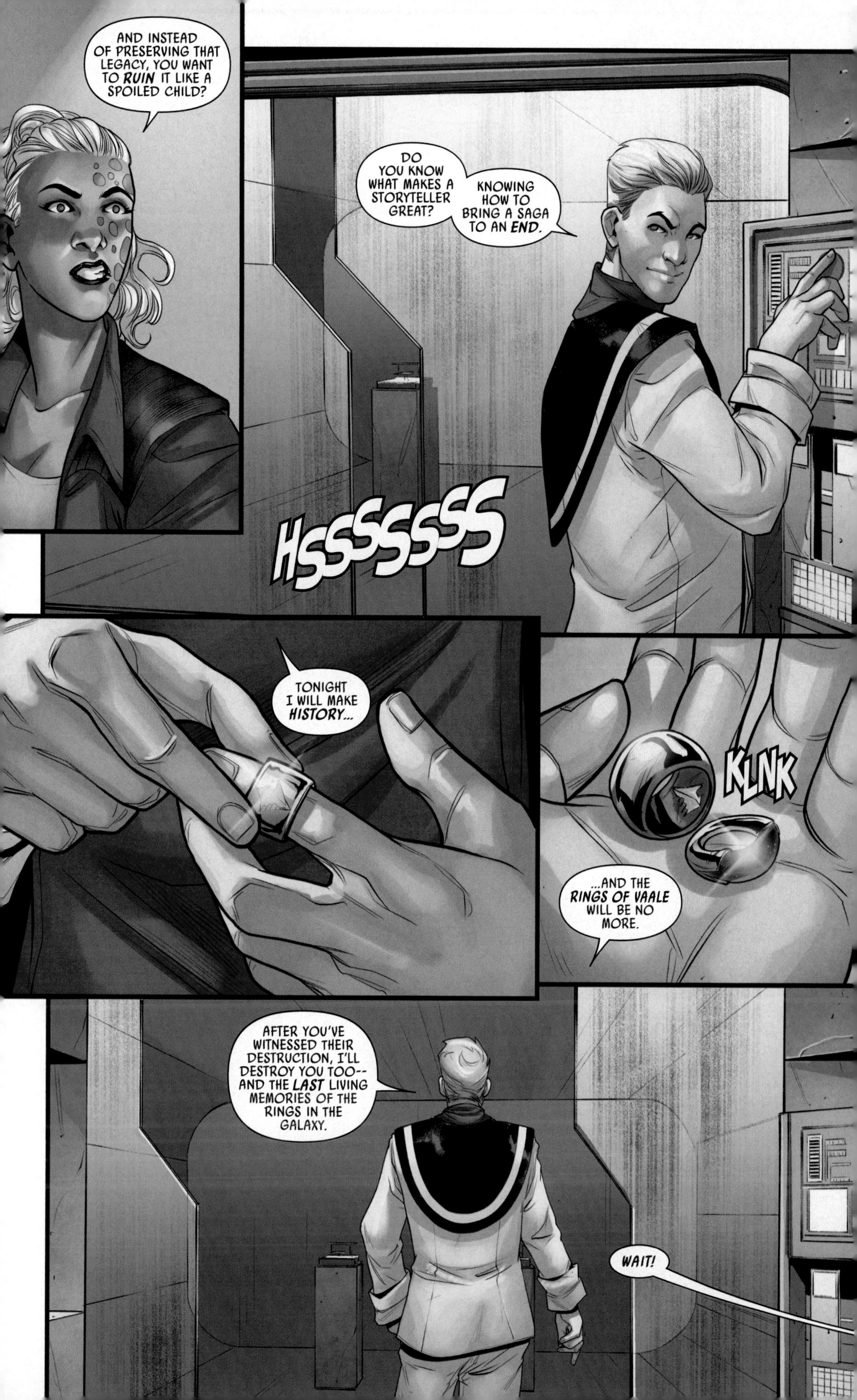
AND INSTEAD OF PRESERVING THAT LEGACY, YOU WANT TO RUIN IT LIKE A SPOILED CHILD?
DO YOU KNOW WHAT MAKES A STORYTELLER GREAT?
KNOWING HOW TO BRING A SAGA TO AN END.
HSSSSSSS
TONIGHT I WILL MAKE HISTORY...
KLNK
...AND THE RINGS OF VAALE WILL BE NO MORE.
AFTER YOU'VE WITNESSED THEIR DESTRUCTION, I'LL DESTROY YOU TOO-- AND THE LAST LIVING MEMORIES OF THE RINGS IN THE GALAXY.
WAIT!

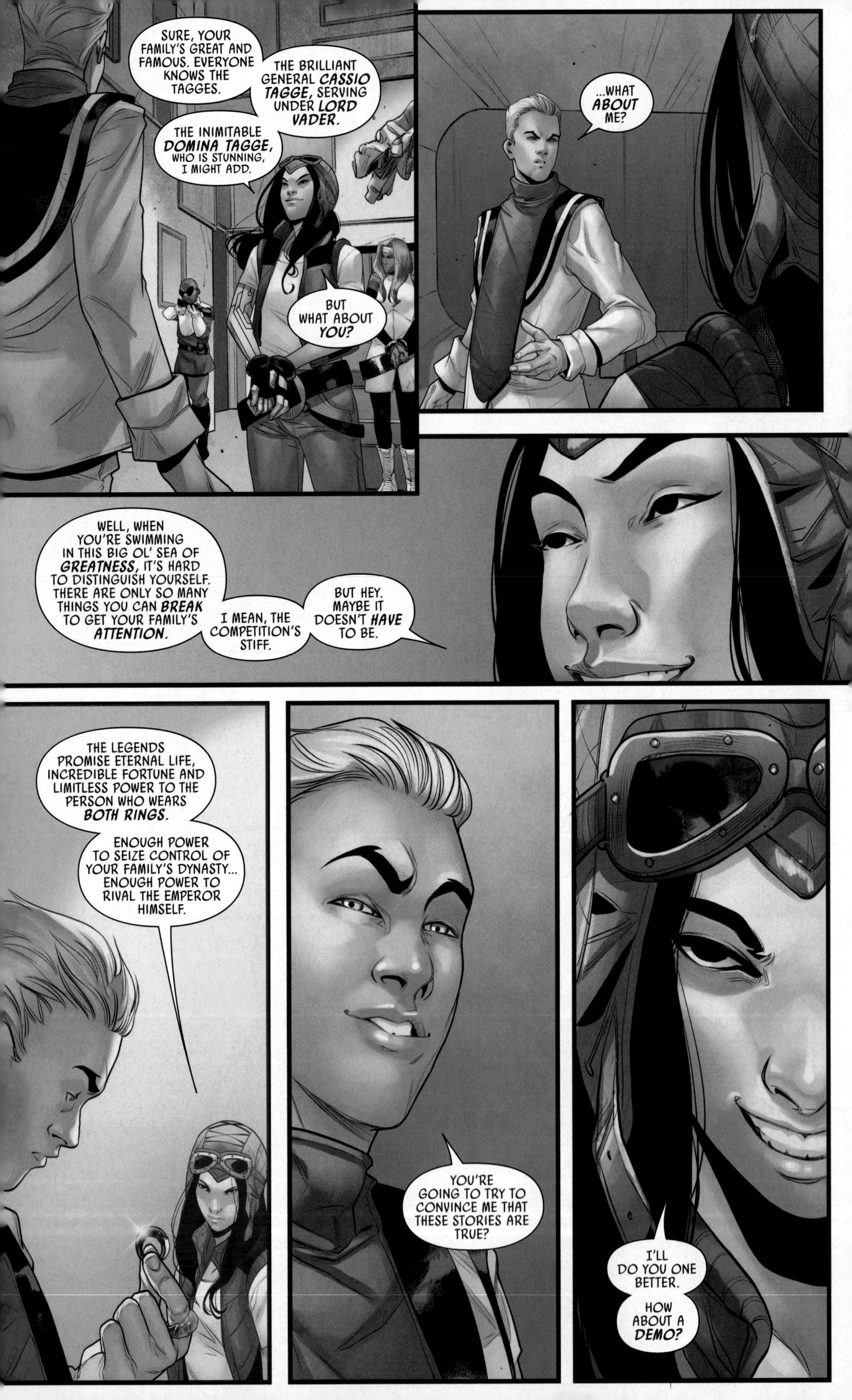
SURE, YOUR FAMILY'S GREAT AND FAMOUS. EVERYONE KNOWS THE TAGGES.
THE BRILLIANT GENERAL CASSIO TAGGE, SERVING UNDER LORD VADER.
THE INIMITABLE DOMINA TAGGE, WHO IS STUNNING, I MIGHT ADD.
BUT WHAT ABOUT YOU?
...WHAT ABOUT ME?
WELL, WHEN YOU'RE SWIMMING IN THIS BIG OL' SEA OF GREATNESS, IT'S HARD TO DISTINGUISH YOURSELF. THERE ARE ONLY SO MANY THINGS YOU CAN BREAK TO GET YOUR FAMILY'S ATTENTION.
I MEAN, THE COMPETITION'S STIFF.
BUT HEY. MAYBE IT DOESN'T HAVE TO BE.
THE LEGENDS PROMISE ETERNAL LIFE, INCREDIBLE FORTUNE AND LIMITLESS POWER TO THE PERSON WHO WEARS BOTH RINGS.
ENOUGH POWER TO SEIZE CONTROL OF YOUR FAMILY'S DYNASTY... ENOUGH POWER TO RIVAL THE EMPEROR HIMSELF.
YOU'RE GOING TO TRY TO CONVINCE ME THAT THESE STORIES ARE TRUE?
I'LL DO YOU ONE BETTER.
HOW ABOUT A DEMO?

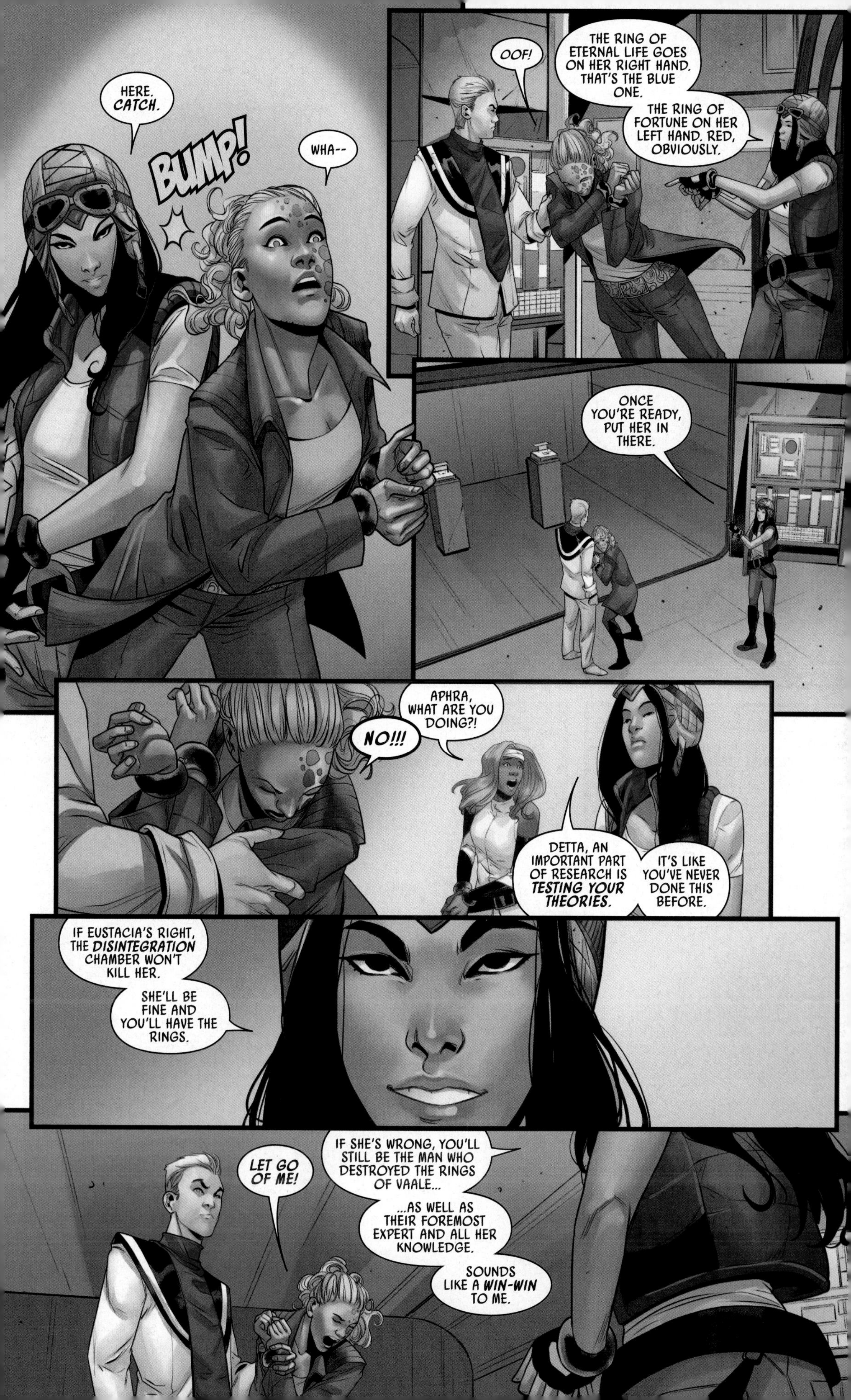
HERE. CATCH.
BUMP!
WHA--
OOF!
THE RING OF ETERNAL LIFE GOES ON HER RIGHT HAND. THAT'S THE BLUE ONE.
THE RING OF FORTUNE ON HER LEFT HAND. RED, OBVIOUSLY.
ONCE YOU'RE READY, PUT HER IN THERE.
NO!!!
APHRA, WHAT ARE YOU DOING?!
DETTA, AN IMPORTANT PART OF RESEARCH IS TESTING YOUR THEORIES.
IT'S LIKE YOU'VE NEVER DONE THIS BEFORE.
IF EUSTACIA'S RIGHT, THE DISINTEGRATION CHAMBER WON'T KILL HER.
SHE'LL BE FINE AND YOU'LL HAVE THE RINGS.
LET GO OF ME!
IF SHE'S WRONG, YOU'LL STILL BE THE MAN WHO DESTROYED THE RINGS OF VAALE...
...AS WELL AS THEIR FOREMOST EXPERT AND ALL HER KNOWLEDGE.
SOUNDS LIKE A WIN-WIN TO ME.

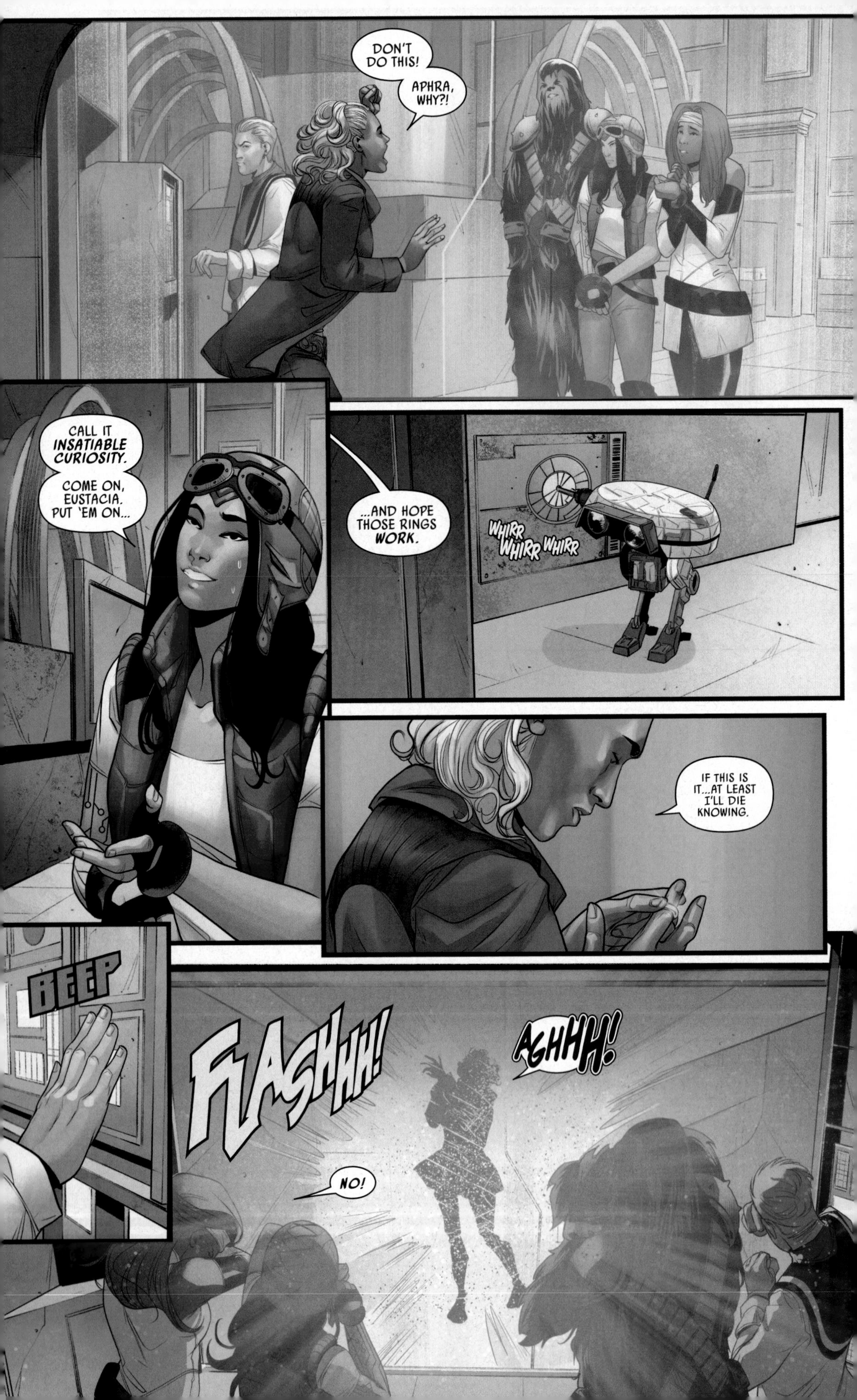
DON'T DO THIS!
APHRA, WHY?!
CALL IT INSATIABLE CURIOSITY.
COME ON, EUSTACIA. PUT 'EM ON...
...AND HOPE THOSE RINGS WORK.
WHIRR WHIRR WHIRR
IF THIS IS IT...AT LEAST I'LL DIE KNOWING.
BEEP
FLASHHH!
AGHHH!
NO!

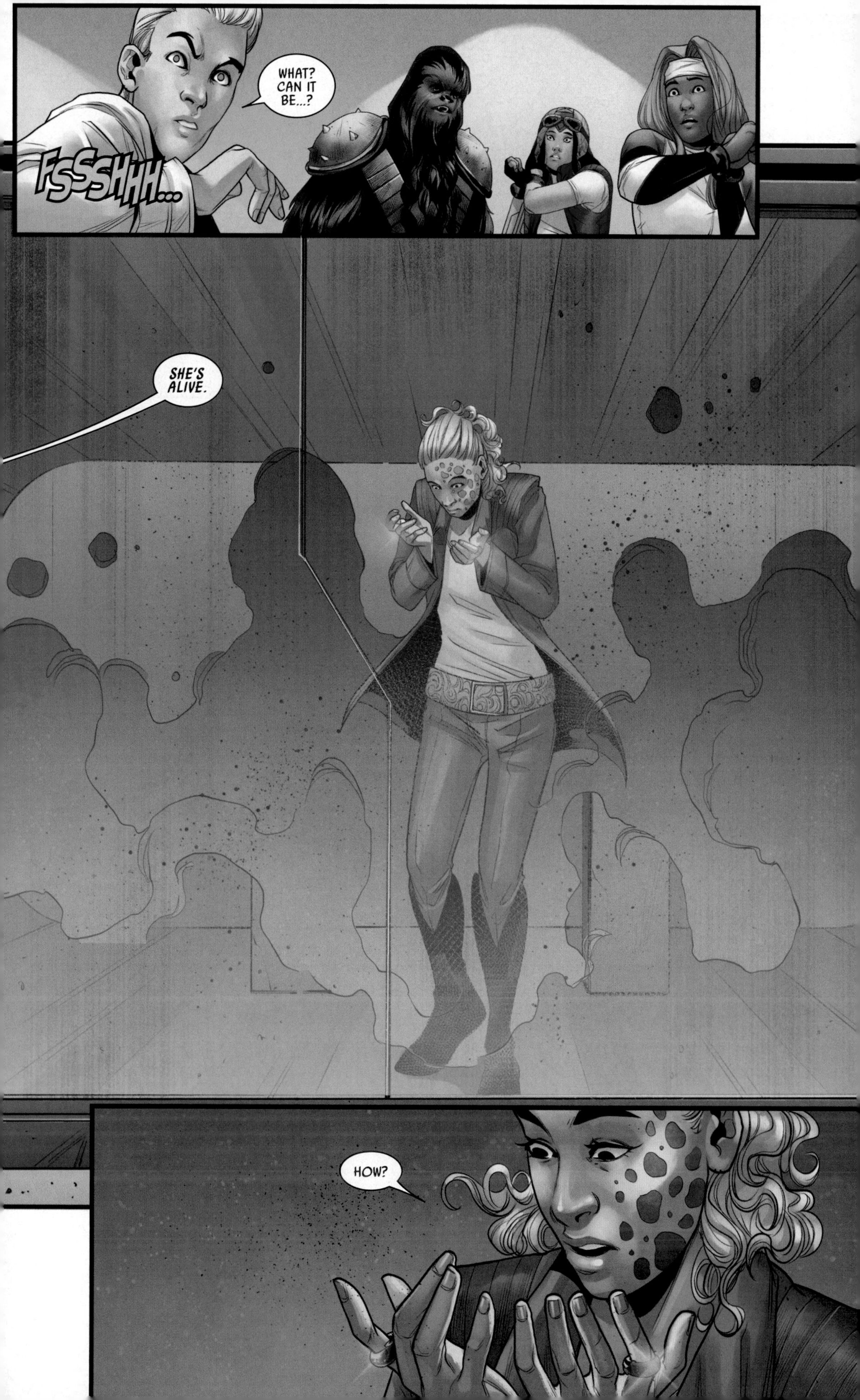
WHAT? CAN IT BE...?
FSSSHHH...
SHE'S ALIVE.
HOW?

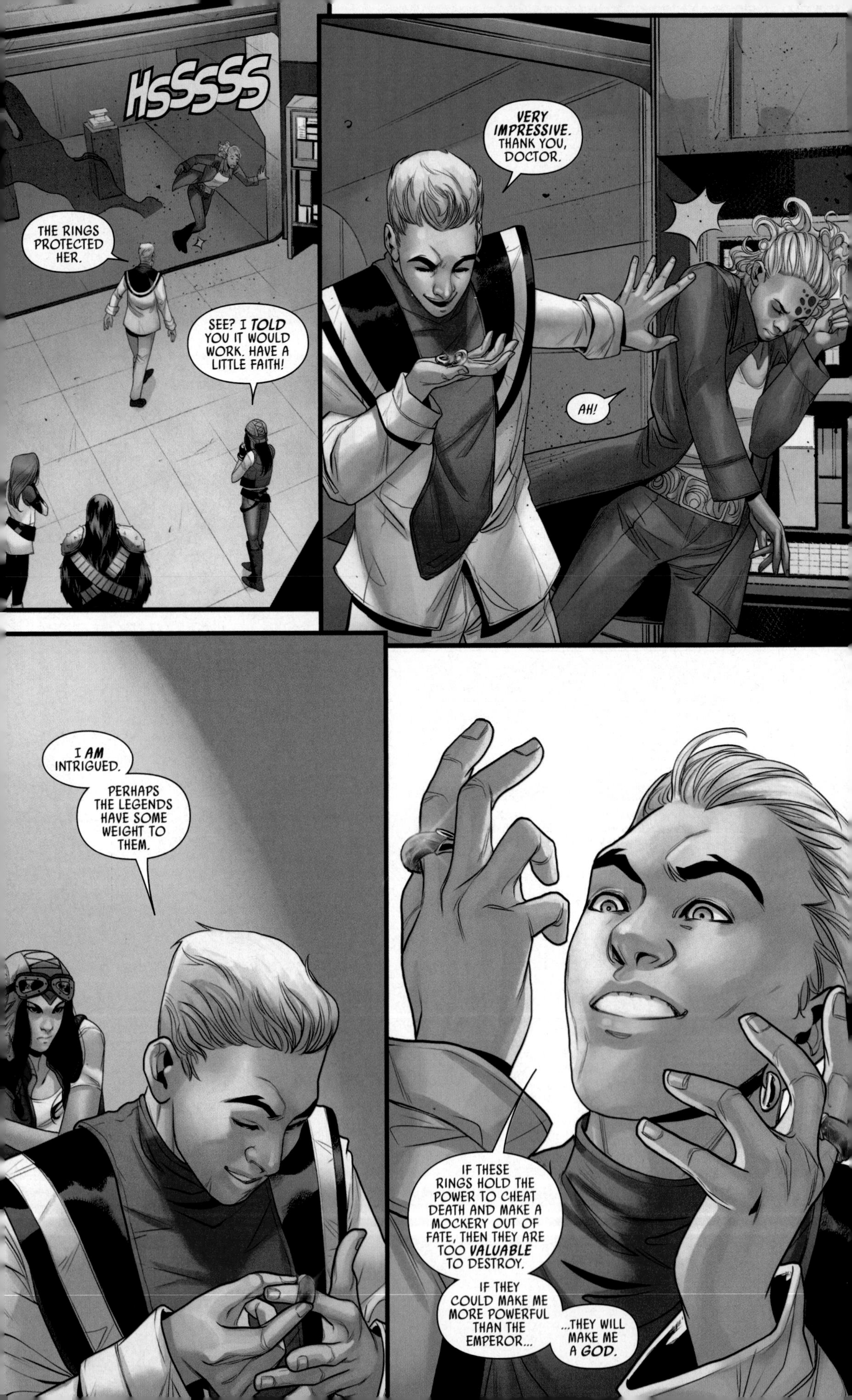
HSSSSS
THE RINGS PROTECTED HER.
SEE? I TOLD YOU IT WOULD WORK. HAVE A LITTLE FAITH!
VERY IMPRESSIVE. THANK YOU, DOCTOR.
AH!
I AM INTRIGUED.
PERHAPS THE LEGENDS HAVE SOME WEIGHT TO THEM.
IF THESE RINGS HOLD THE POWER TO CHEAT DEATH AND MAKE A MOCKERY OUT OF FATE, THEN THEY ARE TOO VALUABLE TO DESTROY.
IF THEY COULD MAKE ME MORE POWERFUL THAN THE EMPEROR...
...THEY WILL MAKE ME A GOD.

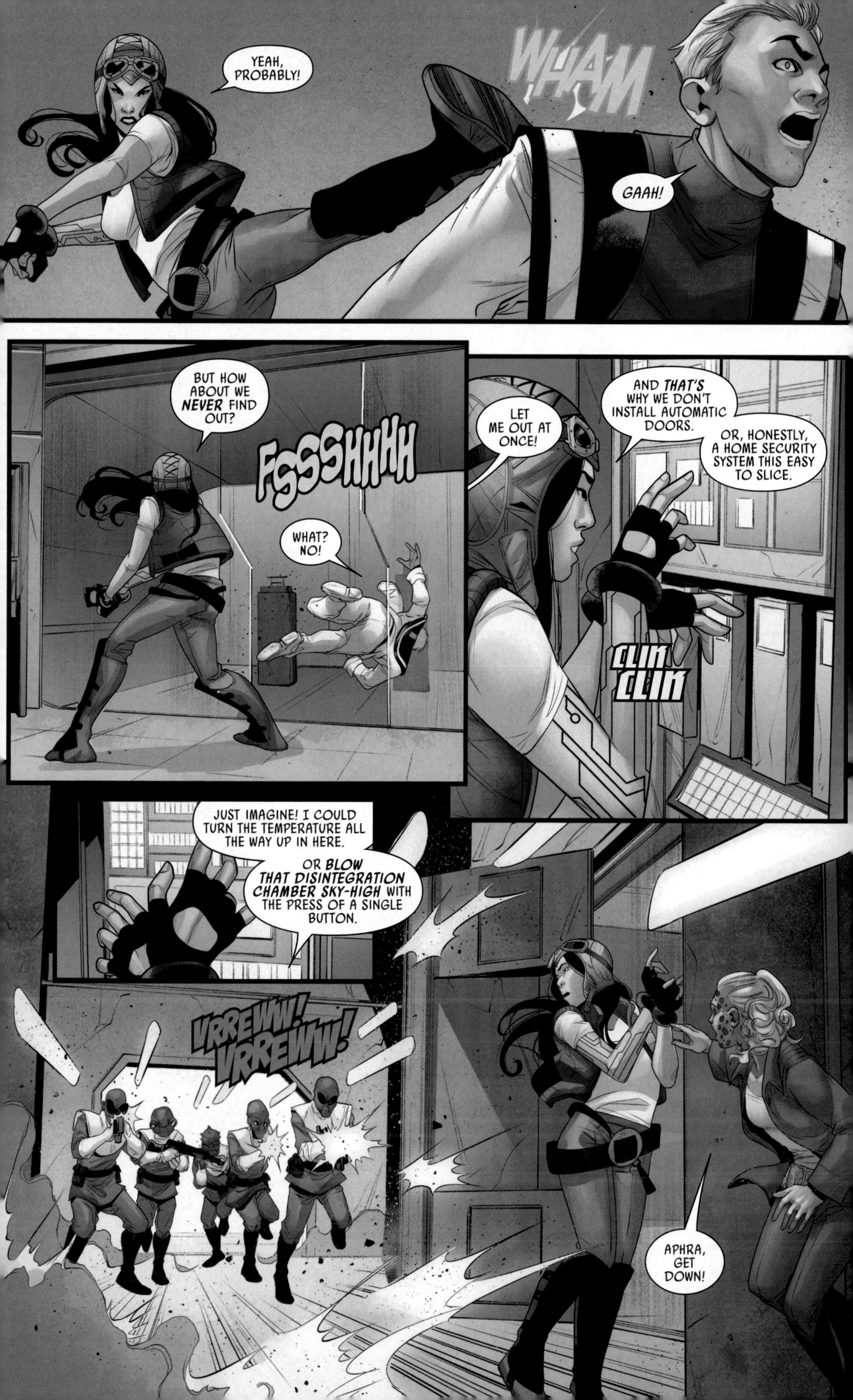

YEAH, PROBABLY!
WHAM
GAAH!
BUT HOW ABOUT WE NEVER FIND OUT?
FSSSHHHH
WHAT? NO!
LET ME OUT AT ONCE!
AND THAT'S WHY WE DON'T INSTALL AUTOMATIC DOORS.
OR, HONESTLY, A HOME SECURITY SYSTEM THIS EASY TO SLICE.
CLIK CLIK
JUST IMAGINE! I COULD TURN THE TEMPERATURE ALL THE WAY UP IN HERE.
OR BLOW THAT DISINTEGRATION CHAMBER SKY-HIGH WITH THE PRESS OF A SINGLE BUTTON.
VRREWW! VRREWW!
APHRA, GET DOWN!

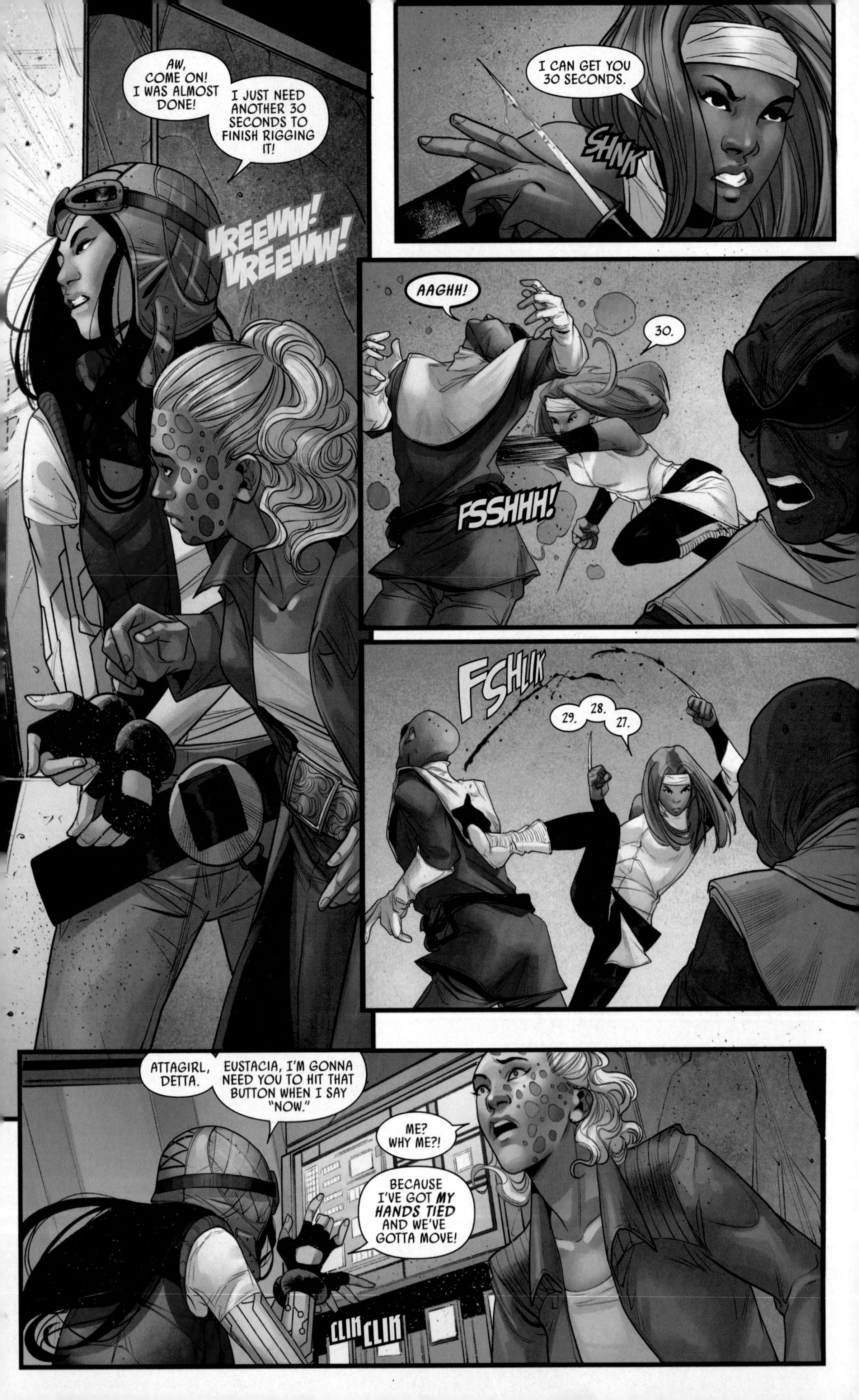
AW, COME ON! I WAS ALMOST DONE!
I JUST NEED ANOTHER 30 SECONDS TO FINISH RIGGING IT!
VREEWW! VREEWW!
I CAN GET YOU 30 SECONDS.
SHNK
AAGHH!
30.
FSSHHH!
FSHLIK
29.
28.
27.
ATTAGIRL, DETTA.
EUSTACIA, I'M GONNA NEED YOU TO HIT THAT BUTTON WHEN I SAY "NOW."
ME? WHY ME?!
BECAUSE I'VE GOT MY HANDS TIED AND WE'VE GOTTA MOVE!
CLIK CLIK

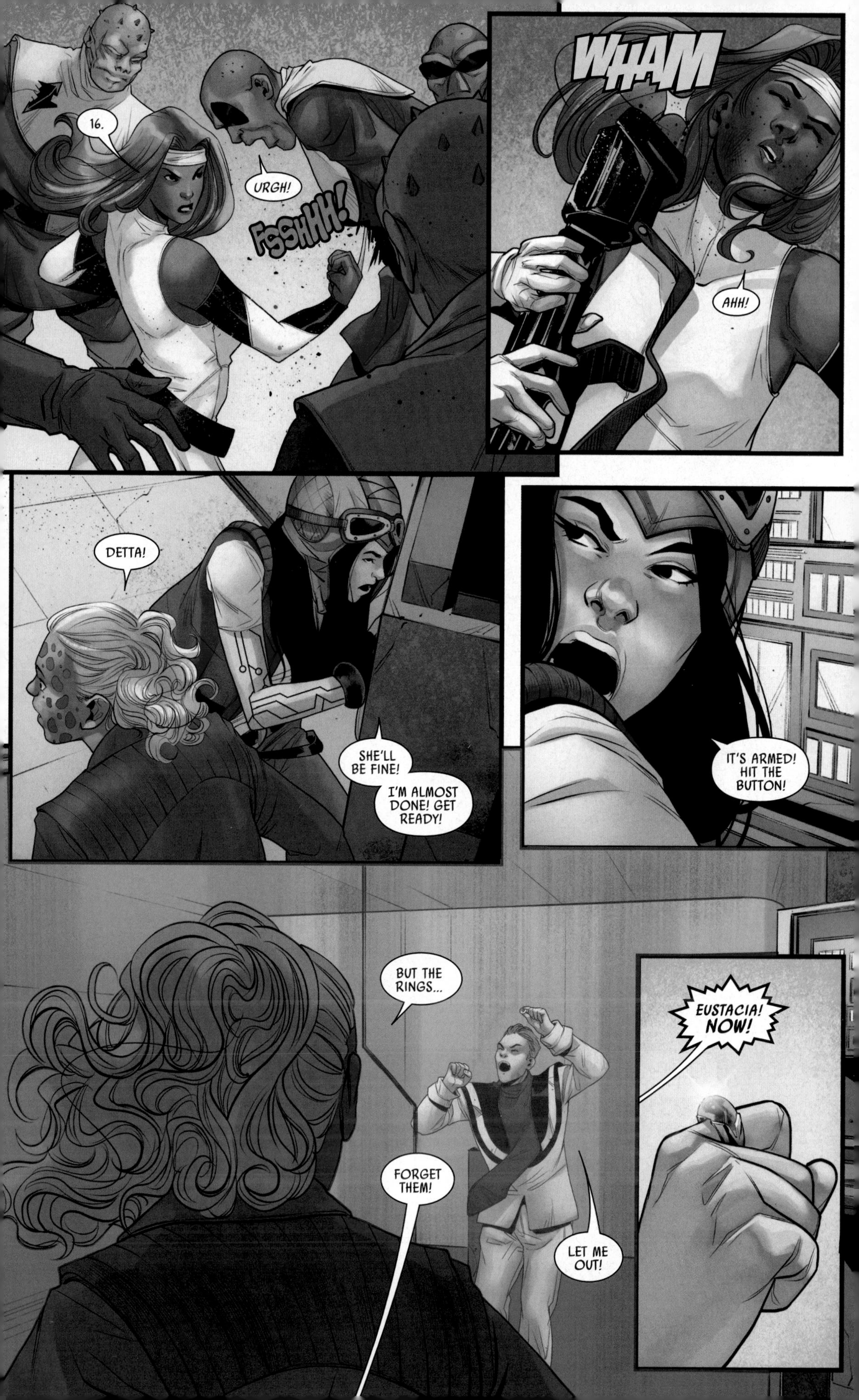
16.
URGH!
FSSHHH!
WHAM
AHH!
DETTA!
SHE'LL BE FINE!
I'M ALMOST DONE! GET READY!
IT'S ARMED! HIT THE BUTTON!
BUT THE RINGS...
FORGET THEM!
LET ME OUT!
EUSTACIA! NOW!

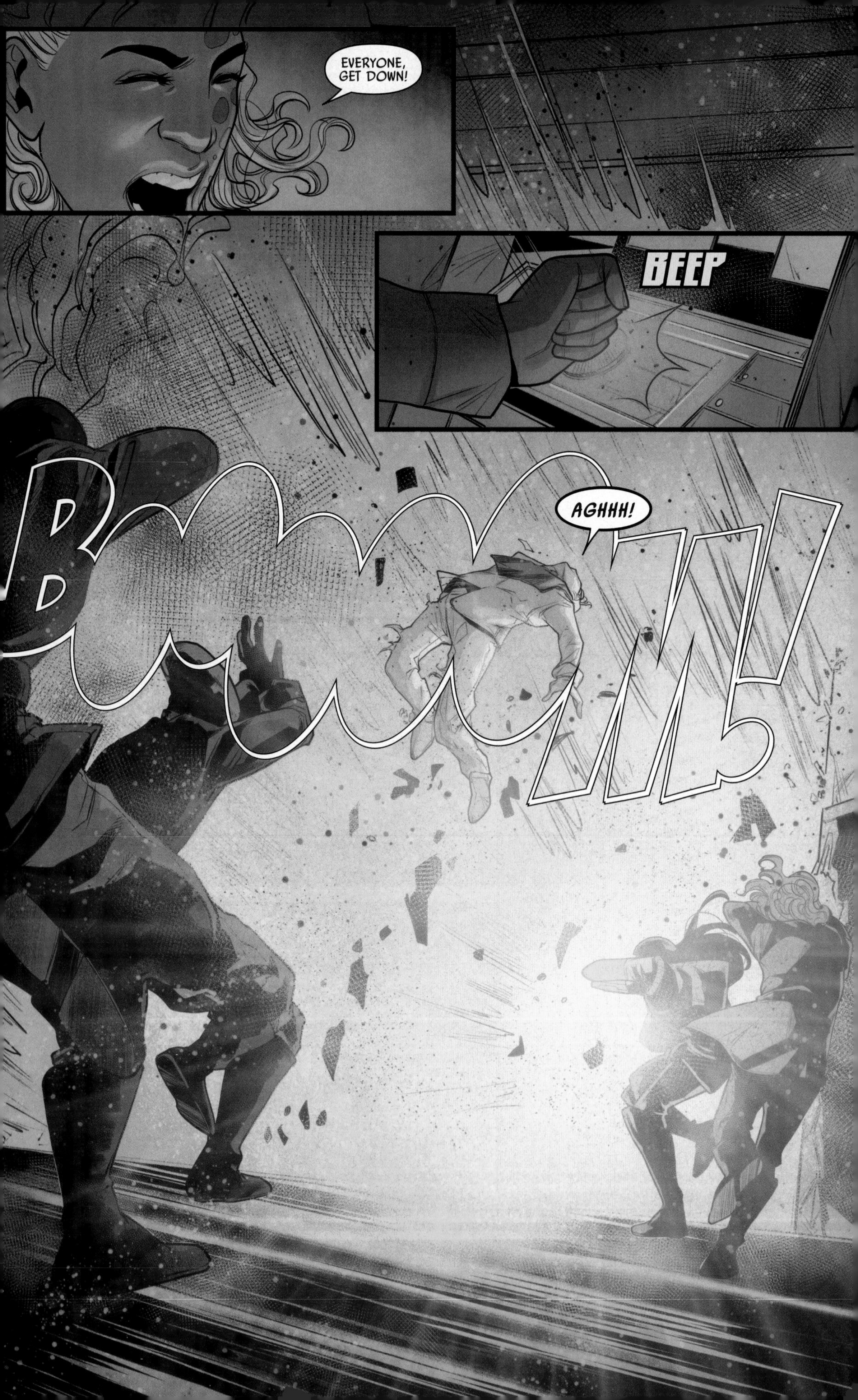
EVERYONE, GET DOWN!
BEEP
BOOOM!
AGHHH!

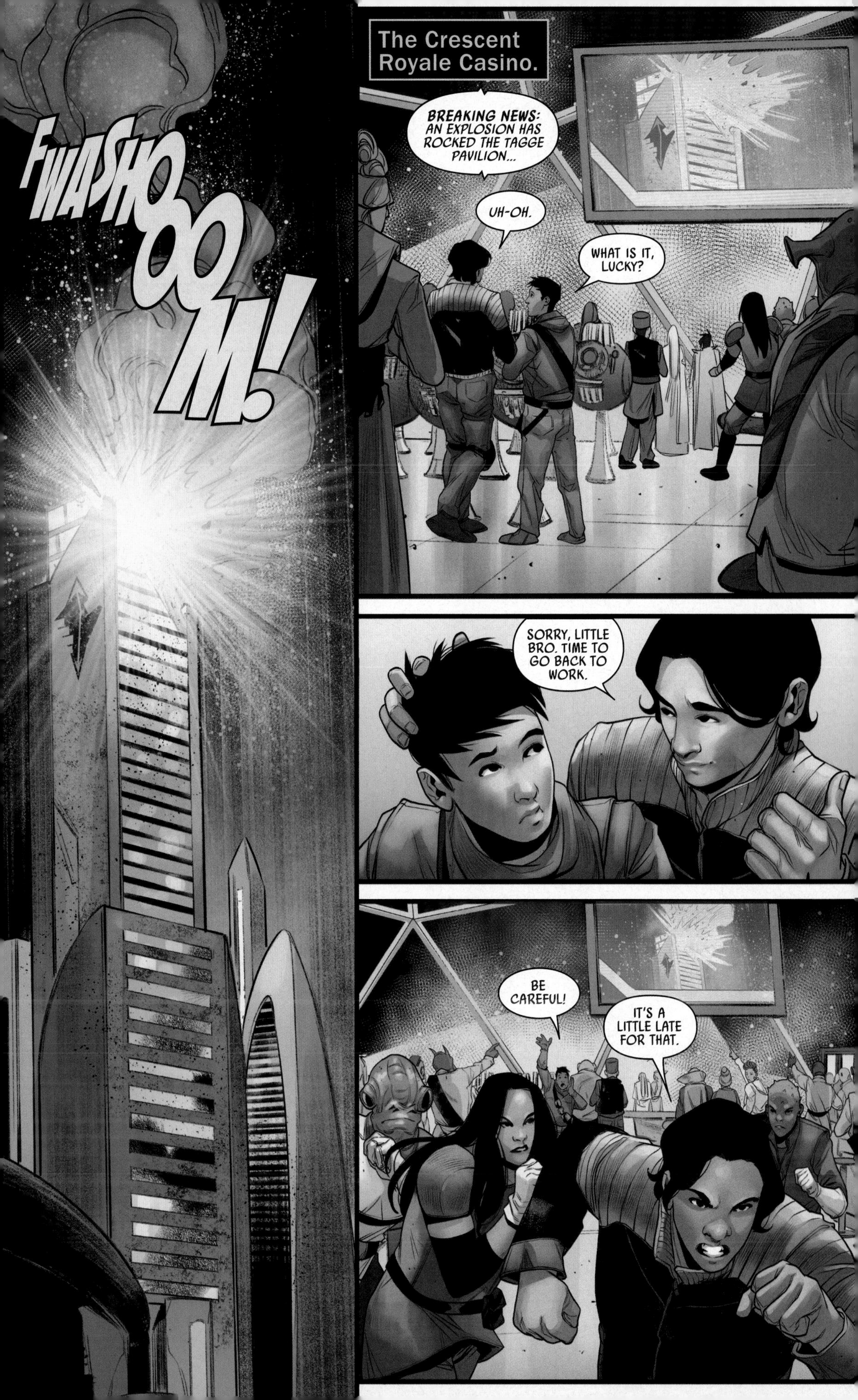
FWASHOOOM!
The Crescent Royale Casino.
BREAKING NEWS: AN EXPLOSION HAS ROCKED THE TAGGE PAVILION...
UH-OH.
WHAT IS IT, LUCKY?
SORRY, LITTLE BRO. TIME TO GO BACK TO WORK.
BE CAREFUL!
IT'S A LITTLE LATE FOR THAT.

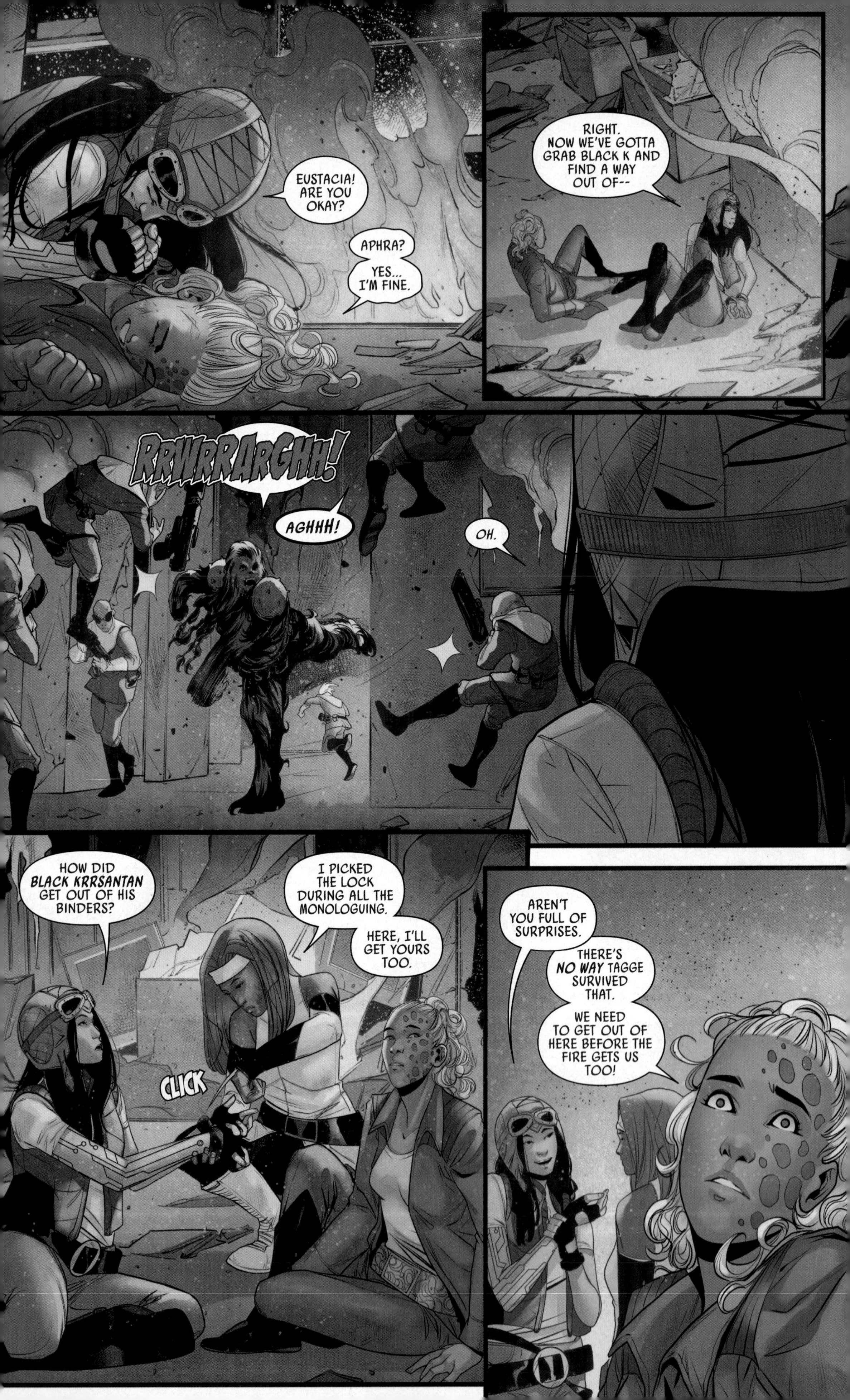
EUSTACIA! ARE YOU OKAY?
APHRA?
YES... I'M FINE.
RIGHT. NOW WE'VE GOTTA GRAB BLACK K AND FIND A WAY OUT OF--
RRWRRARGHH!
AGHHH!
OH.
HOW DID BLACK KRRSANTAN GET OUT OF HIS BINDERS?
I PICKED THE LOCK DURING ALL THE MONOLOGUING.
HERE, I'LL GET YOURS TOO.
CLICK
AREN'T YOU FULL OF SURPRISES.
THERE'S NO WAY TAGGE SURVIVED THAT.
WE NEED TO GET OUT OF HERE BEFORE THE FIRE GETS US TOO!

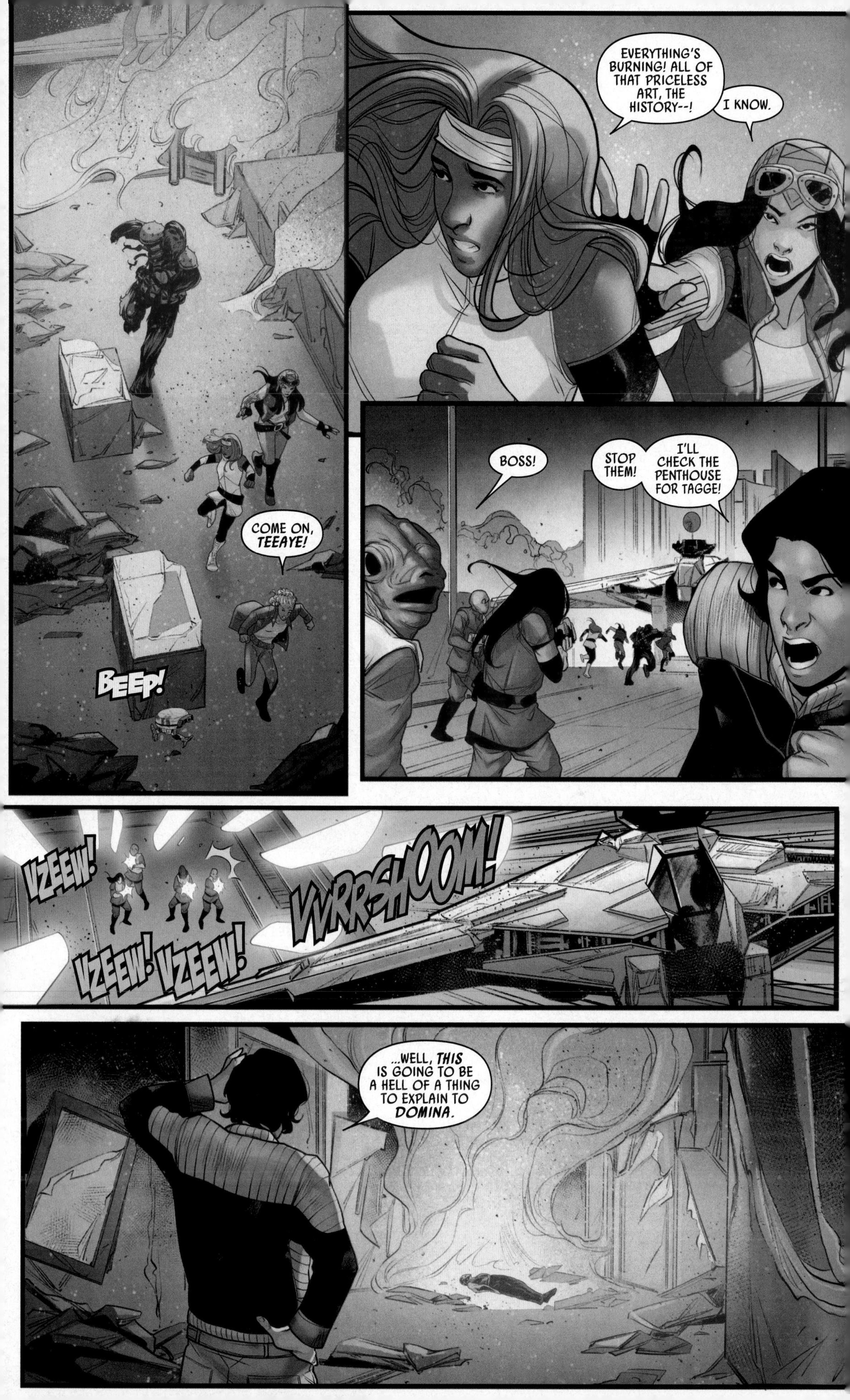
COME ON, TEEAYE!
BEEP!
EVERYTHING'S BURNING! ALL OF THAT PRICELESS ART, THE HISTORY--!
I KNOW.
BOSS!
STOP THEM!
I'LL CHECK THE PENTHOUSE FOR TAGGE!
VZEEW!
VZEEW!
VZEEW!
VVRRSHOOM!
...WELL, THIS IS GOING TO BE A HELL OF A THING TO EXPLAIN TO DOMINA.

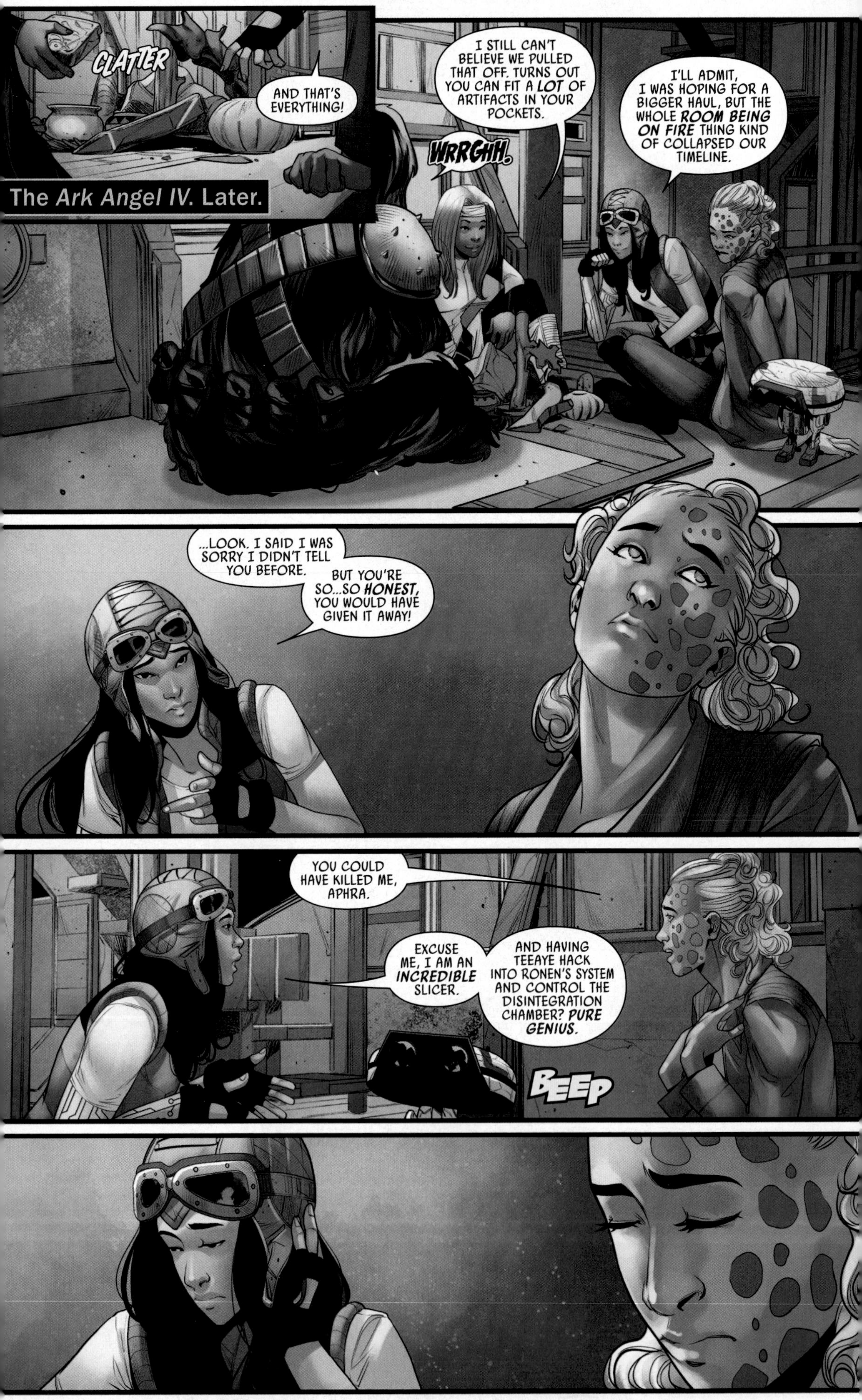
CLATTER
AND THAT'S EVERYTHING!
The Ark Angel IV. Later.
I STILL CAN'T BELIEVE WE PULLED THAT OFF. TURNS OUT YOU CAN FIT A LOT OF ARTIFACTS IN YOUR POCKETS.
WRRGHH!
I'LL ADMIT, I WAS HOPING FOR A BIGGER HAUL, BUT THE WHOLE ROOM BEING ON FIRE THING KIND OF COLLAPSED OUR TIMELINE.
...LOOK. I SAID I WAS SORRY I DIDN'T TELL YOU BEFORE.
BUT YOU'RE SO...SO HONEST, YOU WOULD HAVE GIVEN IT AWAY!
YOU COULD HAVE KILLED ME, APHRA.
EXCUSE ME, I AM AN INCREDIBLE SLICER.
AND HAVING TEEAYE HACK INTO RONEN'S SYSTEM AND CONTROL THE DISINTEGRATION CHAMBER? PURE GENIUS.
BEEP

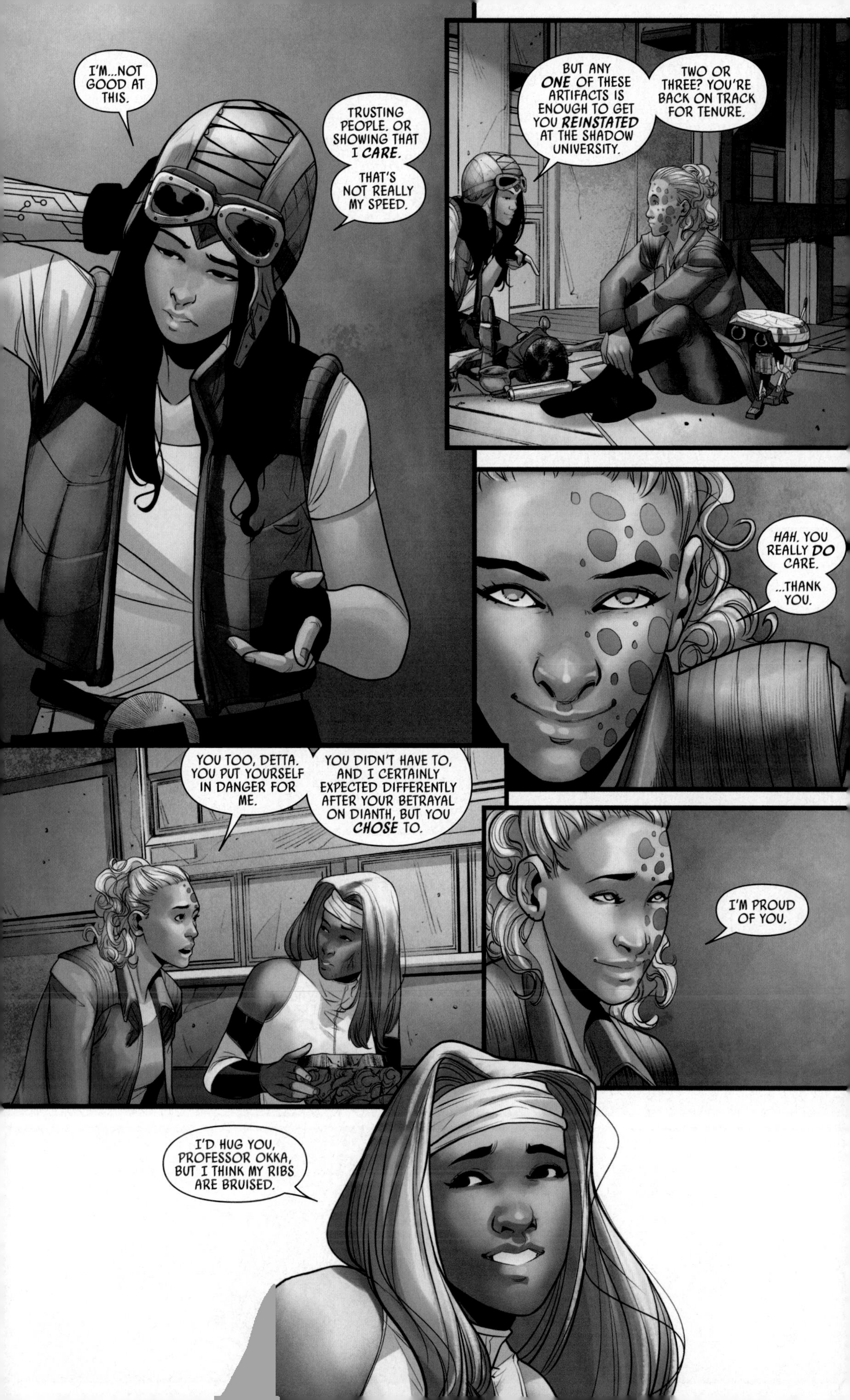
I'M...NOT GOOD AT THIS.
TRUSTING PEOPLE. OR SHOWING THAT I CARE.
THAT'S NOT REALLY MY SPEED.
BUT ANY ONE OF THESE ARTIFACTS IS ENOUGH TO GET YOU REINSTATED AT THE SHADOW UNIVERSITY.
TWO OR THREE? YOU'RE BACK ON TRACK FOR TENURE.
HAH. YOU REALLY DO CARE.
...THANK YOU.
YOU TOO, DETTA. YOU PUT YOURSELF IN DANGER FOR ME.
YOU DIDN'T HAVE TO, AND I CERTAINLY EXPECTED DIFFERENTLY AFTER YOUR BETRAYAL ON DIANTH, BUT YOU CHOSE TO.
I'M PROUD OF YOU.
I'D HUG YOU, PROFESSOR OKKA, BUT I THINK MY RIBS ARE BRUISED.

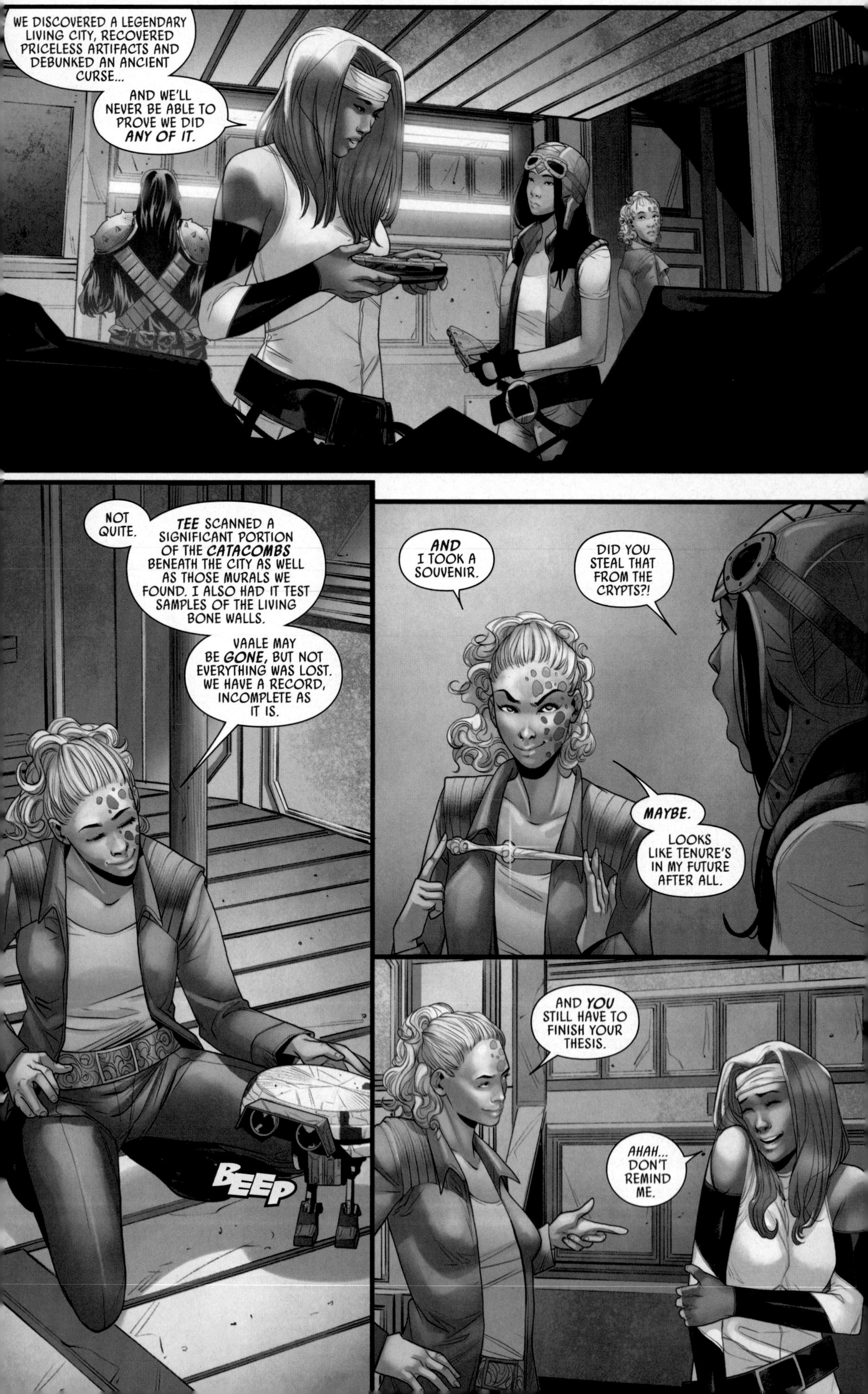
WE DISCOVERED A LEGENDARY LIVING CITY, RECOVERED PRICELESS ARTIFACTS AND DEBUNKED AN ANCIENT CURSE...
AND WE'LL NEVER BE ABLE TO PROVE WE DID ANY OF IT.
NOT QUITE.
TEE SCANNED A SIGNIFICANT PORTION OF THE CATACOMBS BENEATH THE CITY AS WELL AS THOSE MURALS WE FOUND. I ALSO HAD IT TEST SAMPLES OF THE LIVING BONE WALLS.
VAALE MAY BE GONE, BUT NOT EVERYTHING WAS LOST. WE HAVE A RECORD, INCOMPLETE AS IT IS.
BEEP
AND I TOOK A SOUVENIR.
DID YOU STEAL THAT FROM THE CRYPTS?!
MAYBE.
LOOKS LIKE TENURE'S IN MY FUTURE AFTER ALL.
AND YOU STILL HAVE TO FINISH YOUR THESIS.
AHAH... DON'T REMIND ME.

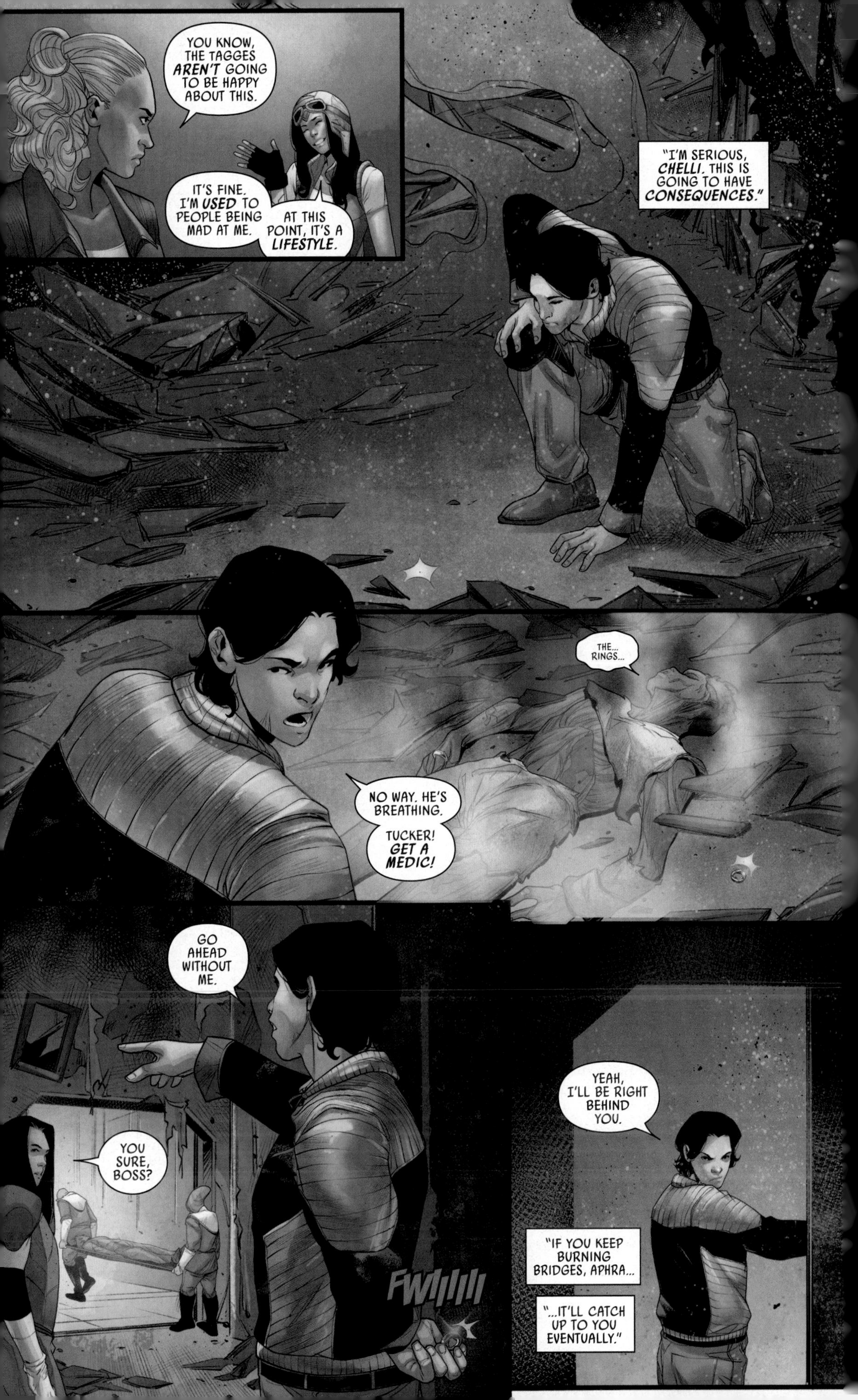
YOU KNOW, THE TAGGES AREN'T GOING TO BE HAPPY ABOUT THIS.
IT'S FINE. I'M USED TO PEOPLE BEING MAD AT ME.
AT THIS POINT, IT'S A LIFESTYLE.
"I'M SERIOUS, CHELLI. THIS IS GOING TO HAVE CONSEQUENCES."
THE... RINGS...
NO WAY. HE'S BREATHING.
TUCKER! GET A MEDIC!
GO AHEAD WITHOUT ME.
YOU SURE, BOSS?
FWIIIIII
YEAH, I'LL BE RIGHT BEHIND YOU.
"IF YOU KEEP BURNING BRIDGES, APHRA...
"...IT'LL CATCH UP TO YOU EVENTUALLY."

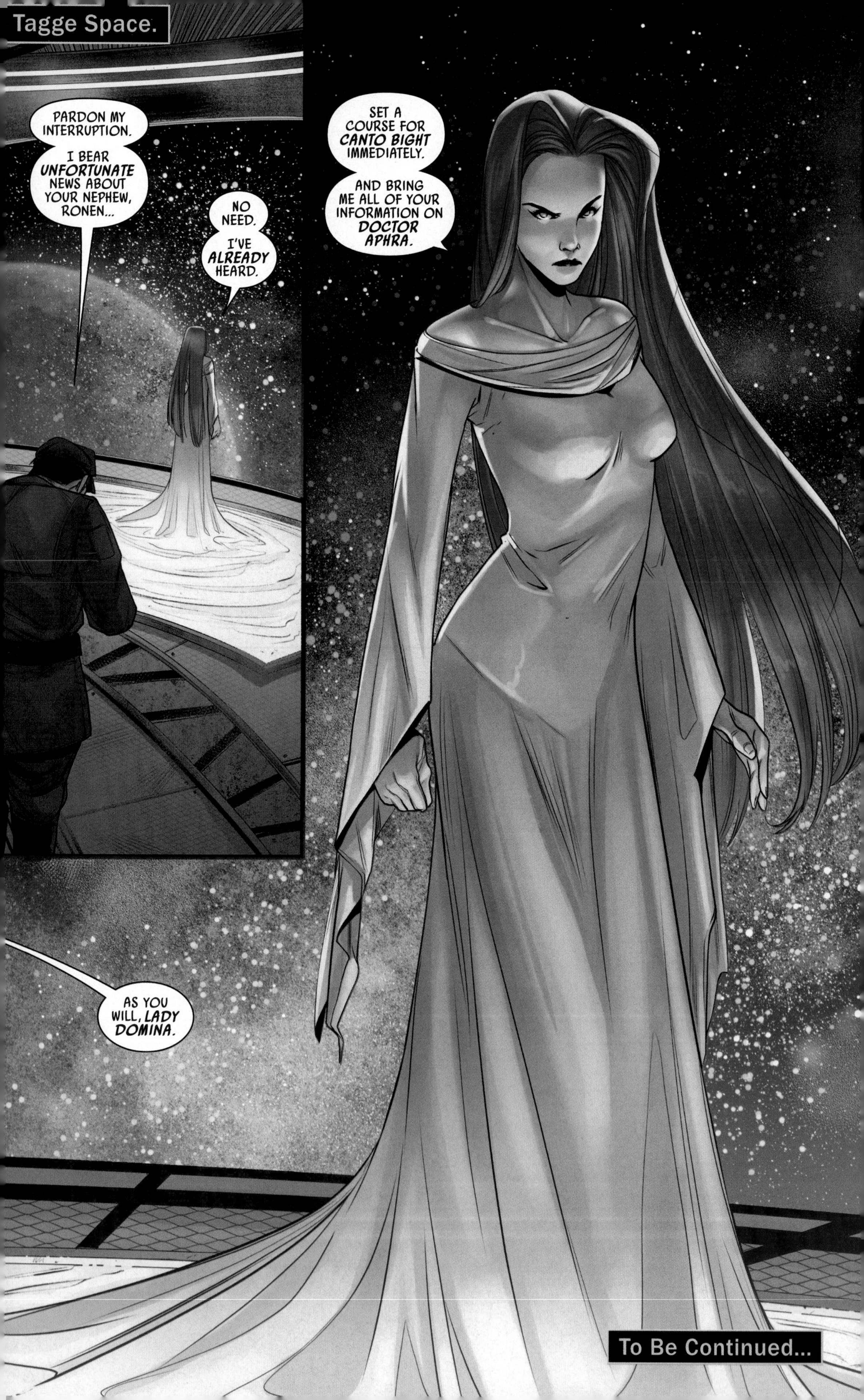
Tagge Space.
PARDON MY INTERRUPTION.
I BEAR UNFORTUNATE NEWS ABOUT YOUR NEPHEW, RONEN...
NO NEED.
I'VE ALREADY HEARD.
SET A COURSE FOR CANTO BIGHT IMMEDIATELY.
AND BRING ME ALL OF YOUR INFORMATION ON DOCTOR APHRA.
AS YOU WILL, LADY DOMINA.
To Be Continued...

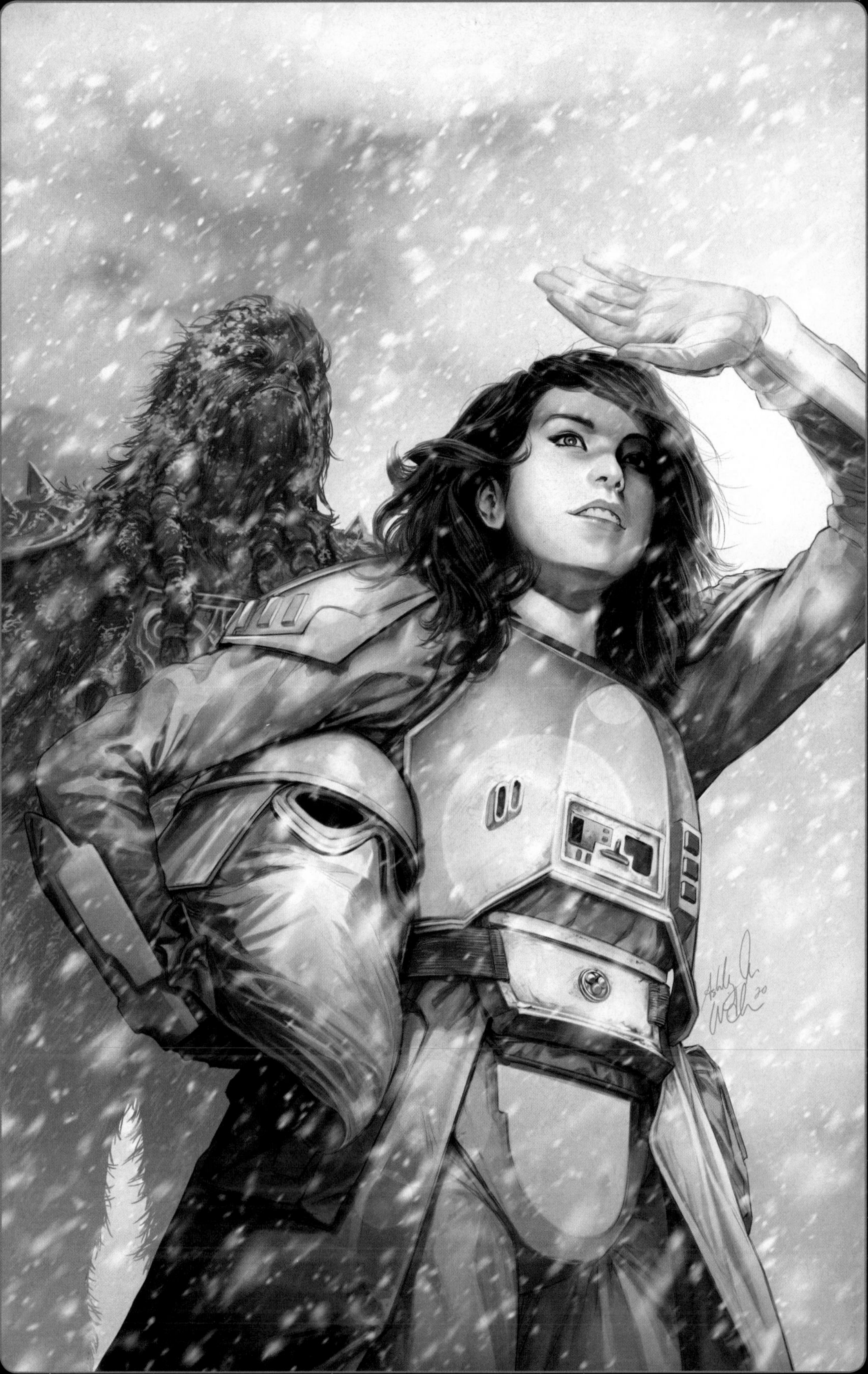

#1 Variant by
ASHLEY WITTER

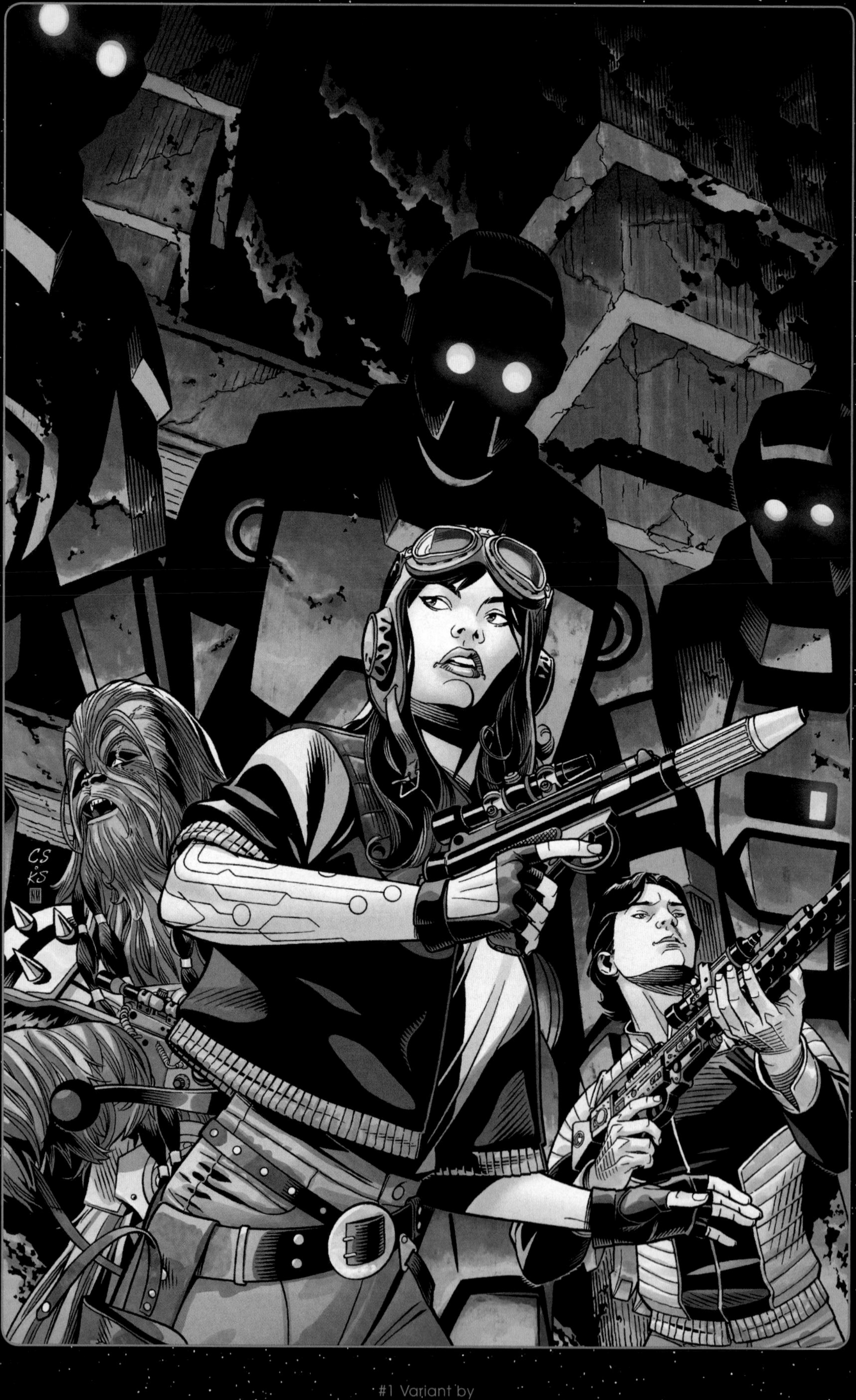
CS
KS
NM

#1 Variant by
CHRIS SPROUSE, KARL STORY & NEERAJ MENON

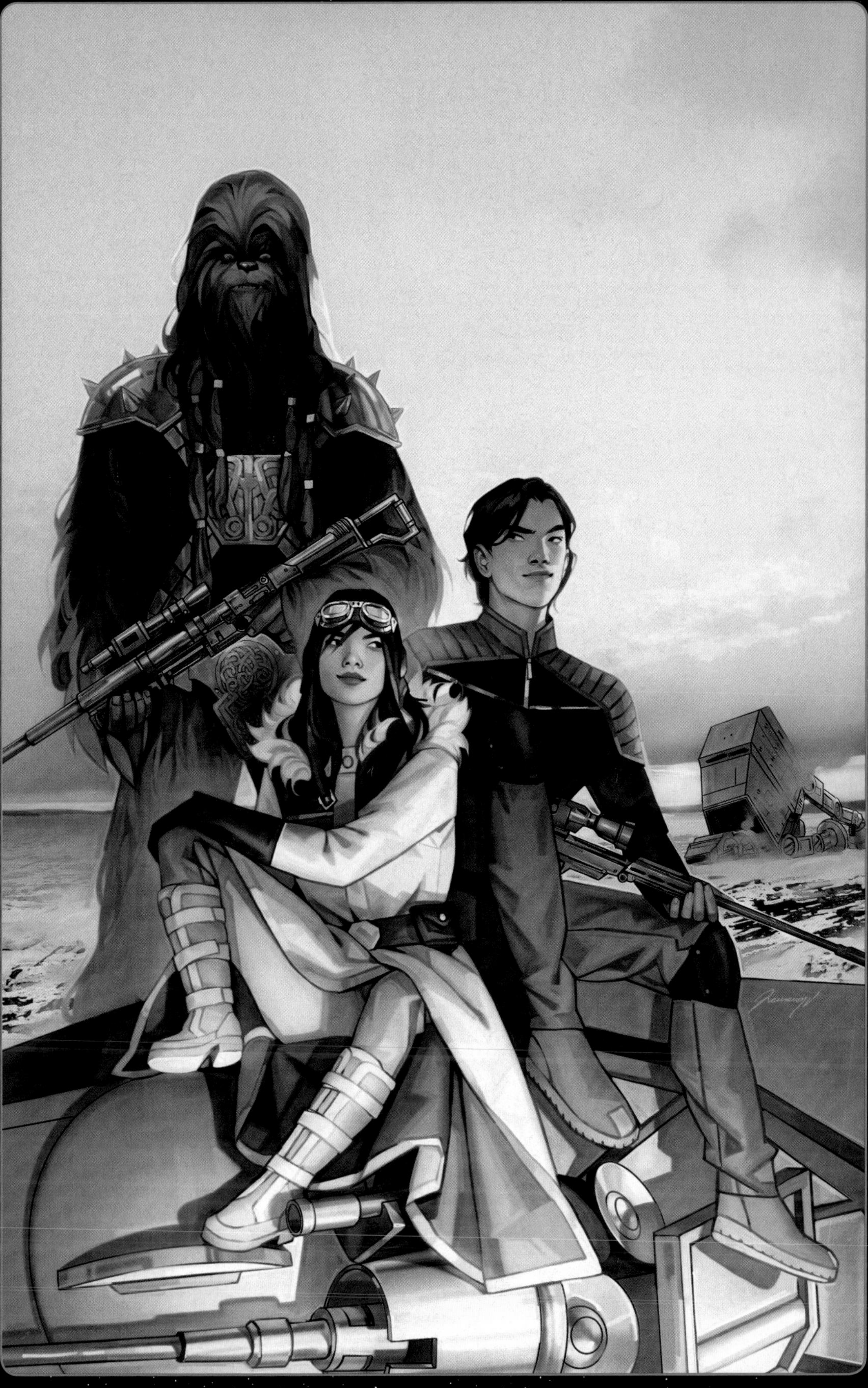

#1 Variant by
VALENTINA REMENAR

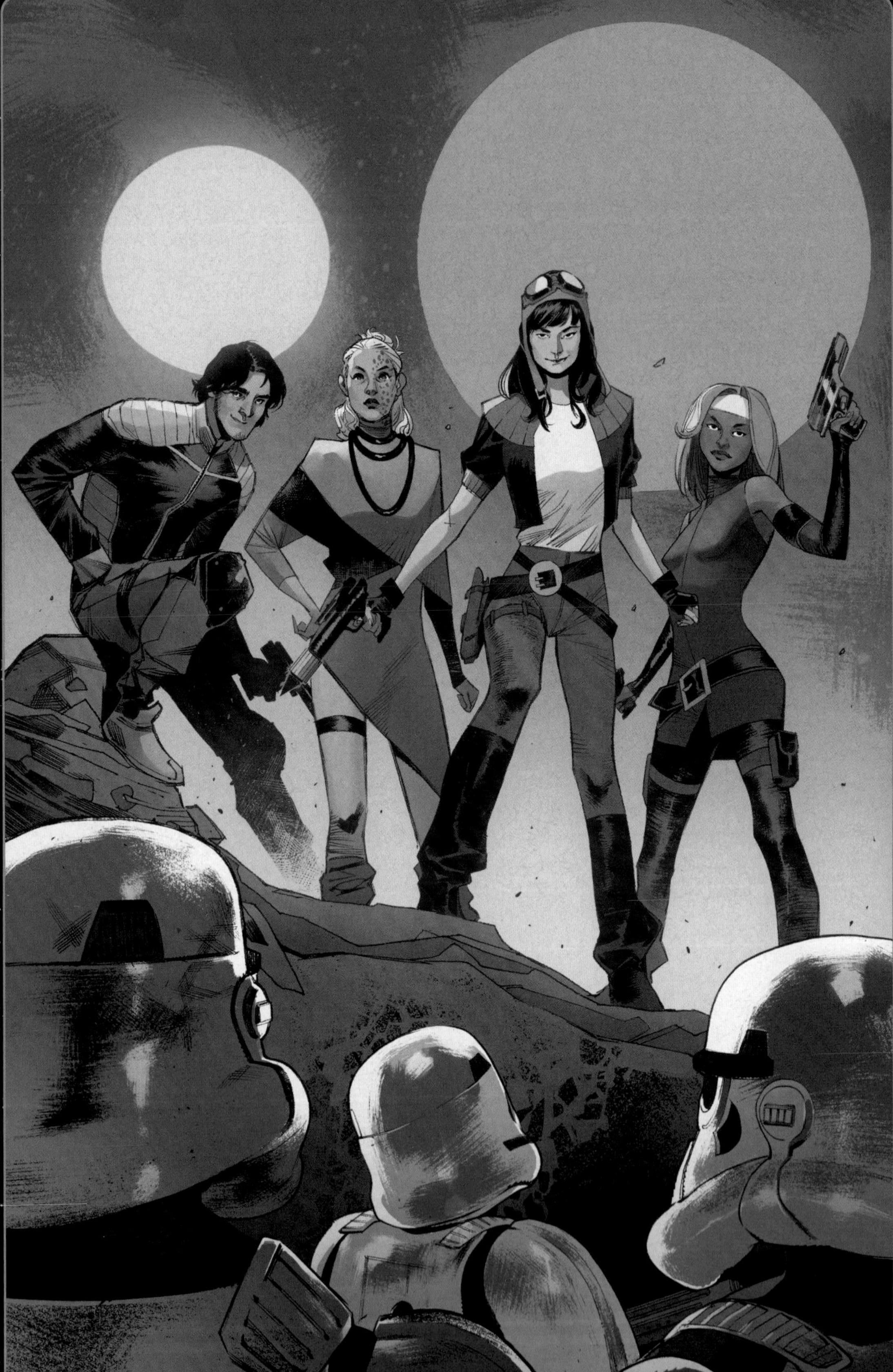

#2 Variant by
SARA PICHELLI & TAMRA BONVILLAIN

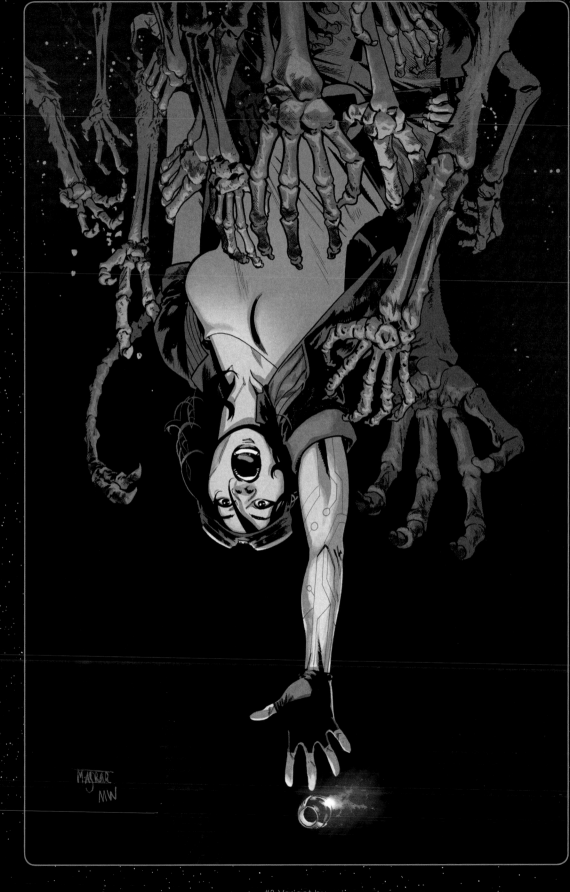

#3 Variant by
MAHMUD ASRAR & **MATTHEW WILSON**

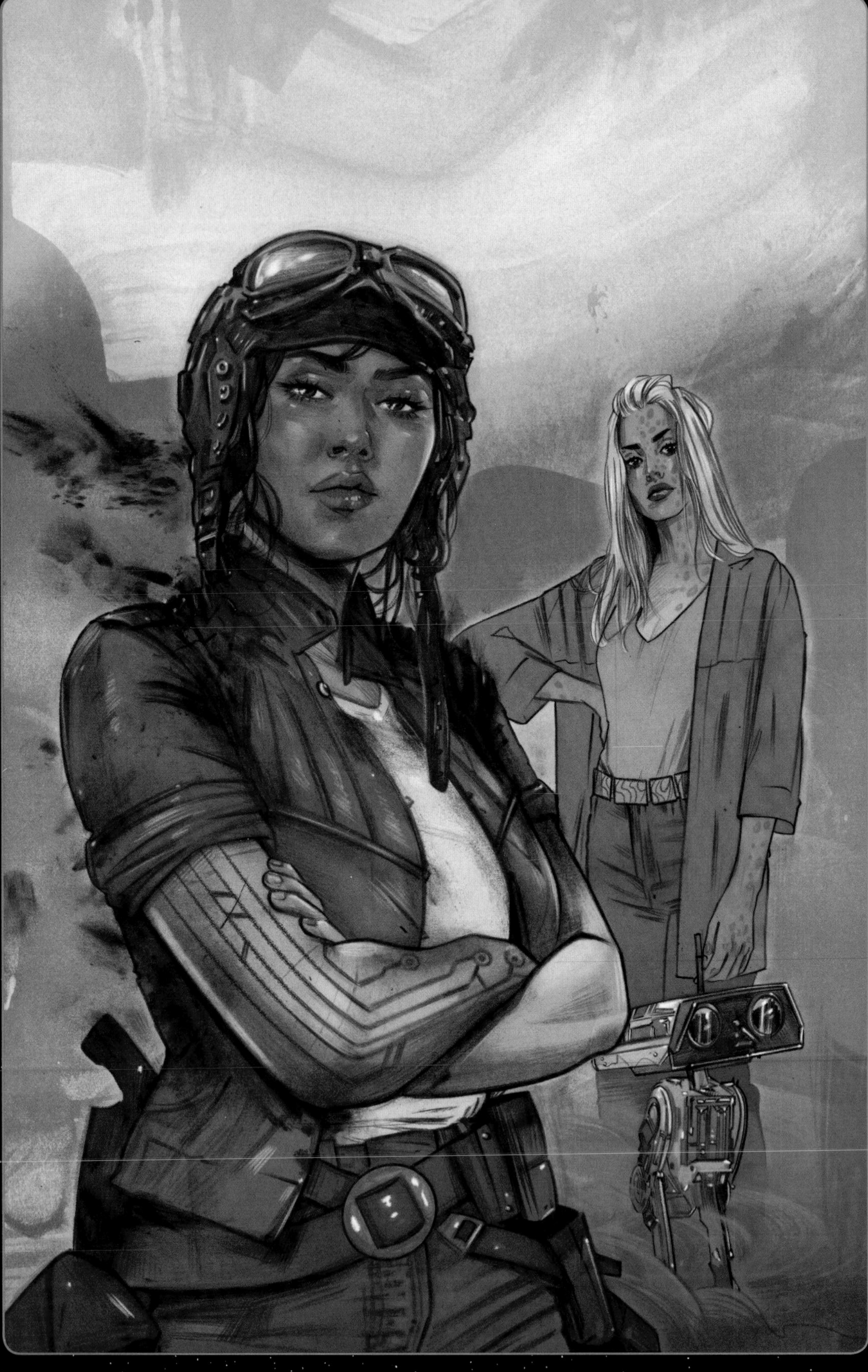

#4 Variant by
TULA LOTAY

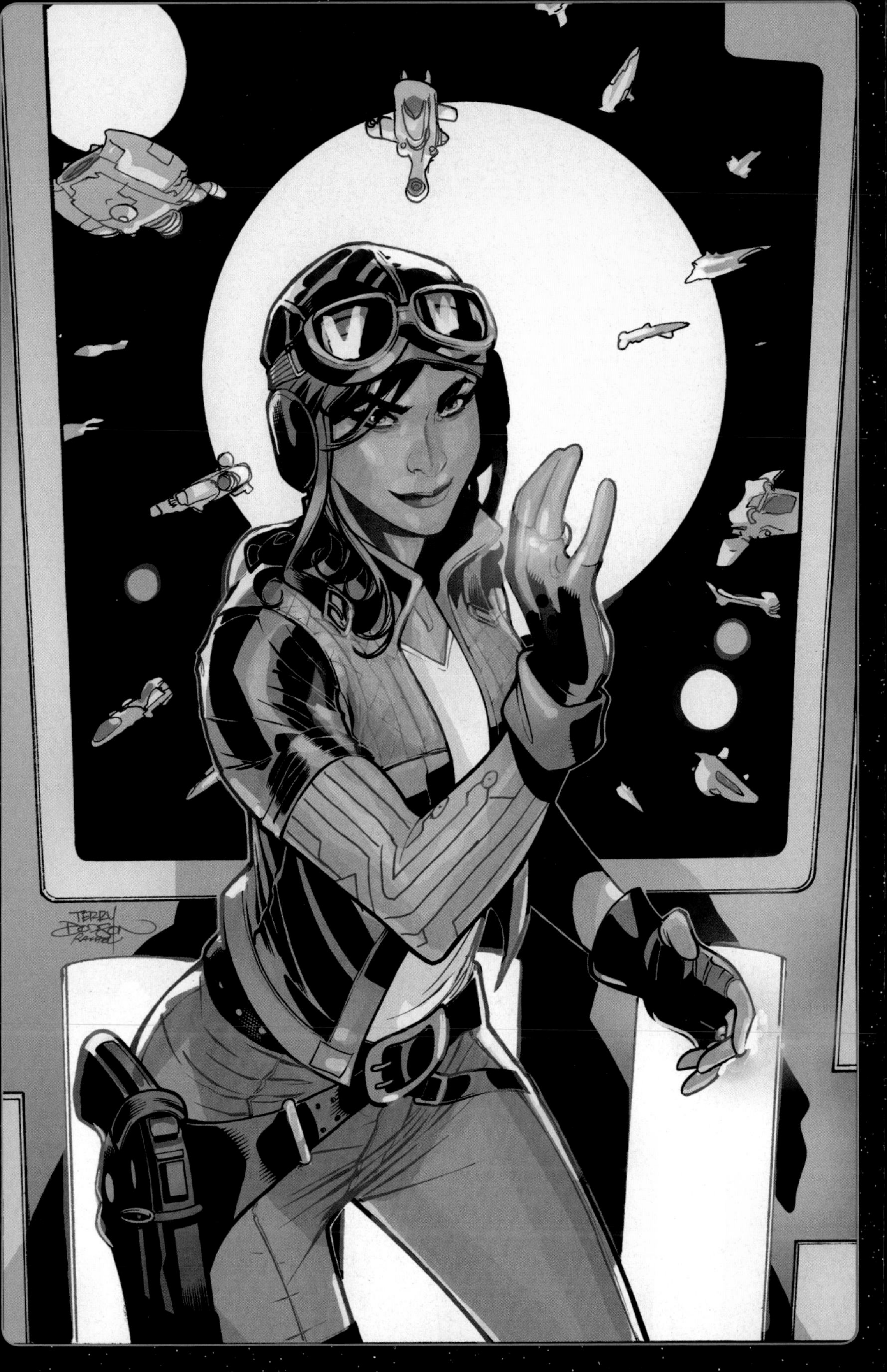

#5 Variant by
TERRY DODSON & RACHEL DODSON

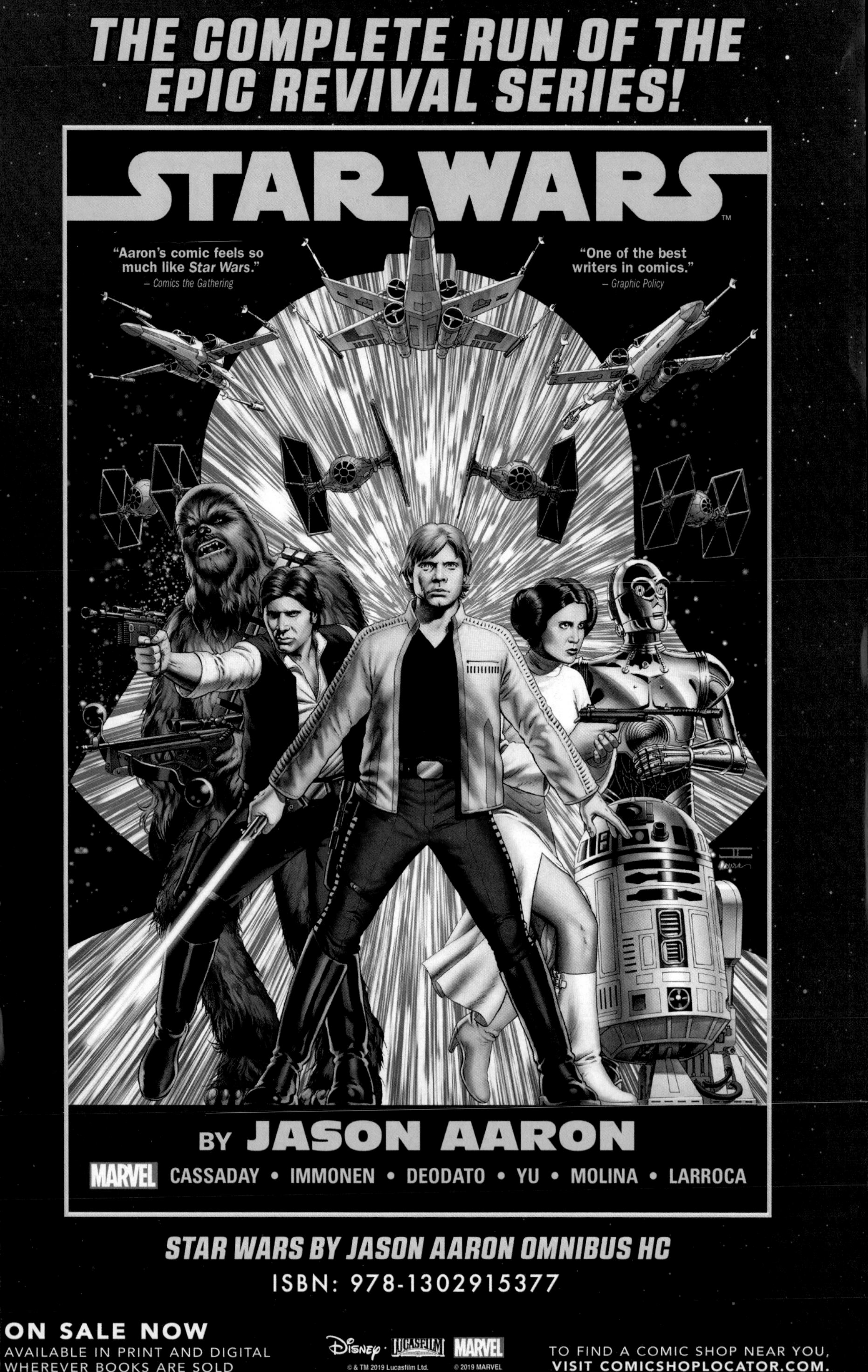

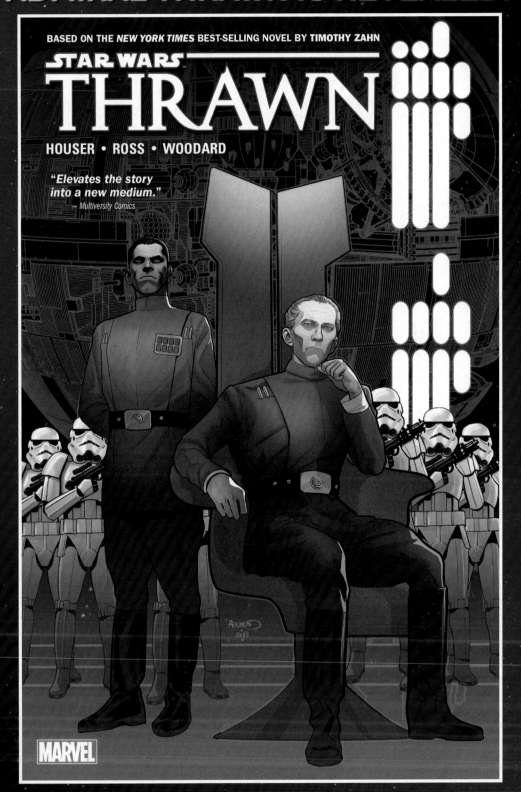

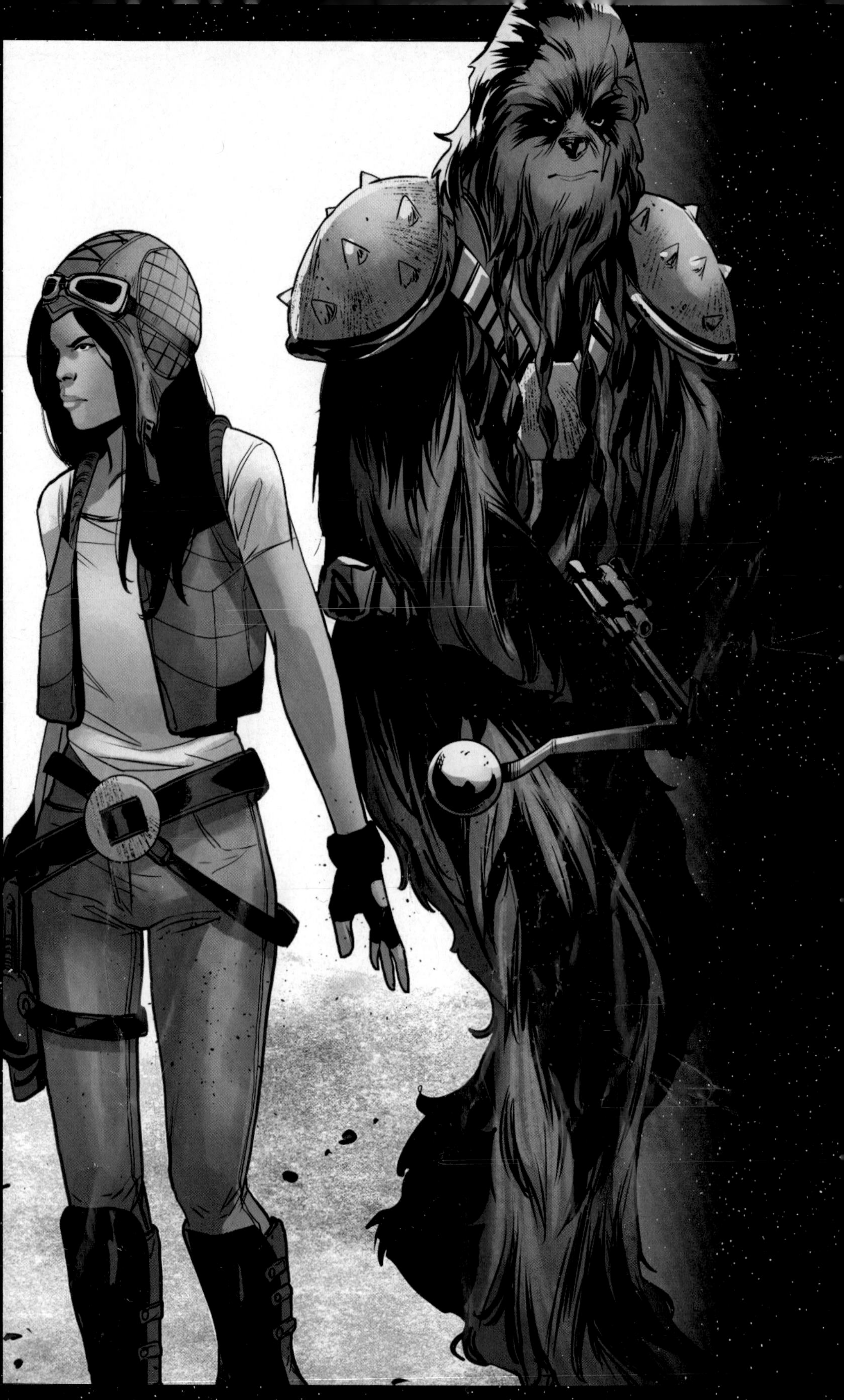

STAR WARS

DOCTOR APHRA

FORTUNE AND FATE